Territories, Environments, Politics

This collection seeks to illustrate the state of the art in territoriological research, both empirical and theoretical. The volume gathers together a series of original, previously unpublished essays exploring the newly emerging territorial formations in culture, politics and society.

While the globalisation debate of the 1990s largely pivoted around a 'general deterritorialisation' hypothesis, since the 2000s it has become apparent that, rather than effacing territories, global connections are added to them, and represent a further factor in the increase of territorial complexity. Key questions follow, such as: How can we further the knowledge around territorial complexities and the ways in which different processes of territorialisation co-exist and interact, integrating scientific advances from a plurality of disciplines? Where and what forms does territorial complexity assume, and how do complex territories operate in specific instances? Which technological, political and cultural facets of territories should be tackled to make sense of the life of territories? How and by what different or combined methods can we describe territories, and do justice to their articulations and meanings? How can the territoriological vocabulary relate to contemporary social theory advancements such as ANT, the ontological turn, the mobilities paradigm, sensory urbanism, and atmospheres research? How can territorial phenomena be studied across disciplinary boundaries? *Territories, Environments, Politics* casts a fresh perspective onto a number of key contemporary socio-spatial phenomena. Refraining from the attempt to ossify territoriology into some disciplinary straightjacket, the collection aims to illustrate the scope of current territoriological research, its domain, its promises, its theoretical advancements, and its methodological reflection in the making.

Scholars interested in social research will find in this collection a rich and imaginative theoretical-methodological toolkit. Students in human geography, anthropology and sociology, socio-legal studies, architecture and urban planning will find *Territories, Environments, Politics* of interest.

Andrea Mubi Brighenti is Professor of Social Theory and Space and Culture at the Department of Sociology, University of Trento, Italy. His research topics broadly cover the relationships between space, power and society. His most recent book is *The Crowd's Common: Towards Canettian epistemology* (forthcoming 2022). His research website is www.capacitedaffect.net

Mattias Kärrholm is Professor of Architectural Theory at the Department of Architecture and the Built Environment, Lund University. His research areas include: architecture, social sciences, territoriality, public space, urban design, architectural theory, space and culture. Monographs include *Animated Lands: Studies in Territoriology*, co-authored with Andrea Mubi Brighenti, and *Retailising Space* (Second edn Routledge 2016).

Space, Materiality and the Normative

Series Editors: Andreas Philippopoulos-Mihalopoulos and Christian Borch

Space, Materiality and the Normative presents new ways of thinking about the connections between space and materiality from a normative perspective. At the interface of law, social theory, politics, architecture, geography and urban studies, the series is concerned with addressing the use, regulation and experience of space and materiality, broadly understood, and in particular with exploring their links and the challenges they raise for law, politics and normativity.

https://www.routledge.com/Space-Materiality-and-the-Normative/book-series/SMNORM

"This thoughtful and rich volume is edited by two of today's foremost scholars of territoriality and the city. It offers a novel re-visioning of issues of territorial complexity and a wide range of urban examples of spatialised social life across different scales and cultural contexts. A very timely and highly original publication that will be a source of inspiration both for researchers and practitioners across disciplines."

Albena Yaneva, *University of Manchester, UK*

"As evinced by the scope and depth of the contributions to this volume, Kärrholm and Brighenti's program for a 'non-reductive territoriology' offers a nuanced and sophisticated understanding of territories which promises to provide inspiration and creative openings for groundbreaking research on the nature and implications of territorialization process and practices for many years to come."

Jonathan Metzger, *KTH Stockholm, Sweden*

"In times of dramatic planetary changes, it is all the more urgent to reflect on the ontological grounds that orient thinking, sensing, and acting in the world. This volume is a convincing move in this direction. Against the grain of decades of reductionist and politically ambiguous interpretations, Brighenti and Kärrholm prompt us to rethink what territories are, how are they made and by whom, by drawing the lineaments of an original Science of Territory that is transversal to hard and soft science, art, politics, and the everyday. This transdisciplinary ambition is reflected on the impressive theoretical, empirical, and methodological diversity of the original contributions that compose the publication, making it an invaluable tool for conjuring new ways of speculating, researching and imagining the material complexity of socio-natural life."

Andrea Pavoni, *Instituto Universitário de Lisboa, Portugal*

Territories, Environments, Politics

Explorations in Territoriology

Edited by
Andrea Mubi Brighenti and Mattias Kärrholm

Routledge
Taylor & Francis Group
LONDON AND NEW YORK

First published 2022
by Routledge
4 Park Square, Milton Park, Abingdon, Oxon OX14 4RN

and by Routledge
605 Third Avenue, New York, NY 10158

Routledge is an imprint of the Taylor & Francis Group, an informa business

British Library Cataloguing-in-Publication Data
A catalogue record for this book is available from the British Library

Library of Congress Cataloging-in-Publication Data
A catalog record has been requested for this book

ISBN: 978-1-032-05166-6 (hbk)
ISBN: 978-1-032-05169-7 (pbk)
ISBN: 978-1-003-19636-5 (ebk)

DOI: 10.4324/9781003196365

Typeset in Bembo
by Taylor & Francis Books

Contents

Figures

Contributors

Sylvaine Bulle is a Professor of Sociology at University of Paris. As a specialist in conflicts, she has written widely on the political sociology of war. Her theoretical research interests also include social theory, critical theory and pragmatism. She has authored many essays and books on the sociology of collective protest movements, and urban phenomena at large. Her last book focuses on the construction of political autonomy in France drawing from the case of the Temporary Autonomous Zones.

Cláudia Casquilho is Assistant Professor at the Lisbon College of Music of the Polytechnic Institute of Lisbon. She is currently conducting her PhD on music education and psychology at the NOVA University of Lisbon.

Paul Draus is a Professor of Sociology in the Department of Behavioral Sciences at the University of Michigan-Dearborn, where he has taught since 2005. From 1992 until 2000, Dr Draus was a public health field worker in New York City and Chicago, and he earned his PhD from Loyola University Chicago. He is the author of *Consumed in the City: Observing Tuberculosis at Century's End* (2004), and he has published more than twenty articles and book chapters on topics ranging from substance abuse and street sex work to urban agriculture and prison education. His most recent research focuses on neighborhood landscape change in Detroit.

Stuart Elden is a Professor of Political Theory and Geography at the University of Warwick. Elden's research is at the intersection of politics, philosophy and geography. He undertakes this work predominantly through approaches from the history of ideas. His work over the past decade or so has been in two main areas – the history, concept and practice of territory; and the history of twentieth-century French thought.

Pedro Gonçalves is a PhD student in Musical Sciences at the NOVA University of Lisbon. He is a member of the Centre for the Study of the Sociology and Aesthetics of Music (CESEM – NOVA). His research interests lie within the study of musical learning by elders and the practice of the traditional cordophones of Madeira: *braguinha, rajão* and *viola de arame*.

Alexis Gonin is a geographer, lecturer at the University of Paris Nanterre, France, and researcher at LAVUE laboratory. His research focuses on appropriation of lands by farming and pastoralism, through territorial ecology-oriented analyses. His latest publication, with G. Filoche and P. Lavigne Delville is: 'Dynamics of Access to Pastoral Resources in a Farming Area (Western Burkina Faso): Unveiling Rights in Open Access Regimes,' *International Journal of the Commons*, 13(2), 2019.

Francisco Klauser is Professor in Political Geography at the University of Neuchâtel, Switzerland. His work explores the socio-spatial implications, power and surveillance issues arising from the digitisation of present-day life, thus bridging the fields of human geography, surveillance studies and risk research. Main research topics include video surveillance, mega-event security, smart cities, airport surveillance, civil drones, and big data in agriculture. Aiming at investigating and conceptualising the intersections between power and space in the digital age, his work also contributes to German, francophone and anglophone socio-spatial theory.

Manfredo Manfredini is Associate Professor in Architecture and Planning at the University of Auckland (NZ) and, since 2016, Honorary Professor at Hunan University, Changsha, China. Manfredo has consistently been involved in fundamental and applied research projects, both locally and internationally. His research spans a wide range of topics in architectural theory and criticism, as well as in design at architectural and urban scales. His current research interests address post-urban spatialisation forms and correlated design aspects, particularly focusing on valorisation, re-qualification and redevelopment of architectural and urban heritage; affordable and special housing; and education in architecture.

Caio Mourão is a PhD student in Musical Sciences at the NOVA University of Lisbon. He concluded his degree and MSc in Musical Sciences at the University of Brasilia. His research in the field of humanities focuses on ethnomusicology, the anthropology of music and music teaching. He is also a guitar player, arranger and a musical producer.

Paula Nunes is a singer, songwriter and musicologist. She is a Professor of Popular Song, History of Popular Brazilian Music and Performance at the Escola de Música de Brasília. She is currently undertaking her PhD in Musical Science at the NOVA University of Lisbon. She holds a MSc in Musicology and a degree in Artistic Education from the University of Brasilia.

Daniel Paiva is a human geographer currently affiliated with the Centre for Geographical Studies of the Universidade de Lisboa. He is undertaking a research project funded by the Fundação para a Ciência e a Tecnologia entitled *Innovative and Creative Practices for Fostering Environmental Awareness,*

Knowledge, and Conservation Action through Direct Experiences of Synanthropic Life in the City (CEECIND/03528/2018).

Kristanti Dewi Paramita has taught architecture at Universitas Indonesia since 2010, becoming Lecturer in 2012. She completed her MA and PhD in Design at the School of Architecture at University of Sheffield, UK. Her current research takes particular interest in situated knowledge produced by spatial and material practice, understanding how such knowledge shapes architectural design methods.

Anna Petersson is Senior Lecturer at the Department of Architecture and the Built Environment, Lund University. Her research includes the way our material culture and built environment both reflect and take part in societal changes concerning cultural diversity in existential meaning-making and in individual networks of support. Petersson is also research member of the Nordic Network of Thanatology, and she has a Master of Fine Arts in Metal Design from Konstfack, University College of Arts, Craft and Design in Stockholm.

Les Roberts is Reader in Cultural and Media Studies at the University of Liverpool. The core focus of his work is situated within the interdisciplinary fields of spatial anthropology and spatial humanities. He is author/editor of a number of books that engage with these research areas, including *Deep Mapping* (2016), *Film, Mobility and Urban Space* (2012), *Liminal Landscapes* (2012), and *Mapping Cultures* (2012). His latest monograph, *Spatial Anthropology: Excursions in Liminal Space*, was published by in 2018 (paperback in 2020).

Juliette Roddy is an Associate Professor of Economics at the University of Michigan-Dearborn. Her research focuses on the economics of substance use, recovery and re-entry. She is an expert on injection drug use, marijuana use and policy, and sex work. She is a trained facilitator in restorative conferencing. She also serves on the University of Michigan-Ann Arbor Institutional Review Board as oversight for human subjects research.

Anke Schwarz is a postdoctoral researcher and lecturer at Technische Universität Dresden's Institute of Geography. An urban geographer, her research has focused on international urbanisation, infrastructures, and everyday practices. Her recent publications include the 2019 *Geographica Helvetica* special issue, *Contested Urban Territories. Decolonized*

Perspectives (co-edited with Monika Streule), and *Demanding Water: A Sociospatial Approach to Domestic Water Use in Mexico City* (2017). Among her present projects, she is conducting research on authoritarian territorialisations and future geographies.

Monika Streule is an urban scholar based at the Department of Architecture at ETH Zürich. She received her PhD in Urban Studies from ETH Zürich and holds a MA in Anthropology, Sociology and Political Sciences from the University of Zurich. Her research engages with the social production of space, urbanisation processes and inventive methodologies of qualitative research. She is also interested in comparative urbanism and a relational understanding of urban territory from post- and decolonial perspectives for a more global approach to understanding cities.

Introduction: The Stake of Territories

Andrea Mubi Brighenti and Mattias Kärrholm

The enduring significance of territories in the current historical context

First conceived in the mid-twentieth century, territoriology – the science of territories – is currently being re-appreciated as a research approach and theory. In this context, this volume seeks to contribute to an on-going conversation revolving around a number of renewed approaches to territories. While not representing a unified disciplinary field, territoriology offers a distinctive take on the possible collaboration between the social and the natural sciences. In the light of contentious contemporary challenges in the fields of politics and the ecology, of environmental changes and newly emerging patterns of urban life, and of an increasingly complex balance between technology and ethics, territoriology offers a contribution to analyse the interplay between space, social interaction, biological processes, social imagination, local attachment and global governance. In the social sciences, territory has been a central tenet of spatial political modernity, in connection to the administration of a population that was supposed to become progressively 'landed,' 'settled,' 'housed,' 'schooled,' etc. In the natural sciences, on the other hand, territory has been extensively investigated by ethological research as a type of behaviour – in this case, 'territoriality' has been defined as the relation the social animal entertains with an environment that appears imbued with social valences. Current territoriology, as we also seek to pursue it through this volume, incorporates all these various insights, and furthers them in the fields of human geography, sociology, anthropology, politics, architecture, urban planning and beyond.

Since 2020, the global pandemic scenario has powerfully brought back the reality of territories into the public debate, not only in terms of managing human mobility and border crossing, but also in terms of structuring healthcare organisations, supporting education and psychological wellbeing, sustaining the economy, adapting lifestyles in ways previously unseen in living memory. Concurrently, however, the continuing significance of territories also inherently reveals the limits of the classic model of the territorial state. More than ever before, our geographical imagination needs to be liberated from the still

DOI: 10.4324/9781003196365-1

dominating state model of territoriality, in order to embrace multiple territorial formations and territory-making activities.[1] Here again, the pandemic has highlighted the significance of territories at multiple scales and in multiple formats, ranging from self-disciplining practices (the control of one's touch and breath) to interpersonal distance management ('social distancing' protocols etc.), from the sorting of access to facilities and spaces ('health passports' etc.), through transformation of entire economic sectors (educational, cultural and recreational activities etc.), to the reconfiguration of global hegemonies (the Chinese model of epidemic control, etc.).

If there is one aspect of territories that comes powerfully to the foreground in the current historical context, it is their *complexity* – where, by complexity, we mean their multidimensional and dynamic nature – their 'immanent constitution,' as we suggest calling it. Facing territorial complexity is the starting point for any serious attempt at analysing contemporary territory-making activities.[2] Whereas the globalisation debate of the 1990s largely pivoted around a 'general deterritorialisation' hypothesis, since the 2000s it has become apparent that, rather than effacing territories, global connections are in fact being superposed onto them: networks do not 'deny' territories, rather, they represent a further factor in the increase of the overall territorial complexity. It is in this sense that the reality of territories has been brought back by not only the pandemic, but more amply, the global ecological and climate crisis, and all the 'anthropocenic' transformations we are living through (with the pandemic being just an instance of a more general critical situation). All these challenges indeed evoke the problem of the 'carrying capacity' of territories, in the context of the demographics of a planet that has never been so populated before[3] – with the population factor, in turn, constituting *only one* among the many issues that, in various ways, today evoke problems of 'measure.'

Once we are able to reframe territories as processes rather than stretches of land, as social programmes and (to borrow from Bachelard) instances of 'material imagination,' they indeed appear as crucial sites for analysis, as they proceed through cycles of production, stabilisation and transformation. Whether one studies the life of an urban street corner or a protest movement that communicates online and then takes to the streets, whether one tackles mundane, everyday shopping wayfaring through urban public space – which again, in pandemic times is not so mundane after all – or the geography of commercial drones as they are deployed in

1 In an oft-quoted piece, Agnew (1994) criticised what he called the 'territorial trap' in political geography. We concur with Agnew, but only to the extent that his critique applies to a classic, restricted model of territory. That same conception is more recently endorsed by Jessop, Brenner and Jones (2008). Our main argument, it should be remarked, goes in the direction of a deep reformulation of such classical social-scientific view on territorial phenomena.

2 On the notion of territorial complexity, see Kärrholm (2005).

3 For a synthesis of the major global demographic trends and their spatial impact, see Forman and Wu (2016).

the aerial milieu of periurban and suburban zones, whether one studies the transhumance of African herders or the action of community-based organisations in Detroit neighbourhoods, one is inevitably confronted with the on-going reformulations of territory-making activities, of territorial politics and management, of territorial significations and feelings, as well as territorial explorations and experimentations. This way, territories appear as, in the end, an intrinsic component of social life: more than places and spaces, they encapsulate practices, rhythms, respirations, patterns, formats, desiderata, expectations, affections, explorations, drifts, dreams, melodies.

The proposition that we and the contributors to this volume advance is that territories need to be conceived of in *not only* legal, political, topographic and 'identitarian' ways (all dimensions that certainly matter!), but must *also* be attended in additional terms: namely, in terms of volumes and depths, in terms of materials and their arrangements – in sum, in terms of the *life* they are capable of enabling, supporting and fostering. Territories are ways in which it becomes possible to establish and strengthen forms of what Les Roberts in this volume calls 'connectedness with the world.' From this perspective, territories appear as social attempts conducted inside shared environments, with unfolding potentials for connections, expectations, observations, and interactions. Contemporary politics, as we know, is haunted by 'possessional,' exclusionary, revanchist and conflictual stances, which nourish a reactionary imagination of territories. While such imagination certainly intersects real concerns and anxieties, it is short-sighted and insufficient. Once we are able to develop a richer notion of territory-making, we come to realise that identitarian, exclusivist and conflictual elements only represent a small fraction of the whole life of territories. What remains excluded from the classic territorial narratives is, accordingly, what we set out to explore here.

The hypothesis that grounds this volume is that territorial complexity acts as a spur to advance new ways of researching spatialised social life.[4] Among other things, territories offer the chance to expand our research methodology. Territorial complexity, as we have seen above, derives from the superposition of a series of plural, incommensurable logics, dynamics, modes of existence within, and engagement with, local environments that are quintessentially *shared* – or *social*, as we are wont to say. This means that research into the many ways of territory-making must be equipped with an adequately rich and imaginative theoretical-methodological toolkit. Here is where the chance is given us to retrieve a wide range of sources of inspiration: whether it is earlier classical social theory or seemingly defunct research programmes such as human ethology, whether it is heterodox research traditions such as psychogeography or more fashionable and contentious epistemologies such as the non-anthropocentric

4 The type of spatiality we evoke here is one deeply enmeshed with temporality. Elsewhere, we have explored this nexus in terms of rhythms and melodies (Brighenti and Kärrholm 2018).

approaches to the social sciences, whether it is the elemental philosophy of Gaston Bachelard or the literary visions of J. G. Ballard, out of which Les Roberts develops his own 'deep territoriology,' we are offered plenty of possibilities.

Theoretical challenges and reformulations of territoriology

The issue of changing territorialities, and indeed the need for an updated perspective as well as an increased theorisation of territorial issues has been noted by contemporary scholars and researchers (see, for example Elden 2005; Brenner and Elden 2009). As mentioned above, in the wake of recent local and global processes of reterritorialisation, territorial issues have recently come to the forefront in projects concerned with the troubled relation between human societies and the Earth. A new interest for territoriality can thus been seen in discussions relating to neologisms such as the Anthropocene, the Capitalocene and the Chthulucene (Malm and Hornborg 2014; Haraway 2016), posthumanism (Braidotti 2013), the notion of Gaia and a New Climatic Regime (Stengers 2015; Latour 2017; 2018). In short (and from the perspective of a territoriologist), the advocates of these new perspectives argue for a move from a classical territorial understanding, focusing on *who* is territorialising *what*, to a broader investigation of entangled territorialisations involving a wide set of both human and non-human actors. In some of his recent work Latour (2017; 2018) has for example suggested that we, in the light of climate change, need 'to rematerialize our existence, which means first of all reterritorializing it or, [...] *reterrestrializing* it' (2017: 223). Latour argues that we must leave the modernist idea that we can, or ever have been, 'discovering new land' and instead focus more on the complexity of the Earth. This means that we need to direct our attention to the intensity of the Earth, rather than to its extension, and to rediscover it as different layers of territorialisation rather than as a two-dimensional mosaic of power relations. For Latour, the question is here a pragmatic one: What do we (living things of all sorts) depend on for our existence, as terrestrials? Territories are produced by social relations and we always depend on others to form a territory or a dwelling place if we want it to sustain over time (Latour 2018: 87). Accepting that territories are always entangled with other times and places means that they are, as we also have argued (Brighenti and Kärrholm 2020), phenomenological as well as ecological entities. This also means that we must accept that a territory cannot be seen as a spatial container. It is embedded in the world in a richer way: we can hit a territory just as much by cutting its supplies as by actually invading it.

Living in the ruins of capitalism, and struggling to sustain a habitable land (Tsing 2015), it has become increasingly apparent that we have a responsibility to respond (Haraway 2016) and to care (Puig de la Bellacasa 2017), not only for the living, but for all actors associated with life, as we produce and maintain our territorial world. This also implies that we constantly need to find new ways of representing territories and territorial actors. As we run out of water, or as the flood takes our home, we might realise that water is an actor that needs to be better accounted for, it needs a representative with a seat at the table (Latour 2017: 272 f.). In fact, one might argue that it has become an urgent matter to find the silent actors with whom we always shared our territories, before it is too late. This is also where a territoriological approach can be important. The state of the world and its territorial complexity – which we have yet to fully understand – brings a new challenge to science and research. Science has in general tended to see itself as territorial in the classical sense, i.e. as sitting firmly within a disciplinary field to be expanded and protected from intrusions, although sometimes of course also entering temporarily into more or less controlled relationships with other parties. Disciplinary fields are of course also here for a reason, they have over time become effective and embodied as they have become associated with certain methods, instruments, laboratories and seminar rooms, tools of the trade, concepts, etc. The territoriological practice is not to undo these territorialisations; rather, it is to see what entanglements are already there, connecting different disciplines, sometimes in subterraneous and unnoticed ways, as well as investigating new entanglements and new relations to be made – it is, in other words, about engaging less in the frontlines of a discipline and more with the intensities of critical issues that might have become invisible through the disciplinary division of the world.

Our hope is here for a non-reductive territoriology that is rich in sources so as to allow for abstraction as well as for concrete and very precise sightings, to happen side by side. The type of territoriology that is being proposed here wants to focus on both empirical and theoretical sides of territo-realities, and not least how the two strands of inquiry can draw from each other.[5] Furthermore, it looks to tackle territorial issues in an encompassing and open-minded way without reducing the perspective to a certain fixed repertoire of methods and techniques, or to be a concern of a certain discipline alone (and only on its own). This anthology can hopefully be seen as a small step in this direction. The contributors of this volume come from a wide range of different disciplines including, for example, anthropology, applied aesthetics, architecture, anthropology, criminology, culture and media studies, economy, human geography, political geography, sociology and urban studies. It also counts affiliations and empirical field studies from all over the world, including Burkina Faso, France, Germany, Indonesia, Mexico, New Zealand, Poland, Portugal, Sweden, Switzerland, UK and USA. Our hope is that this heterogeneity of sources and perspectives might give the reader an idea of the rich and diverse field that is territoriology.

Outline of the volume

In this volume, we present ten original essays that have been commissioned by us editors to give a wide-ranging illustration of the state of the art and current

5 For a more thorough discussion on the scope of territoriology, see Brighenti and Kärrholm (2020).

directions in territoriological research, both empirical and theoretical. The eleventh essay of the volume, by Stuart Elden, is instead – as credited – a republication.[6] We are most happy to include it here, thanks to Stuart's benign consent, as the opening piece of the collection. Indeed, we believe that 'The State of Territory Under Globalization' is a most apposite contribution to set the stage for current territoriological elaboration, containing as it does a wide-ranging reflection on the theoretical 'situation' of territory. Elden retraces the 'deterritorialisation–reterritorialisation–territorialisation' scheme that subtends Deleuze and Guattari's (1980) analysis in *Mille Plateaux*, arguably one of the richest sources of inspiration for a dynamic territoriology, and discusses how this conceptual scaffolding has been employed by Hardt and Negri (2000) in their attempt to explain the model of sovereignty under globalisation. Besides the fact that, by 2020, *Empire*'s overall thesis reads a bit out-dated (since we clearly live in times of new struggles for hegemony), Elden takes issue with the fact that Hardt and Negri, like most of the globalisation literature they criticised, 'do not seem to have a fully worked through notion of what territory itself might be.' Examining closely such a shortcoming, Elden concludes that Hardt and Negri's borrowing from the French theorists lost sight of 'the push–pull, almost dialectical, balance of de- and reterritorialization.' Elden also sounds a note of caution when it comes to trading notions across the line between the social and natural sciences and, although we do not believe that Deleuze and Guattari can be charged of reductionism, twentieth-century history proves abundantly that, on this terrain, the conflation of natural and social dimensions can easily end up producing monsters.

In the second chapter, the sociologist Sylvaine Bulle also emphasises the political import of territories. More specifically, in her 'How the non-human turn challenges the social sciences,' she reconstructs recent theoretical debates in sociology and anthropology highlighting the role of the 'non-humans' in social life. Together with the diffusion of ANT and its call for a 'symmetrical epistemology,' the more recent debate in anthropology – sometimes discussed under the catch-phrase of 'ontological turn' – has repositioned the role of human agency within a larger set of natural-ecological coordinates. Bulle argues that, however much such an enlarged context and the inclusion of ecological, environmental and spatial issues into the sphere of contentious politics is welcome, the new approaches run, on their turn, the risk of missing important dimensions in the logic of political mobilisation, which both social movement studies and a pragmatically inspired political sociology are better equipped to account for. As a case study where all these dynamics become quite visible, Bulle discusses her fieldwork about the environmental struggles conducted at Notre-Dame-des-Landes in France, in one of the most iconic 'Zones to

6 Elden's essay originally appeared in 2006; a 2021 afterword has been added by the author on the occasion of the inclusion of his essay in this volume.

defend' ever launched.[7] There, in 2014 started the occupation of the agricultural land and the squatting of soon-to-be-torn-down buildings as a form of protest against the construction of a new major airport – a plan which the French government eventually dropped in 2018, while however simultaneously launching a forcible and rather violent expulsion of the squatters that resulted in many being seriously wounded. Bulle deliberately picks this case because many of the activists themselves embrace a seemingly 'post-humanist' stance, celebrating, with their lifestyle, the elements of the forest, the animals and the spirits of the land ('We are Nature defending itself' being one of their most declarative mottos). However, Bulle warns us, the demise of the social science has occurred too hastily – indeed, she reverses the lens and shows how, in fact, the social science on its turn challenges the non-human turn: one could not understand much of the vicissitudes at Notre-Dame-des-Landes without understanding how the political state and its legal infrastructure operate, without taking into account the multiple ways in which territories are organisationally managed, and how even post-humanist resistance has to take a specifically anthropic logic of politics seriously if it wants to achieve any result. Not simply, but sociological analysis also proves necessary to examine how the front of the Zadists itself was never homogeneous, as it became apparent after 2018, when different ideological factions took different paths according to their willingness, or lack thereof, to negotiate patterns towards the legalisation of their settlements (interestingly then officially reframed as 'projects').

The third chapter also proposes a theoretical discussion and advancement based on a case study, this time in human geography. In 'Commercial drones and the territorialisation of the air' Francisco Klauser examines the deployment of drone use in Switzerland, showing how the classic geographical imagination of territory proves insufficient for explanatory purposes in this case. The aerial realm, Klauser argues, must be examined as an 'aero-volumetric' reality endowed with a multiplicity of social, economic and political underpinnings. The new forms of territorialisation produced by a specific technology such as the drone, emphasise the role played by a whole politics of verticality that emerges under current conditions. Unfolding such a perspective, the author initiates an important reflection into how the very notion of territory gets enmeshed with, and enriched by, elemental, sensory, and affective aspects. While traditionally the land and the air – just as the land and the sea for Carl Schmitt – constituted fundamentally distinct domains, with territorialisation only fully functioning on the land, the introduction of new technologies of mobility – of which the drone is one instance – reconfigures the domains and the modes of territorialisation, creating new contested realms of interaction. Retrieving Claude Raffestin's approach to territorialisation as mediation, Klauser contributes to such a line of thinking going beyond bi-dimensionality, so as

7 Basic information about this story is provided by Wikipedia: https://en.wikipedia.org/wiki/ZAD_de_Notre-Dame-des-Landes

to encounter and include the deeper 'elementality' of the air: while technology imparts a striation onto the aerial space in terms of its 'parametrisation,' the making of airy territories necessarily still differs from landed territoriality, both in terms of affection and, again, in terms of material imagination.

Contemporary anthropological research illuminates the dynamics of territorialisation in a further sense. Here Alexis Gonin contributes a chapter on the relations between pastoralism and agriculturalism in Sub-Saharan West Africa, particularly the Sudanian savanna in Burkina Faso. In previous work, Gonin (2018) has explored the peculiar territoriality of nomad herders leading cattle through seasonal transhumance. With his chapter for this collection, 'Inhabiting Together,' he now more specifically shows that territories are always forms of composition between different projects, different visions, and different practices of land and spatial use. Territories, the author suggests, are attempts to answer questions concerning cohabitation. This insight resonates very much with what we have argued above, namely that territories in practice are more often about inclusion than about exclusion, although certainly exclusion represents one extreme (and most often doomed) attempt to close the question. Thanks to his ethnographic fieldwork, Gonin is capable to analyse the emergence of pastoral-agricultural 'territorial compositions' in the Sahelo-Sudanian pasturelands: in that context, territories appear as shaped by relations that might be either of alliance or of conflict, but whose existence is made necessary on account of a series of mutual ecological and economic interdependencies. Territories thus operate upon these nets of relations and expectations by subjecting them to an operation of 'consolidation:' 'The goal of territorialization – Gonin writes – is to bind other actors in one's network by making them interested in participating to a common territory.' In a space of multiple mobilities and unstable agencies, and in a context characterised by high ecological fragility, making territories may therefore become a vital matter, particularly for the nomadic herders Gonin has followed.

On the threshold between spatial anthropology and literary studies we encounter the essay contributed by Les Roberts, 'Territory Glimpsed Through Lache Eyes,' a subtle and visionary excursion into the experiential side in the life of territories – a veritable exercise in *deep territoriology*. Tracing his theoretical heritage from pataphysics, psychogeography, soundscape studies, as well as from J. G. Ballard's fiction, and interspersing them with his own poetry, Roberts sets his exploration during the period of the 2020 lockdown in the UK. He recalls, to begin, the peculiar sense of psycho-social-spatial disorientation that contradistinguished that period. The feeling of being on uncharted terrain (as indeed is the case also for the global climate crisis) lets emerge a series of personal and cultural memories with which Roberts tries to mediate, and remediate, his own embodied ties to the spaces of the lockdown. In particular, Ballard's short story, 'The Enormous Space' (1989) – together with its BBC TV adaptation (*Home*, 2003) – is evoked by the author as a striking precedent where the confusion of scales and the inversion of exterior and interior lead the protagonist's twisted design into a veritable line of flight, or journey with no return (his 'mind may have drifted into a realm without yardsticks or sense of scale,' wrote Ballard). The Ballardian raving adventure is mobilised by Roberts to lay out the coordinates of what a deep mapping of home spaces might look like. Another literary companionship to these territories is offered by René Daumal's pataphysical novella *Mount Analogue* (published posthumously in 1952). Roberts manages to compound these earlier territoriologists into a fruitful and imaginative dialogue that carries them and us with him into an exploration of the marshland known as Lache Eyes, located in the outskirts of the village of Saltney, across Flintshire and Cheshire, in the UK. This way, the author invites us to consider the potential for an enlarged spatial anthropology capable of embracing what he calls the 'affective sensorium' of a territory.

The first five chapters of the volume, which we have introduced so far, deal with territorial formations and modes of territorialising that are deliberately quite disparate, set in different geographies and at different scales. We found this a convenient start, precisely to unsettle the regular geographical imagination of territories. The following six chapters, as will become apparent, are specifically engaged with the urban scale. Of course, such an urban dimension is itself quite heterogeneous, including as it does instances of public space ranging from local neighbourhoods to planetary urbanism. Yet, we believe the reader will easily understand why we have decided to arrange the chapters into this order.

In chapter six, Manfredo Manfredini proposes to interpret contemporary market-led urban renewal as a peculiar form of deterritorialisation. To do so, the author engages in an intense discussion with twentieth-century French philosophy, particularly the works of Lefebvre, Deleuze and Guattari, and Rancière. Seeking ways to expand the scope for an emancipatory and egalitarian approach to urbanism, Manfredini highlights how most mainstream interpretations of the French theoretical legacy are not radical enough in accounting for the dominant trends in urban restructuring. He identifies three such worrying developments, namely, the pre-eminence of top-down spatial production over the enactment of counter-spatialisations, the increased homogenisation of social-spatial assemblages against their spontaneous diversification, and the overemphasis on policed consensus as opposed to the manifestation of political disagreement. Reading through these tensions, Manfredini contends that deterritorialisation itself is not univocal, but can bring about either affirmative or, contrarily, 'overcoding' outcomes. On the basis of his studies in Auckland and Wellington, Aotearoa/New Zealand, he then identifies how the increase in overcoding deterritorialisation is enhanced by processes of mediatisation and financialisation of urban space. Particularly visible is the case of privately owned and privately designed retail spaces, where a series of public and civic functions are inscribed in a way that now includes, the author writes,

> instagrammably styled pedestrian squares and lanes artistically counter-pointed à la Camillo Sitte, segmented sets of transindividually subprofiled

> active lifestyle precincts eventfully curated à la Greg Richards and Robert Palmer, mediatised pacificatory cappuccino made-places à la Fred Kent, and various multiplatform and cross-identification cultural installations celebrating Richard Florida's 3Ts.

However, Manfredini also makes his point illustrating how these developments do not completely stop affirmative deterritorialisations from occurring, the latter coming about either as everyday spontaneous usages, or through more explicitly political movements.

Chapter seven is signed by Anke Schwarz and Monika Streule, who report from their fieldwork research in Mexico. In San Salvador Atenco, a municipality in the North-Western periphery of Mexico City, a social movement known as *Frente de Pueblos en Defensa de la Tierra* (FPDT) has developed and engaged in a decade-long mobilisation against the land expropriation carried out for the projected construction of a new airport and related large-scale real estate speculation (known as *Ciudad Futura* development – a project that also came to a halt in 2018). In 2006, the police committed an infamous bloodshed in Atenco, killing and raping the protesters and on top of that, fabricating false proofs to jail other innocents.[8] In 'Rendering territory (in)visible,' Schwarz and Streule document how urban struggles articulate different understandings of territorial existence. They highlight how the land conflict over the area opposes two fundamentally incompatible conceptions of land use: the public–private neoliberal model on the one hand, and the communal land stewardship known as *ejido*, practiced by the local *campesinos*. In their approach, situated at the intersection of human geography, sociocultural anthropology, architecture, planning and sociology, the authors bring in notable contributions from the perspective of Latin American Indigenous, Afrodescendant and feminist scholarship, also drawing inspiration from the Italian territorialist school that analyses territory as a palimpsest of temporally subsequent, stratified uses. All these approaches seem to converge towards a processual and relational understanding, where power dynamics appear as precipitated spatially in 'contested urban territories.' Schwarz's and Streule's chapter thus offers an apt illustration of how the visibility of territories can turn into a crucial stake in the public sphere of contentious politics: stories of voice and erasure, of repression, impunity and resistance, are materially encapsulated in the removal by the authorities of a mural painting that represented a symbolic reference for *Frente* movement – painting that, however, subsequently reappeared in various guises and different places, on different material supports.

With the following chapter, we move to Europe and we shift to the analysis of everyday territories. Mattias Kärrholm and Anna Petersson discuss in their chapter 'Territorialisation of the Grocery Shopper' a micro-territoriology of shopping in *Västra Hamnen* (Western Harbour), a newly developed district of

8 Relevant documentation updated to 2021 can be found here (in Spanish): https://www.albora.mx/la-lucha-no-tiene-tiempo/

Malmö explicitly designed for ecological sustainability. The stabilisation of a territory can proceed in different ways, but here Kärrholm and Petersson focus on the routes and the routines that progressively lead one to territorialise one's 'role' as grocery shopper. When considering even such an apparently mundane activity as going to shop, a number of dimensions must be attended, which are of interest to an area of study known as consumer mobility or 'consumer logistics.' The chapter, however, privileges an experiential vantage point, following a number of residents as they make, change, adapt and refine their shopping routines and decisions. In a scenario dominated by supermarkets, and where local groceries and delicacies do not survive for long, the choice range might initially appear slim, but is in fact quite subtle: where to go is weighted against factors such as the type of eco-friendly products available at what price, but also in terms of how many trips are needed to complete one's list, in terms of the complementarity between supermarket food and one's garden production, in terms of the location of recycling stations along the way, and so on. The authors thus show how ethical considerations mix with a number of additional variables, including the atmosphere of the neighbourhood and its shops (some parts of the district being still dusty, noisy and under redevelopment), the mobility infrastructures that are available (the district not being yet fully functionally connected to the rest of the city), and even meteorological qualities (some parts of the district being known for exceedingly strong winds, etc.). This shows how the territoriology of even a small and relatively historyless neighbourhood can be incredibly rich and complex. An interesting theoretical advancement provided by Kärrholm and Petersson concerns the notion of 'territorial role.' There is indeed a zone of indistinction between the two terms: if roles always have a territorial element to them, in the sense that they stabilise interactional expectations, on their turn territories are themselves always imbued with multiple roles, without which they would be unusable. Roles are not simply performed; they can also be emphasised, or 'intensified.' Here in particular, the authors relate territorial roles to a process of 'self-improvement as consumers,' which has also been described as an 'asceticism of consumption' – where asceticism must be understood not in terms of renouncement to consumption, but literally in terms of exercise and training.

Chapter nine advances a comparative perspective on Warsaw and Lisbon as concerns a peculiar territoriality, namely, the soundscape. Based on the assumption that 'sound can be a crucial medium for the expressive components of territories,' in their chapter, titled 'The territories of music in public space,' Cláudia Casquilho, Pedro Gonçalves, Caio Mourão, Paula Nunes and Daniel Paiva consider the case of music as an element in urban branding strategies. Music in the streets is often used to promote cosy and 'hip atmospheres,' yet it is not uncontroversial, and can at times even backfire, sparking conflicts between music promoters and local residents. The authors therefore set out to explore these controversies surrounding the territorialisation of music. To do so, they contrast two vignettes, the former from Poland – where the Warsaw municipality has 'equipped' a number of public benches located in its central district with loudspeakers playing Chopin. The latter is from Portugal – where a resident in a central Lisbon square engaged in a private 'sonic fight' against performers of street music stationed in the square where he lived, by playing loud salsa music out of a speaker so as to spoil their performance. The authors draw attention to the peculiar geographies of these sonic territorialities. The vignettes they report from their fieldwork indeed concern very specific urban places, contradistinguished by not only established cultural-historical meaning (such as Warsaw's 'Royal Route') but also peculiar (sometimes pleasant, sometimes less pleasant, as in Lisbon's Carmo Square quarrel) sensory atmospheres. Atmospheres, in turn, are themselves condensing around diverging interests, with the street musicians, but also restaurant managers, catering to the flow of tourists, and the resident in question staging an atmospheric disruption to air his complaints about a perceived lack of quiet in the zone. The authors suggest we consider sonic compositions of public spaces as 'transterritorial, in the sense that they emerge within the transient experience of multiple territories.' Music, sound and territory thus contribute to make each other, in immersive and affective ways – a fertile ground for further investigation.

We continue the analysis of small-scale urban territories with a chapter that, just like Kärrholm's and Petersson's, focuses on the everyday. The context, however, is manifestly different, so that a comparative perspective might become fruitful. The chapter contributed by Kristanti Dewi Paramita, reports from her study into how domestic territories are composed and managed in the context of an informal urban settlement in Jakarta known as Kampung Pulo. In Indonesia, similar *kampung* settlements are densely populated, mostly lower-class neighbourhoods comprising various degrees of makeshift buildings and a bustling public space. Following Richard Sennett, Paramita calls the residents' territorial assemblages 'passage territories,' to stress the multiple regions and settings that are being coordinated together. Indeed, the *kampung* residents deploy multiple territorial strategies to cope with a fragile environment subject to power cuts, period flooding, lack of basic municipal services and infrastructures, beside a number of additional sources of economic uncertainty. These informal and inventive territorial strategies are examined by Paramita in activities that comprise rearing children (where the extended family is involved), running business (most commonly food stalls), securing access to sanitation and waste disposal facilities, and the need to keep life going when the settlement is flooded and partly inaccessible. Paramita reveals how all these requirements scatter home territories across the space of the *kampung*, so as to manage the available resources in the best possible way. As can be seen, the practices of dwelling unfold not only at the location of home, but also along the entangled 'passages' through which the local residents connect their places of interest, ensuring their to-and-fro mobility.

In the final chapter, Paul Draus and Juliette Roddy offer a rich narrative and experiential account on conducting research in various Detroit neighbourhoods.

In 'Dodging rocks and baseball bats,' they recount their lived experiences over more than a decade spent analysing quite peculiar urban territories, including industrial, post-industrial, declined and depopulated neighbourhoods – those spaces that the classic Chicago school had once called 'zones in transition.' It is important to mention that the authors had an almost unique access to the field-work, in their role of, respectively, healthcare worker and social worker. Thanks to such a knowledgeable perspective of the social microterritorialities of the neighbourhoods, the reader is allowed a way into these places that goes beyond the usual stereotypes circulating about Detroit. Certainly, these neighbourhoods are affected by social and economic problems – including poverty, addiction, violence, and so on – but the complexity of territorial life cannot wholly be resolved through the social-problems lens. Moving in the uncertain space between official institutions (beginning, of course, with law enforcement agencies) and the informal life of a spread-out, low-density urban space with plenty of vacant structures, on-going informal business and redevelopment projects, Draus and Roddy highlight how the local population has evolved a number of tools to fill in the (huge) gaps in welfare provision and secure much-needed resources. Concurrently, the authors also develop a reflection into the ethics of conducting social research in contexts such as popular urban neighbourhoods undergoing rapid transition, where the lines between official and unofficial, legal and illegal, fair and unfair, respectful and disrespectful, are thin and not always easy to draw. In particular, they raise a concern that the researcher might end up occupying the awkward position of an urban 'tourist' heading off to places where residents already have enough problems on their own.

References

Agnew, J. (1994) The Territorial Trap: The Geographical Assumptions of International Relations Theory. *Review of International Political Economy* 1 (1): 53–80.

Braidotti, R. (2013) *The Posthuman*. Cambridge: Polity Press.

Brenner, N., and S. Elden (2009) Henri Lefebvre on State, Space, Territory. *International Political Sociology*, 3 (4): 353–377.

Brighenti A. M. and M. Kärrholm (2018) Beyond Rhythmanalysis: Towards a Territoriology of Rhythms and Melodies in Everyday Spatial Activities. *City, Territory and Architecture* 5 (1): 1–12.

Brighenti A. M. and M. Kärrholm (2020) *Animated Lands, Studies in Territoriology*. Lincoln: University of Nebraska Press.

Deleuze, G. and F. Guattari (1980) *Mille Plateaux*. Paris: Minuit.

Elden, S. (2005) Territorial Integrity and the War on Terror. *Environment and Planning A* 37 (12): 2083–2104.

Elden, S. (2006) The State of Territory under Globalization. In M. Margaroni and E. Yiannopoulou (Eds), *Metaphoricity and the Politics of Mobility*. Leyden: Brill, 47–66.

Forman, R. T. T. and J. Wu. 2016. Where to Put the Next Billion People. *Nature* 537: 6081–6011.

Gonin, A. (2018) Des pâturages en partage Territoires du pastoralisme en Afrique de l'Ouest. *Revue internationale des études du développement* 233: 21–40.

Haraway, D. J. (2016) *Staying with the Trouble, Making Kin in the Chthulucene*. Durham: Duke University Press.

Hardt, M. and T. Negri (2000) *Empire*. Cambridge, MA: Harvard University Press.

Jessop, B., N. Brenner and M. Jones. (2008) Theorizing Sociospatial Relations. *Environment and Planning D* 26 (3): 389–401.

Kärrholm, Mattias (2005) Territorial Complexity in Public Places. *Nordisk Arkitekturforskning* 18 (1): 99–114.

Latour, B. (2017) *Facing Gaia: Eight Lectures on the New Climatic Regime*. Cambridge: Polity Press.

Latour, B. (2018) *Down to Earth: Politics in the New Climatic Regime*. Cambridge: Polity Press.

Malm, A. and A. Hornborg (2014) The Geology of Mankind? A Critique of the Anthropocene Narrative. *The Anthropocene Review*, 1 (1): 62–69.

Puig de la Bellacasa, M. (2017) *Matters of Care, Speculative Ethics in more than Human Worlds*. Minneapolis: University of Minnesota Press.

Tsing, A. L. (2015) *The Mushroom at the End of the World*. New York: Princeton University Press.

Stengers, I. (2015) Accepting the Reality of Gaia: A Fundamental Shift? In C. Hamilton, F. Bonneuil and C. Bonneuil (Eds), *The Anthropocene and the Global Environmental Crisis: Rethinking Modernity in a new Epoch*. London: Routledge, 134–144.

Chapter 1

The State of Territory Under Globalization

Empire and the Politics of Reterritorialization

Stuart Elden

'Mais un jour, peut-être, le siècle sera deleuzien.'

(Foucault 1994: 76).

Michel Foucault's suggestion is often misconstrued. The usual translation, found in the *Language, Counter-Memory, Practice* collection, is 'perhaps one day, this century will be known as Deleuzian' (1977: 165). Unsurprisingly, it is regularly referenced in books on Gilles Deleuze (see, for example, Marks 1998: 79, Dumoncel 1999: 67), and indeed there was a special issue of the journal *SAQ* entitled 'A Deleuzian Century?' (Buchanan 1997).[1] But as James Faubion notes, following a lead from Paul Rabinow, the *double entendre* is neglected – *le siècle* can also mean the circle of courtiers, and the phrase can therefore be translated as 'some day, the in-crowd will be Deleuzian' (1998: xix, xxxix n. 30). We might be content with this, laughing gently at Foucault's prophetic irony. Deleuze himself certainly saw the suggestion as a joke, or at least as provocative (1995: 4, 88–89).[2] But there is yet more in this polysemantic phrase. *Le siècle*, especially in religious contexts, can mean the worldly life or the world as a whole, an exchange of a temporal marker for a spatial signifier.

Attempts to understand the world as Deleuzian have been widespread in recent years, with a range of studies taking up his concepts with alacrity. Of course, the 'his' obscures the way in which many of his most used concepts are those he developed in congress with Félix Guattari, in four important works. Indeed, in *What is Philosophy?* he and Guattari describe the task of the philosopher as formulating concepts (1994: 5) and, in his well-known interview with Foucault, Deleuze suggested that 'a theory is exactly like a box of tools… it must be useful. It must function' (Foucault 1977: 208). Does this mean that we should merely sit back and watch as the terms of schizoanalysis, hybridity,

1 That Dumoncel writes in French shows that this is not merely an issue of translation.
2 See also the comment made at the very beginning of *A Thousand Plateaus*: 'The two of us wrote *Anti-Oedipus* together. Since each of us was already several, there was already quite a crowd' (Deleuze and Guattari 1988: 3).

DOI: 10.4324/9781003196365-2

smooth and striated space, the molar and the molecular, the rhizome, the refrain and others are paraded for the entertainment and edification of the multitude? Conceptual policing might seem to go against the very nature of the Deleuzian enterprise.

Despite this, it seems to me to be instructive to slow down, to hesitate, to read and to think, before such an appropriation. That was certainly the way that Deleuze approached his thinkers in studies of, among others, Nietzsche, Spinoza and Leibniz. Here, I am particularly concerned with thinking about the notion of deterritorialization, developed in some of the collaborative works with Guattari. This term has been widely used in recent literature on globalization (for a critique see Elden 2005), but there it is usually divorced from its conceptual partner of reterritorialization. What is interesting about these terms in Deleuze and Guattari is the way they function in both a linguistic medium and in terms of organisms and their movement. Metaphoricity and mobility are therefore intertwined in important and complicated ways. Perhaps the most important recent study utilizing these terms has been Michael Hardt and Antonio Negri's *Empire*, where sometimes they are used together and at times separately. The separation raises a number of problems, but in utilizing and developing these terms in a much more explicitly political way, they make space for potential utilizations. Taking this forward, the conclusion of the essay stresses not the politics of deterritorialization, but the politics of reterritorialization. It suggests we can see this at play in recent events, but that before we speak too freely of either deterritorialization or reterritorialization we need to think much more carefully about territory itself, conceptually, historically and politically.

Deterritorialization/Reterritorialization

There are a number of ways in which these terms are used in the work of Deleuze and Guattari. As Ronald Bogue has usefully cautioned, the concept of *territory* is discussed 'in its narrow ethological sense in *Thousand Plateaus*,' but 'is inseparable from the general notions of territorialization, reterritorialization and deterritorialization, which play through their thought in a wide range of contexts' (2002: 114). These contexts have been helpfully discussed in some of Bogue's own works, but in the wider literature they can often seem to be largely run into each other. Bogue notes that the first use of the terms is in 1966, in Guattari's work on group psychology (Guattari 1972, Bogue 1997: 466). As Holland has also noted, the use of deterritorialization/reterritorialization 'derive from Lacanian usage' (1996: 241).[3] Territorialization, in Lacan, describes the way in which parental care structures and organizes the child's body, where feeding and cleaning focus behavior to specific zones or sites of the body (the mouth, the genitals, the anus, etc.). As Holland notes, in Deleuze and Guattari,

3 We should remember that Guattari was trained by Lacan.

deterritorialization shows how this centering on particular sites can be made elsewhere. Holland gives the examples of movement from the mother's breast or the Oedipal complex (1996: 241–42; see also 1991).

The point though, for both Bogue and Holland, is that this is not just a move in the psychological register, but also one in the social, where the terms can describe something going on within capitalism, 'the disconnection and reconnection of working bodies and environments – for example, the disconnection of peasants from grazing land by the Enclosures Acts in England, and their reterritorialization onto textile looms as wage-labor in the nascent garment industry' (Holland 1996: 242). For Bogue, the aim of Guattari's early work 'is to extend to the domain of the social Lacan's essentially psychological use of "territorialization",' a process which is continued in *Anti-Oedipus*, when 'deterritorialization' and 'reterritorialization' 'figure prominently in tandem with the concepts of "decoding" and "recoding"' (1997: 466). In *Anti-Oedipus* Deleuze and Guattari discuss different ways in which the world has been configured, as primitive-territorial, barbarian-despotic, civilized-capitalist (1984; see Marks 1998: 95). What is significant about the capitalist machine is that it 'seeks to multiply deterritorialised schizophrenic flows, never reaching a limit' (Marks 1998: 96). For Marks, following Lyotard (1972), 'Marx was the first to locate the fluidity and deterritorialisation which is axiomatic of capitalism,' but it is Deleuze and Guattari who are able to reveal this (Marks 1998: 97). As Marx and Engels famously proclaimed, 'all that is solid melts into air' (1973a: 70).

But although the term deterritorialization is found in places of *Anti-Oedipus*, it is in the book on Kafka (1986, originally 1975) that it takes on a central role. Here Kafka's writings in German are seen as disruptive because of his position outside of Germany itself, as a Czech Jew. Kafka himself, in a diary entry from Christmas Day 1911, discusses these issues: the springboard for the reflections of Deleuze and Guattari (see Kafka 1964: 148–153; Bogue 2002: 114–115). Other studies that Deleuze in particular undertook emphasized these disruptive tendencies in writers such as Marcel Proust, Jack Kerouac, Samuel Beckett, Herman Melville and Henry Miller (1993, Deleuze and Parnet 1987; see also Goodchild 1996: 55, Bryden 2002, Buchanan and Marks 2000). Some of Deleuze's work on Nietzsche functions in a similar way. Indeed here, in a piece written a couple of years before the book on Kafka, he explicitly relates the two: 'The only parallel I can find here is with Kafka, in what he does to German, working with the language of Prague Jewry: he constructs a battering ram out of German and turns it against itself' (1985: 143; see Marks 1998: 58–59).

This is a distinct understanding of the concept of deterritorialization, based on the notion of a minor literature (1986: 16–17; see also Deleuze and Guattari 1988: 97–98, 104–105). The notion of minor literature, which rather than coming from a minor language is that which "a minority constructs within a major language" (1986: 17), has been developed in recent work in the areas of sociology, literary and cultural studies (for example Appadurai 1996, Papastergiadis 2000). For Papastergiadis, for example, 'the concept of deterritorialization has been a useful mode of understanding the fissures within language and cultural identity' (118). As he notes,

> the cultural dynamic of deterritorialization has decoupled previous links between space, stability and reproduction; it has situated the notion of community in multiple locations; it has split loyalties and fractured the practices that secure understanding and knowledge within the family and social unit.
>
> (117)

It is essential to note that these are quite narrow understandings, interesting in their own right, but limited to specific issues. Bogue notes it is only really in '1837: Of the Refrain' in *A Thousand Plateaus* that Deleuze and Guattari discuss 'territory *per se*, engaging the subject via an analysis of music's relation to animal ethology' (2002: 125; see also 1997: 466). Bogue then leads us through a range of discussions of animal territoriality, touching on the work of Henry Eliot Howard, Bernard Altum, J. S. Huxley, Konrad Lorenz, Jacob von Uexküll, and Raymond Ruyer among others, spending most time on the last two, because of their importance to Deleuze and Guattari (Bogue 1997: 466–475). It is worth citing Bogue at length here:

> In essence, what Ruyer is describing at such length are biological instances of de/reterritorialization, of the detachment or unfixing of elements and their reorganisation within new assemblages. Ruyer's work, then, supports Deleuze and Guattari's contention that a *territory*, in the biologic sense of the term, is created through the general process of *deterritorialization*, whereby milieu components are detached and given greater autonomy, and *reterritorialization*, through which those components acquire new functions within the newly created territory.
>
> (1997: 475)

In this we can stress one key thing: the continual process of de- and reterritorialization. In other words, the reconfiguration of spatial relations rather than their end. This is often missed: deterritorialization is part of a process. We find this insisted upon in several places in *A Thousand Plateaus*. They are 'always connected, caught up in one another,' deterritorialization 'always occurs in relation to a complementary reterritorialization' (1988: 10, 54; see also 181, 508; 1994: 67–68). Indeed, they make this point more strongly when they stress the territoriality that is the condition for the change: 'we must therefore take a number of factors into consideration: relative territorialities, their respective deterritorializations, and their correlative reterritorializations' (1988: 303; see also 203). In this we see that deterritorialization, in spite of its name, does not mean the end of the importance of territory. Indeed, far from it, as territory is both its condition of possibility and, in some newly configured form, its necessary outcome.

In this light, it is worth turning our attention to Deleuze and Guattari's discussion of the nomad in *A Thousand Plateaus*. Contrary to visions of the nomad as without territory, they emphasize how nomads too follow 'customary paths... from one point to another,' noting the water, dwelling and assembly points. But these points are reached only in order to be left behind, they are stages on a life's way, 'strictly subordinated to the paths they determine, the reverse of what happens with the sedentary.' This is in distinction to the migrant, 'for the migrant goes principally from one point to another, even if the second point is uncertain, unforeseen or not well localized' (1988: 380). Deleuze and Guattari make a distinction here between a closed space and an open one. In the first, land is parceled out, divided between people; in the second, people are distributed in space. This leads them to suggest the difference between these understandings of space, a distinction between striated and smooth space (1988: 380–81, 474ff).

The migrant moves in striated space, space that is divided and limited – 'walls, enclosures, and roads between enclosures.' Every deterritorialization is partnered by a reterritorialization (1988: 381). Agriculture therefore is a form of both, with land distributed between people (rather than the other way round), and, for Deleuze and Guattari, 'earth, unlike other elements, forms the basis of a striation, proceeding by geometry, symmetry, and comparison' (1988: 441). For the nomad, '

> there is no reterritorialization *afterward* as with the migrant, or upon *something else* as with the sedentary,' instead, 'it is deterritorialization that constitutes the relation to the earth, to such a degree that the nomad reterritorializes on deterritorialization itself. It is the earth that deterritorializes itself, in a way that provides the nomad with a territory.'
>
> (1988: 381)

Even here, with the stress on the deterritorialization, there is an insistence on the importance of reterritorialization. The nomad has a territory, but it is a territory in the process of making and remaking, one in which they are always changing, without a final resting point. The distinction between smooth and striated space is an important one, and relatively well known. What is sometimes neglected is the stress they make 'that the two spaces in fact exist only in mixture'. Despite the important qualification that 'the de facto mixes do not preclude a de jure, or abstract, distinction between the two spaces' (1988: 475), they note that 'smooth space is continually being translated, transversed into a striated space; striated space is constantly being reversed, returned to a smooth space' (1988: 474). This point seems to be crucial in actually comprehending the ways in which contemporary events are played out in space, and the way in which the spaces of Empire operate. It is a point to which I will return.

In terms of the project here, the other issue is the wide historical scope of the book. It is no surprise that the various plateaus all carry datings, given the range of examples given. From Kleisthenes' reforms in ancient Athens, through the Roman Empire and the Crusades, to the discovery of the New World, we see that deterritorialization and reterritorialization (in Deleuze and Guattari's terms) are not a new phenomenon. Rather, the continual remaking and reshaping of spatial relations may take on, indeed must take on, different forms in different times and places, but this is not a vision of a static world of fixed territories suddenly thrown into flux, as it is in much of the literature on deterritorialization. Here I would sound a note of caution, suggesting that, though undoubtedly spatial relations and territorial configurations have been continually under a process of review, this does not mean that earlier periods had anything like a sense of 'space' or 'territory.' There is a weak version of this argument – that suggests that they had different senses of these, and other terms – and a strong version – which argues that they did not have senses of them at all (on Kleisthenes in this context, see Elden 2003a).

There are other uses of these terms in Deleuze and Guattari, indeed in *What is Philosophy?* thinking itself is a form of deterritorialization (1994; see Patton 1996: 9), but this is hopefully a useful enough survey to take forward (see also Colebrook 2004). The terms emerge from an engagement with Lacan, and function as a way of moving from the psychological to the social sphere; they are used to analyze minor literatures and the potential for disruption; they re-emerge through engagement with ethology and ideas of nomads and migrants. For Paul Patton, the political implications are great: 'Minority provides an element capable of deterritorialising the dominant social codes. Conversely, it is the process of deterritorialisation which constitutes the essence of revolutionary politics for Deleuze and Guattari' (2000: 7). For Philip Goodchild, who defines deterritorialization as 'leaving home and travelling in other parts,' and reterritorialization as 'making a new dwelling place' (1996: 218–219), they are, despite the title of his book, largely apolitical. In his view, issues around desire are more important. Indeed, following the suggestions in *What is Philosophy?*, he suggests that 'Deleuze and Guattari's concepts are entirely deterritorialized: they have no meaning, and only express a kind of nonsense – "deterritorialized" means "outlandish"' (1996: 56; citing Deleuze 1993: 93).

Empire, Sovereignty and Territory

One of the most interesting adaptations of these ideas is found in Michael Hardt and Antonio Negri's *Empire*. As they state in an early note, 'two interdisciplinary texts served as models for us throughout the writing of this book: Marx's *Capital* and Deleuze and Guattari's *A Thousand Plateaus*' (2000: 415 n. 4). But this is not an idle claim, Hardt having written one of the best introductions to Deleuze's thought (1993; see also Negri 1995) and Negri having corresponded and written with both Deleuze and Guattari (Deleuze 1995, Negri 1989, Guattari and Negri 1990). Equally, a few years before, Negri argued that he had found in *A Thousand Plateaus* 'the fundamental elements of the renewal of historical materialism, in function of the new dimensions of capitalist development' (1995: 104, cited in Patton 2000: 6; see also Negri 1989: 95 n.). He also admitted that his own work on Spinoza would have been impossible without Deleuze's (1991: 267, cited in Patton, 2000: 143 n. 1).

Empire is perhaps the philosophically most sophisticated attempt to come to terms with the new world order that has partnered "an irresistible and irreversible globalization of economic and cultural exchanges" (2000: xi). At its root it is a reformulation of understandings of sovereignty, with a recognition that models of sovereignty developed in the early modern period – Hobbes, for example – are no longer valid. There is a "new form of sovereignty," and it is Empire that is the political subject that "effectively regulates these global exchanges." Instead of the sovereignty of nation-states, we now have sovereignty of the world. This is important, because it underlines the way in which Hardt and Negri dismiss claims that sovereignty itself has declined (2000: xi). It is a new *logic* of rule that is under investigation here. That rule might be exercised in different ways, in different places, and by a range of bodies, but the underlying "single logic of rule" is consistent (2000: xii).

Hardt and Negri claim that the concept of sovereignty, in its modern sense, evolved in tandem with that of modernity. It was tied to both conflict within Europe and the colonial project, where it was formulated through Europe's relation to its outside. It was also tied to developments in modern science (2000: 70). Elsewhere I have discussed how sovereignty, political theory and scientific practices come together particularly in the seventeenth century, with the Thirty Years War and the English Civil War showing the problems of divided rule and overlapping territoriality, with theoretical solutions in Hobbes and Leibniz, respectively. While Hobbes' solution to the question of sovereignty is to concentrate it in one place, unlimited and undivided; Leibniz proposes a distinction between sovereignty and majesty, with the Emperor having the latter, meaning the power to command obedience and loyalty, and the princes of the Empire have sovereignty, tied explicitly to territory (Leibniz 1969: VI, 347; for a discussion, see Elden 2005).

Hardt and Negri draw upon Weber and Foucault to theorize the emergence of modern sovereignty, but, contra Foucault, suggest that instead of a development from sovereignty to governmentality there is 'a passage *within* the notion of sovereignty' (2000: 88). Citing the famous principle from the 1555 Diet of Augsburg they argue that 'cuius regio, eius religio' means that 'religion had to be subordinated to the territorial control of the sovereign' (2000: 94). The real issue here though is in danger of being missed in the speed of their progress.[4] Augsburg laid down a principle that the territorial princes in the Holy Roman Empire had religious freedom, that they could fix the religion of their subjects. This was only partly upheld at Westphalia a hundred years later,

4 Tellingly, when they discuss this in *Multitude* (2004: 16) they entirely neglect the spatial content.

which proclaimed the 'free exercise of territorial right' to the princes. In other words, rather than sovereignty being exercised over territory and then over religion, it is territory that makes the sovereign. Sovereignty, in this weak sense that is the first modern version of the term, is 'territorial superiority,' in distinction to the majesty proposed by Bodin and claimed by the Emperor. Hobbes' absolute version proposed just a few years after Westphalia should not blind us to the way in which it was Leibniz's formulation that was a more accurate reflection of the situation at the time.

Nevertheless, Hardt and Negri recognize that the model of sovereignty in the imperial period was tied to boundaries, strictly defined and demarcated territories, with the parceling up of the world into discrete portions. 'Wherever modern sovereignty took root, it constructed a Leviathan that overarched its social domain and imposed hierarchical territorial boundaries, both to police the purity of its own identity and to exclude all that was other' (2000: xii). Modern sovereignty is framed in terms of its territory and its relation to an outside (2000: 187); 'the spiritual identity of the nation rather than the divine body of the king now posed the territory and population as an ideal abstraction' (2000: 95). In contrast, they argue that

> Empire establishes no territorial centre of power and does not rely on fixed boundaries or barriers. It is a *decentred* and *deterritorializing* apparatus of rule that progressively incorporates the entire global realm within its open, expanding frontiers. Empire manages hybrid identities, flexible hierarchies, and plural exchanges through modulating networks of command... Capital seems to be faced with a smooth world – or really, a world defined by new and complex regimes of differentiation and homogenisation, deterritorialization and reterritorialization.
>
> (2000: xii–xiii)

There is obviously much here that derives from and parallels the ideas of Deleuze and Guattari. Perhaps even more so, when they suggest that Empire is a concept not a metaphor (2000: xiii), and that the book's aim is to be 'a general theoretical framework and a toolbox of concepts' (2000: xvi).

However, in places they can seem to be proposing an understanding of the world as deterritorialized alone, without the concomitant process of remaking, of reterritorialization.[5] In part this is because, like many other theorists of globalization, they do not seem to have a fully worked through notion of what territory itself might be. The best I can find, from Negri alone in an earlier work, is that 'in advanced capitalism *territory* becomes the framework of productive potential; that is, it becomes the spatial ontology of the productive society' (1989: 90). But in *Empire*, for example, we find a discussion of the 'deterritorializing capacities of

5 On this criticism of *Empire*, see Painter 2003; more generally Minca 2003; Balakrishnan 2003.

communication,' bringing about both the 'dissolution of territorial and/or national sovereignty,' but also 'the very possibility of linking an order to a space' (2000: 346–47). They recognize the analysis hits the buffers here: 'At this point we cannot conceive of this relationship except in *another space*, an elsewhere that cannot in principle be contained in the articulation of sovereign acts,' but they do claim that 'the space of communication is completely deterritorialized' (2000: 347). They attempt to justify this by suggesting that it does not fit the pattern of space analyzed in 'terms of the monopoly of physical force and the definition of monetary measure' (2000: 347), but this perhaps simply reveals the problem of that very definition.

Elsewhere we find the suggestion that the 'deployments of the imperial machine are defined by a whole series of new characteristics, such as the unbounded terrain of its activities' (2000: 35). They also argue that 'perhaps the fundamental characteristic of imperial sovereignty is that *its space is always open*' (2000: 167). While they are right in noting that political sovereignty in the modern period 'conceived space as bounded, and its boundaries were always policed by the sovereign administration' (2000: 167), this seems to me to get things somewhat misplaced. Space was understood in such a way in the modern period as to allow it to be bounded, which then allowed it to be policed. Space was conceived as something extended in three dimensions, qualitatively measurable and thereby amenable to partition, regulation and order. The sense of 'space', of *spatium*, that emerges in the late medieval period and which finds its most clearly worked through argument in Descartes, is not *necessarily* something that is bounded and divided politically into separate sovereign entities. But this sense of space is a necessary *condition* for such a political system: it makes it possible.

In contrast, rather than the strict differentiation of an earlier time, 'the world market both homogenizes and differentiates territories, rewriting the geography of the globe' (2000: 310). It is clear that this phrase rests on the inclusive logic of 'both… and….' New changes both homogenize *and* differentiate. If the homogenization is a process of deterritorialization, the differentiation and indeed the homogenization itself evoke a passage of reterritorialization. This may not be what we commonly understand by territory, but the spatial context is clear. We find this most strikingly illustrated in a central passage:

> The striated space of modernity constructed *places* that were continually engaged in and founded on a dialectical play with their outsides. The space of imperial sovereignty, in contrast, is smooth. It might appear to be free of the binary divisions or striation of modern boundaries, but really it is crisscrossed by so many fault lines that it only appears as a continuous, uniform space. In this sense, the clearly defined crisis of modernity gives way to an omni-crisis in the imperial world. In this smooth space of Empire, there is no *place* of power – it is both everywhere and nowhere. Empire is an *ou-topia*, or really a *non-place*.
>
> (2000: 190; see 2004: 101–102)

There is much going on here, and its conceptual prevarication can easily lead us to misconstrue its purpose. There is a danger that striated and smooth space are looked at as polar opposites, and that we are supposedly seeing the passage from one to the other. For here, even if smooth space only *appears* to be free of striation, it is still being conceived in such a way that it is different from, and seen in opposition to, striated space in the strict sense. While striated space is scored, chamfered, grooved, channeled and divided into shapes of various sizes, the smooth space of Empire is crisscrossed with lines, overlapping and jumbled, points in a web of connections. Politically, we have the nation-state map of ordered Europe, progressively eradicating the overlapping sovereignties of medievalism, redistributing land to remove almost all the enclaves and exclaves, in contrast to the globalized world of the third millennium, a world of far flung points connected in a network society, nodes in a system. But as Sparke puts it,

> Hardt and Negri fail to distinguish between the globalist enframing of smooth space and the much more messy, uneven and asymmetrical political-economic geography of globalization that the vision of a decentred and deterritorialized globe serves simultaneously to obscure and enable.
> (2003: 385)

In other words, there may be a conceptual division within globalization, rather than a passage from a prior mode of spatial ordering. Indeed, it seems to me to make more sense to think of the two spaces as overlapping, the smooth space of Empire imposed over the striated spaces of modernity, the nation-states still attempting to cling to their sovereignty and territorial integrity in an age of globalizing markets and culture and emergent global modes of governance. The unevenness and asymmetry show the messiness, the incomplete, the striation of the smooth. In other words, deterritorialization partnered with reterritorialization.

A Politics of Reterritorialization

I am not convinced that Deleuze and Guattari's understandings of de- and reterritorialization, important and interesting though they are, are the most useful ways of understanding what is happening at the moment. In particular, I think that there is a danger of using ethological understandings of territoriality as a basis for understanding territory. In *A Thousand Plateaus* Deleuze and Guattari analyze how birdsong is used to mark a territory, broadening this into a discussion of how the refrain functions as a 'territorial assemblage [*agencement*]'. What this means is whatever other functions it has, 'it always carries earth with it; it has a land (sometimes a spiritual land) as its concomitant' (1988: 312, see also 326–327). Earth [*terre*] and territory [*territoire*] are not the same, but as they describe it, earth 'is the intense point at the deepest level of the territory or is projected outside it like a focal point, where all the forces draw together in close embrace' (1988: 338–339). Territory 'is the product of a territorialization of milieus and rhythms' (1988: 314), and they give examples of birds and fishes, rabbits and monkeys, in the process drawing upon a wide range of ethological literature (see also 1994: 67). My concern is that not only is there a latent vitalism here, despite the critique of some of this literature, notably Konrad Lorenz's work on aggression (1966),[6] but that in this understanding all periods of human behavior have exhibited some sense of territoriality. It seems to me that territory is something rather more historical and limited. In other works I have tried to develop an understanding of space (as opposed to place) as both a historical development and one centrally tied to understandings of calculation, in particular a new mode of geometry that emerges from late scholasticism and finds its central exponent in Descartes (2001a, 2001b, 2003b, 2005; see also Casey 1997; Malpas 2003). Territory is, I think, the political corollary of the notion of space – much more about calculation than boundedness; boundaries being a consequence of, and made possible by, 'space' and the emergence of new techniques in cartography and surveying.

But even if we are to use Deleuze and Guattari as a tool, it seems important to see the push–pull, almost dialectical, balance of de- and reterritorialization. As Deleuze and Guattari insistently argue, every deterritorialization is partnered by a reterritorialization; striated and smooth space can theoretically be dis-associated, but are practically continually entwined. To the present, such a dialectical understanding of Deleuze and Guattari's territorial politics remains underdeveloped. In one of the most interesting discussions of the politics of Deleuze's work, Patton suggests that 'Deleuze and Guattari's mature political philosophy might be regarded as a politics of deterritorialisation' (2000: 136).

> The concept of deterritorialisation implies a contrast between 'earth' and 'territory' (*terre* and *territoire*) understood as the two fundamental dimensions of nature. Territory is in the first instance territorialised earth, but it produces its own movements of deterritorialisation, while conversely the earth gives rise to processes of reterritorialisation and the constitution of new territories. Stable identities or territories are therefore secondary formulations upon the mobile earth. Deleuze and Guattari describe a world in which the overriding tendency is deterritorialisation.
>
> (2000: 9)

By contrast, I want to argue that perhaps in the current climate, as we try to come to terms with both *Empire* and Empire, it is rather a politics of reterritorialization that we need to think about and articulate. How is the globe being reconfigured, remade, re-divided?

David Harvey's recent book *The New Imperialism*, a book that explicitly understands itself as operating in the wake of *Empire*, makes a persuasive

6 This would not have concerned Deleuze. See his suggestion that 'everything I've written is vitalistic, at least I hope it is' (1990: 5; 1995: 143, cited in Smith 1998: xiii).

distinction between two contrasting elements within capitalist imperialism: its fundamental basis in state politics and the flow of capital between and beyond such strict territorial boundaries. This he calls the logic of territory and the logic of capital (2003: 26, 33). Trading upon his earlier writings (for example 1999, 2001), Harvey discusses the strains between these two logics. For example, the endless accumulation of capital creates tensions with the territorial logic because of a need to 'create a parallel accumulation of political/military power' (2003: 183). The boundaries of the state are necessarily exceeded by the capitalist demand for bigger and better markets, a tendency Marx perceptively noted in the *Grundrisse*: 'capitalism by its nature drives beyond every spatial barrier... to conquer the whole world for its market' (1973b: 524, 539). Political demands, especially when the state takes on the role of protecting and promoting the internal economy on the world stage, what Lefebvre called the state mode of production (1976–78; see Elden 2004: 222–226, 231–335), may require military solutions.

Harvey is certainly on the right track when he suggests that 'imperialism cannot be understood, therefore, without first grappling with the theory of the capitalist state in all its diversity' (2003: 183), but this must be understood to include the state's territorial foundation. By this I mean more than a simple cataloguing of its material base, but a deeper understanding of territory itself. Indeed, the recent events in Afghanistan and Iraq have shown the way in which it became easier for the US to fight a territorially identifiable foe rather than the Al-Qaeda 'network of networks.'[7] A deterritorialized challenge was reterritorialized, situated by the US government, forced onto a geographically located base. Baghdad could be found and targeted and Saddam located more easily than a dispersed and splintered organization. Harvey identifies this clearly when he suggests that 'with most of the American public uncaring and uninformed about almost anything geographical, it proved fairly easy to parlay the hunt for terrorists into a campaign to hunt down and remove Saddam' (2003: 15; see Leaman 2004). In a quote variously attributed to Ambrose Bierce or Paul Rodriguez, war is supposedly 'God's way of teaching Americans geography.' Reversing Marx, this is comedy replayed as tragedy (1973c: 146).

But the territorial aspects of the war on terror go beyond these straight-forward, if important, geographies.[8] One of the key issues is the way the term "territorial integrity" is being used. Territorial integrity is a term with two interlinked and usually compatible meanings. The first is that states should not seek to promote border changes or secessionist movements within other states. This also applies to attempts to seize territory by force. The second meaning is the standard idea that

7 I owe this phrase to Burke 2004: 14.

8 There is a key question, raised by Meiksins Wood, as to whether the thesis of *Empire* can 'accommodate the military actions of an imperial nation-state, and least of all the "democratic" U.S.A.?' (2003: 71). Hardt and Negri's answer can be found in 2004, the first part of which is entitled 'War,' although it seems to require quite a lot of conceptual back-pedalling to do so.

within its own borders, within its territory, a state is sovereign. Territorial integrity in this sense can be found enshrined in the UN Founding Charter:

> All Members shall refrain in their international relations from the threat or use of force against the territorial integrity or political independence of any state, or in any other manner inconsistent with the Purposes of the United Nations.
>
> (Charter of the United Nations, Chapter 1: Purposes and Principles, Article 2 Paragraph 4)

It is also found in numerous Security Council Resolutions, and in the constitutions of several countries. States are supposed to recognize the equal legal standing of other states, and therefore respect their sovereignty within the limits of their boundaries.

In recent years though, this notion of non-intervention in the internal affairs of other states has come under scrutiny. Tony Blair was one of the first to make this assumption problematic, notably in a speech in Chicago in April 1999, where he called for a 'new doctrine of international community.' Under this doctrine intervention could be justified, not on the basis of 'any territorial ambitions but on values' (1999). At the time this was a justification of the actions in Kosovo, but was used soon after to legitimize British involvement in Sierra Leone. Since the war on terror commenced, however, several other examples have been given. One of the most striking is that given by Richard Haass, Director of Policy at the US State Department, in April 2002:

> Sovereignty entails obligations. One is not to massacre your own people. Another is not to support terrorism in any way. If a government fails to meet these obligations, then it forfeits some of the normal advantages of sovereignty, including the right to be left alone inside your own territory. Other governments, including the United States, gain the right to intervene. In the case of terrorism, this can even lead to a right of preventive, or peremptory, self-defense. You essentially can act in anticipation if you have grounds to think it's a question of when, and not if, you're going to be attacked.
>
> (Lemann 2002)

Blair too, has warmed to this theme:

> So, for me, before September 11th, I was already reaching for a different philosophy in international relations from a traditional one that has held sway since the treaty of Westphalia in 1648; namely that a country's internal affairs are for it and you don't interfere unless it threatens you, or breaches a treaty, or triggers an obligation of alliance…
>
> The best defence of our security lies in the spread of our values…

> But we cannot advance these values except within a framework that recognises their universality. If it is a global threat, it needs a global response, based on global rules.
>
> (2004a)

Blair has similarly called for revisions to the UN charter that allow this changed position (2004b).

While there are clearly numerous problems with such positions, not least the Euro-centric projection of universal values, it is notable that the notion of 'territorial integrity' in the other sense is continually stressed by Blair and others. In fact, Blair has usually gone out of his way to underline the importance of the territorial integrity of just about everywhere he has later bombed. Security Council resolutions stressed the territorial integrity of Yugoslavia, even as their government complained to the UN that it was being violated; it has similarly been underlined for Sierra Leone and Afghanistan, and even, recently, for Sudan. Challenges to it have been identified as terrorism: China has used the notion to protest against Muslim separatists in Xinjiang province calling for a separate East Turkestan; Russia has stressed its importance in relation to Chechnya; and India has long insisted on it in relation to Kashmir. The US has generally gone along with these recodings. As I write these lines the outcome of the Ukraine election is still in doubt, and worries about the viability of that country's unity are being voiced. Most notably, the term has been insisted upon in relation to Iraq. Despite the artificial construction of a country out of three provinces of the Ottoman Empire – Mosul, Baghdad, Basra – under British mandate following World War One, the most important territorial issue in Iraq can now not even be mentioned. Bush, Blair and Aznar stressed that they envisaged 'a unified Iraq with its territorial integrity respected' as an outcome of the war (2003), and subsequent UN resolutions and the express wishes of several of Iraq's neighbors have supported this. Only dissident voices such as Naqishbendi in *The Kurdistan Observer* (2004), have suggested that the maintenance of the arbitrary unity is the root of the problem, proposing three states – Kurdish, Sunni, Shiite from north to south – with the Kurds and Shiites providing some kind of financial recompense to make up for the uneven distribution of oil reserves.

While dominant powers are therefore able to suggest that the precepts of international law should be revised in accordance to their values, it seems that the other side of the coin is that secessionist movements, that is those who want to challenge any notions of territorial integrity, are increasingly being recoded as terrorists. This can be profitably related to Weber's famous definition of the state: 'The state is that human community, which within a certain area or territory [*Gebietes*] – this "area" belongs to the feature – has a (successful) monopoly of legitimate physical violence' (1971: 510–511). The point here is not just that standard discussion of the state neglects the territorial aspect; nor that this definition renders any use of violence by non-state actors necessarily illegitimate; but that any potential redrawing of the borders of a state limits the extent of the state's ability to use violence, and is therefore, in itself, necessarily violent and illegitimate. As Blair noted in 2002, 'today boundaries are virtually fixed. Governments and people know that any territorial ambition threatens stability, and instability threatens prosperity.'

This explicit linking of territorial issues, stability and prosperity is revealing. It is a concern which is important in the various strategies that the US, notably, has taken in recent years to safeguard its interests. Of the many strategies one is particularly worth noting, because it makes the territorial issues implicit in globalization explicit. This is the 'Pentagon's New Map', a map of a world where 'disconnection defines danger' (Barnett 2003, 2004).

Barnett's map shows a world with a 'functioning core' and a 'non-integrating gap,' that is, those countries which share American values and can be seen as part of a globalized world, and those which do not. The map is represented in two ways. One is a picture of the globe in two halves, showing its physical geography, but with a dark 'stain' spreading over the center, across the equator and running north and south to various degrees. On the other map 'major US military operations 1990–2003,' these 'excluding humanitarian operations,' are plotted. These operations are subdivided into combat; show of force, contingent positioning, reconnaissance; evacuation, security; and peacekeeping (see 2004: 144–145). A line snakes around these plotted areas, demarcating the 'non-integrating gap,' a lasso thrown around the problem places, the hole in the global ozone layer. This gap is a contiguous area, including Central and South America, with the exception of Brazil, Argentina, Uruguay and Chile; Africa (except for South Africa); the Middle East and the Balkans; the Central Asian Republics of the former USSR; South-East Asia, Indonesia and the Philippines. There are but a few exceptions to the inclusion of all the places the US military has been involved since the end of the Cold War, notably North Korea (2004: 149). For Susan Roberts, Anna Secor and Matthew Sparke, 'the map is both that which is to be explained and the explanation itself, descriptive of the recent past and predictive of future action' (890; see Barnett 2004: 153). These authors usefully discuss how the 'common neoliberal imagined geography of the globe as a smooth, de-centred, borderless, level playing field' is seemingly in tension with this model of the world as divided and orientated around a new US hegemony, what we might perceive as striated and scarred. For them, following Thomas Friedmann (1999: 373), the tension is implicit in the neoliberal project; the US as the hidden fist that enables the hidden hand of the economy (894). Barnett talks of shrinking the gap, effectively tightening the noose around the non-globalized world. What is significant is that the map operates with no outside: the gap is within the core.

Conclusion

What these and other examples show is the concomitant reterritorialization that partners the deterritorialization. New geographies, maps and territorial configurations are emerging. If John Locke founded his seventeenth century argument for property accumulation on the basis that 'in the beginning all the World was *America*' (1988: II §49), perhaps today we are seeing an attempt to turn the clock back. Indeed, Barnett's solution to the global malaise is 'more Locke' (2004: 166). Although Hardt and Negri are careful to argue against seeing Empire as an American venture, the organization Project for the New American Century, set up during the Clinton years by a number of prominent conservatives, including Jeb Bush, Dick Cheney, Francis Fukuyama, Donald Rumsfeld, Dan Quayle, and Paul Wolfowitz seems determined to mould it in its own image. In its founding Statement of Principles it calls for 'a Reaganite policy of military strength and moral clarity,' which although it 'may not be fashionable today… is necessary if the United States is to build on the successes of this past century and to ensure our security and our greatness in the next' (1997). They subsequently laid out the military program required for this new century in a major report (2000), which has clearly influenced The National Security Strategy of the United States of America (The White House 2002).

If the century is indeed defined in this way, the world will be reshaped. This shift is worth stressing: a persuasive point made by Neil Smith is that Henry Luce's 1941 editorial for *Life* magazine, 'The American Century,' masks its territorial, imperial ambitions through a temporal aspiration (Smith 2003: 18–20). As Harvey notes, PNAC 'deliberately repeats, therefore, all the evasions that Smith exposes in Luce's presentation' (Harvey 2003: 191).

Perhaps then, in the current global climate (and however loosely we define ourselves as a crowd of followers of such thought as Deleuze and Guattari's), we need both to articulate a response to such geographical obfuscation and understand what is actually taking place. Although some important steps have been taken along this path, by geographers and other spatially minded social theorists, it seems to me that discussions of deterritorialization and reterritorialization require more than a straight-forward deployment. In attempting here to demonstrate how these terms are utilized in the work of Deleuze and Guattari, to show how they are deployed in a more explicitly political sense in *Empire*, and to highlight some contemporary territorial issues, I have essentially opened up a much deeper and more difficult problematic. That is, that before we attempt to understand deterritorialization, and to articulate a politics of reterritorialization, we need to undertake a more detailed – that is conceptual, historical and political – analysis of territory itself. In other words, what precisely is it that we have supposedly gone beyond?

This is a long-term project investigating the interrelation of mathematical, philosophical and political conceptions of space. The guiding theme is that there is a relation, but that this is not a strict, causal relation, but rather a complicated set of shifts and developments that needs to be investigated carefully. What is at stake in this project is to understand the ways advances in geometry and calculus allowed more exact mapping of the territories of states in Europe and increasingly abstract geometries of division in the New World. For if territory can be re-thought not as a bounded space, but as the political form of the type of conceptualization of space that makes boundaries possible, we may well find that contemporary events are a variant within an existing spatial-political configuration, rather than the ontological shift they are often supposed to be.[9]

References

Appadurai, Arjun. *Modernity at Large: Cultural Dimensions of Globalisation*. Minneapolis: University of Minnesota Press, 1996.

Balakrishnan, Gopal (ed.) *Debating Empire*. London: Verso, 2003.

Barnett, Thomas P. M. 'The Pentagon's New Map.' *Esquire*, March 2003 issue. Now available at http://www.thomaspmbarnett.com/published/pentagonsnewmap.htm Last accessed 29th November 2004.

Barnett, Thomas P. M. *The Pentagon's New Map: War and Peace in the Twenty-First Century*. New York: G. P. Putnam's Sons, 2004.

Blair, Tony Speech to the Chicago Economic Club, 22 April, 1999. Full text at http://www.pbs.org/newshour/bb/international/jan-june99/blair_doctrine4-23.html Last accessed 29 November 2004.

Blair, Tony Speech at George Bush Senior Presidential Library, Texas, 8th April 2002. Full text at http://politics.guardian.co.uk/speeches/story/0,11126,680866,00.html Last accessed 29 November 2004.

Blair, Tony Speech in Sedgefield, 5 March2004a. Full text at http://politics.guardian.co.uk/iraq/story/0,12956,1162991,00.html Last accessed 29 November 2004.

Blair, Tony Mansion House Speech on Foreign Policy", 16 November2004b. Full text at http://politics.guardian.co.uk/foreignaffairs/story/0,11538,1352442,00.html Last accessed 29 November 2004.

Bogue, Ronald. 'Art and Territory.' *A Deleuzian Century?* Ed. Ian Buchanan. Spec. issue of *The South Atlantic Quarterly* 96. 3 (1997): 465–482.

Bogue, Ronald. 'Minority, Territory, Music.' *An Introduction to the Philosophy of Gilles Deleuze*. Ed. Jean Khalfa. London: Continuum, 2002, 114–132.

Bryden, Mary. 'Deleuze and Anglo-American Literature: Water, Whales and Melville.' *An Introduction to the Philosophy of Gilles Deleuze*. Ed. Jean Khalfa. London: Continuum, 2002, 105–113.

Buchanan, Ian, ed. *A Deleuzian Century? Special Issue of The South Atlantic Quarterly* 96. 3 (1997).

Buchanan, Ian and John Marks. *Deleuze and Literature*. Edinburgh: Edinburgh University Press, 2000.

Burke, Jason. *Al-Qaeda: The True Story of Radical Islam*. Harmondsworth: Penguin, 2004.

Bush, George W., Blair, Tony, and Aznar, Jose Maria '*Azores Summit Statement*,' 16 March 2003. Full text at http://news.bbc.co.uk/2/hi/middle_east/2855567.stm Last accessed 29 November 2004.

9 I am grateful to Paul Harrison for some very useful conversations in the early development of this essay, and Antonis Balasopoulos and Effie Yiannopoulou for their useful comments. A version of this paper was given as a lecture at the Comparative Cultural Studies and Globalization workshop, University of Cyprus, 19–20 November 2004. I owe a particular debt to Maria Margaroni for this invitation, and for continually encouraging me to develop its claims through successive versions.

Casey, Edward S. *The Fate of Place: A Philosophical History*. Berkeley: University of California Press, 1997.
Colebrook, Claire. "The Sense of Space: On the Specificity of Affect in Deleuze and Guattari", *Postmodern Culture* 15. 1 (2004): http://www.iath.virginia.edu/pmc/current.issue/15.1colebrook.html Last accessed 29 November 2004.
Deleuze, Gilles. "Nomad Thought." *The New Nietzsche*. Ed. David B. Allison. Cambridge: MIT Press, 1985, 142–149.
Deleuze, Gilles. "Lettre-préface." *Sahara: L'esthétique de Gilles Deleuze*. Mireille Buydens. Paris: Vrin, 1990, 5.
Deleuze, Gilles. *Critique et clinique*. Paris: Éditions de Minuit, 1993.
Deleuze, Gilles. *Negotiations, 1972–1990*. Trans. Martin Joughlin. New York: Columbia University Press, 1995.
Deleuze, Gilles and Félix Guattari. *Anti-Oedipus: Capitalism and Schizophrenia*. Trans. Robert Hurley, Mark Seem and Helen R. Lane. London: Athlone, 1984.
Deleuze, Gilles and Félix Guattari. *Kafka: Toward a Minor Literature*. Trans. Dana Polan. Minneapolis: University of Minnesota Press, 1986.
Deleuze, Gilles and Félix Guattari. *A Thousand Plateaus: Capitalism and Schizophrenia*. Trans. Brian Massumi. London: Athlone, 1988.
Deleuze, Gilles and Félix Guattari. *What is Philosophy?* Trans. Hugh Tomlinson and Graham Burchill. London: Verso, 1994.
Deleuze, Gilles and Clare Parnet. *Dialogues*. Trans. Hugh Tomlinson and Barbara Habberjam. London: Athlone, 1987.
Dumoncel, Jean-Claude. *Le Pendule du Docteur Deleuze: Une introduction à l'Anti-Œdipe*. Paris: Cahiers de l'Unebévue, 1999.
Elden, Stuart. 'The Place of Geometry: Heidegger's Mathematical Excursus on Aristotle.' *The Heythrop Journal* 42. 3 (2001a): 311–328.
Elden, Stuart. *Mapping the Present: Heidegger, Foucault and the Project of a Spatial History*. London: Continuum, 2001b.
Elden, Stuart. 'Another Sense of Demos: Kleisthenes and the Greek Division of the Polis.' *Democratization* 10. 1 (2003a): 135–156.
Elden, Stuart. 'The Importance of History: A Reply to Malpas.' *Philosophy and Geography* 6. 2 (2003b): 219–224.
Elden, Stuart. *Understanding Henri Lefebvre: Theory and the Possible*. London: Continuum, 2004.
Eldon, Stuart. 'Missing the Point: Globalisation, Deterritorialisation and the Space of the World.' *Transactions of the Institute of British Geographers* 30. 1 (2005).
Faubion, James D. 'Introduction.' *Aesthetics, Method, and Epistemology*. By Michel Foucault. Ed. James D. Faubion. Harmondsworth: Penguin, 1998, xi–xli.
Foucault, Michel. *Language, Counter-Memory, Practice*. Ed. Donald F. Bouchard. Oxford: Basil Blackwell, 1977.
Foucault, Michel. *Dits et écrits 1954–1988*. Ed. Daniel Defert and François Ewald.
Vol. II. Paris: Gallimard, 1994.
Friedmann, Thomas L. *The Lexus and the Olive Tree: Understanding Globalization*. New York: Farrar Straus Giroux, 1999.
Goodchild, Philip. *Deleuze and Guattari: An Introduction to the Politics of Desire*. London: Sage, 1996.
Guattari, Félix. *Psychanalyse et transversalité*. Paris: François Maspero, 1972.

Guattari, Félix and Toni Negri. *Communists Like Us: New Spaces of Liberty, New Lines of Alliance*. Trans. Michael Ryan. New York: Semiotext(e), 1990.

Hardt, Michael. *Gilles Deleuze: An Apprenticeship in Philosophy*. Minneapolis: University of Minnesota Press, 1993.

Hardt, Michael and Antonio Negri. *Empire*. Cambridge: Harvard University Press, 2000.

Hardt, Michael and Antonio Negri. *Multitude: War and Democracy in the Age of Empire*. New York: The Penguin Press. 2004.

Harvey, David. *The Limits to Capital*. London: Verso, 1999.

Harvey, David. *Spaces of Capital: Towards a Critical Geography*. Edinburgh: Edinburgh University Press, 2001.

Harvey, David. *The New Imperialism*. Oxford: Oxford University Press, 2003.

Holland, Eugene W. "Deterritorializing Deterritorialization: from the Anti-Oedipus to A Thousand Plateaus." *SubStance* 66 (1991): 55–65. http://people.cohums.ohio-state.edu/holland1/deterritorializing.htmDepartment of French and Italian, Ohio State University. Last accessed 29 November 2004.

Holland, Eugene W. '*Schizoanalysis and Baudelaire: Some Illustrations of Decoding at Work.*' *Deleuze: A Critical Reader*. Ed. Paul Patton. Oxford: Blackwell, 1996, 240–256.

Kafka, Franz. *The Diaries of Franz Kafka*. Ed. Max Brod. Harmondsworth: Penguin, 1964.

Lefebvre, Henri. *De l'État*, four volumes. Paris: UGE, 1976–1978.

Leibniz, Gottfried. *Œuvres de Leibniz*, seven volumes. Ed. Louis Alexandre Foucher de Careil. Hildesheim: Olms Verlag, 1969.

Leaman, George. 'Iraq, American Empire, and the War on Terrorism,' *Metaphilosophy* 35. 3: (2004) 234–248.

Lemann, Nicholas 'The Next World Order,' *The New Yorker*, 1 April2002. http://www.newyorker.com/fact/content/?020401fa_FACT1 Last accessed 29 November 2004.

Locke, John. *Two Treatises of Government*. Ed. Peter Laslett. Cambridge: Cambridge University Press, 1988.

Lorenz, Konrad. *On Aggression*. London: Methuen, 1966.

Lyotard, Jean-François. 'Capitalisme énergumène.' *Critique* 306 (1972): 923–956.

Malpas, Jeff. 'On the Map: Comments on Stuart Elden's Mapping the Present: Heidegger, Foucault and the Project of a Spatial History.' *Philosophy and Geography* 6. 2 (2003): 213–218.

Marks, John. *Gilles Deleuze: Vitalism and Multiplicity*. London: Pluto, 1998.

Marx, Karl and Friedrich Engels. 'Manifesto of the Communist Party.' *The Revolutions of 1848: Political Writings*, Vol. I. Ed. David Fernbach. Harmondsworth: Penguin, 1973a, 62–98.

Marx, Karl. *Grundrisse: Foundations of the Critique of Political Economy (rough* draft). Trans. Martin Nicolaus. Harmondsworth: Penguin, 1973b.

Marx, Karl. 'The Eighteenth Brumaire of Louis Bonaparte.' *Surveys from Exile: Political Writings*, Vol. II. Trans. David Fernbach. Harmondsworth: Penguin, 1973c, 143–249.

Meiksins Wood, Ellen. 'A Manifesto for Global Capitalism.' Ed. Gopal Balakrishnan. *Debating Empire*. London: Verso, 2003: 61–82.

Minca, Claudio. 'Empire Goes to War, or, The Ontological Shift in the Transatlantic Divide.' *ACME: An International E-Journal for Critical Geographies* 2. 2 (2003): 227–235. < www.acme-journal.org/vol2/minca.pdf > Last accessed 29 November 2004.

Naqishbendi, Rauf. 'Maintaining Iraq's Territorial Integrity Is Causing United States' Failure and Continuing Hardship For The Iraqi People." *The Kurdistan Observer*, 8

September2004. http://home.cogeco.ca/~kurdistan/8-9-04-opinion-naqishbendi-us-failure-irq-integrity.html Last accessed 29 November 2004.

Negri, Antonio. *The Politics of Subversion: A Manifesto for the Twenty-First Century*. Trans. James Newell. Cambridge: Polity Press, 1989.

Negri, Antonio. *The Savage Anomaly: The Power of Spinoza's Metaphysics and Politics.* Trans. Michael Hardt. Minneapolis: University of Minnesota Press, 1991.

Negri, Antonio. 'On Gilles Deleuze and Félix Guattari, A Thousand Plateaus.' Trans. Charles T. Wolfe. *Graduate Faculty Philosophy Journal* 18. 1 (1995): 93–109.

Painter, Joe. 'Empire and citizenship.' *ACME: An International E-Journal for Critical Geographies* 2. 2 (2003): 248–253. < www.acme-journal.org/vol2/painter.pdf > Last accessed 29 November 2004.

Papastergiadis, Nikos. *The Turbulence of Migration: Globalisation, Deterritorialization and Hybridity*. Cambridge: Polity Press, 2000.

Patton, Paul. 'Introduction.' *Deleuze: A Critical Reader.* Ed. Paul Patton. Oxford: Blackwell, 1996, 1–17.

Patton, Paul., *Deleuze and the Political.* London: Routledge, 2000.

Project for the New American Century. "Statement of Principles." 1997. <http://www.newamericancentury.org/statementofprinciples.htm > Last accessed 29 November 2004.

Project for the New American Century. *Rebuilding America's Defenses: Strategy, Forces and Resources for a New Century*. Washington DC: Project for the New American Century, 2000. http://www.newamericancentury.org/RebuildingAmericasDefenses.pdf Last accessed 29th November 2004.

Roberts, Susan, Anna Secor and Matthew Sparke. 'Neoliberal Geopolitics.' *Antipode* 35. 5 (2003): 886–897.

Smith, Daniel W. '"A Life of Pure Immanence:" Deleuze's "Critique et Clinique" Project,' *Essays Critical and Clinical.* Gilles Deleuze. Trans. Daniel W. Smith and Michael A. Greco. London: Verso, 1998, xi–liii.

Smith, Neil. *American Empire: Roosevelt's Geographer and the Prelude to Globalization.* Berkeley: University of California Press, 2003.

Sparke, Matthew. 'American Empire and Globalisation: Postcolonial Speculations on Neocolonial Enframing,' *Singapore Journal of Tropical Geography* 24. 3 (2003): 373–389.

United Nations. *Charter of the United Nations*, 1945. http://www.un.org/aboutun/charter/index.html Last accessed 29 November 2004.

Weber, Max. 'Politik als Beruf. *Gesammelte Politische Schriften*. Ed. Johannes Winckelmann. Tübingen: Mohr, 1971: 505–560.

White House, The. *The National Security Strategy of the United States of America*, Washington DC: The White House, 2002. http://www.whitehouse.gov/nsc/nss.pdf Last accessed 29 November 2004.

2021 Afterword

In September 2002 I joined Durham University's Department of Geography as a lecturer in political geography. With an undergraduate degree in politics and modern history and a PhD in political theory, this was perhaps a surprising move, but it made sense to me – and clearly to Durham – for at least two reasons. The first was the work I had done on the spatial thinking of, particularly, Heidegger, Foucault and Lefebvre; the second was the developing interest I had in the question of territory.

Territory was the main focus of the 11 years I spent at Durham, being the main topic of my teaching in a course on Territory and Politics, and my research. Quite early in my time at Durham I worked with friends and colleagues Luiza Bialasiewicz and Joe Painter on the role of territory in the EU constitution (2005), and wrote two pieces on the territorial aspects of some of the theoretical questions I was interested. One of those articles, 'Missing the Point' was published in the flagship journal *Transactions of the Institute of British Geographers* (2005), the other was the piece reprinted here. These two articles were written in parallel and there is some overlap in their themes, formulations and references.

This piece developed out of a conference paper presented in Cyprus in November 2004 on the invitation of Maria Margaroni, and the book she co-edited with Effie Yiannopoulou, Metaphoricity and the Politics of Mobility, was its natural home.

This chapter and 'Missing the Point' were written in the early years of the 'war on terror,' and this piece in particular begins to think about that contemporary political situation through a territorial lens. I would go on to write several more pieces on this topic, culminating in the 2009 book *Terror and Territory: The Spatial Extent of Sovereignty*. But I always intended for my major contribution to be a historical study of the development of the concept and practice of territory in Western political thought, a book which was eventually published in 2013 as *The Birth of Territory*.

This piece already gives some indications of those projects. People who know some of my later work on territory might recognise some of the themes discussed here – Bush, Blair and the challenge to territorial integrity, Thomas Barnett's The Pentagon's New Map, the Project for a New American Century, Max Weber's famous definition of the state and relative neglect of its territorial dimension, and the relation between mathematical, philosophical and political conceptions of space. But it also indicates some work that was useful to me in writing those books, and related papers, but which didn't end up being emphasized in them. This would include at least three themes of this paper – the reading of Deleuze and Guattari, the critical engagement with Hardt and Negri's work on Empire, and the discussion of animal ethology.

I have resisted the temptation to revise the piece, which appears here in its original form. But I'm interested and intrigued that I was already beginning to think about what has become my key recent focus in work on territory, its materiality, which I've been trying to think about in relation to the question of terrain (2017, 2021). So perhaps some of the questions I think about here should spur me to further thought in the future.

References

Luiza Bialasiewicz, Stuart Elden and Joe Painter 2005 'The Constitution of EU Territory,' *Comparative European Politics*, Vol 3 No 3, pp. 333–363.

Elden, Stuart 2005 'Missing the Point: Globalisation, Deterritorialisation and the Space of the World,' *Transactions of the Institute of British Geographers*, Vol 30 No 1, pp. 8–19.

Elden, Stuart 2009 *Terror and Territory: The Spatial Extent of Sovereignty*. Minnesota: University of Minnesota Press.

Elden, Stuart 2013 *The Birth of Territory*. Chicago: University of Chicago Press.
Elden, Stuart 2017 'Legal Terrain: The Political Materiality of Territory,' *London Review of International Law*, Vol 5 No 2, pp. 199–224.
Elden, Stuart 2021 'Terrain, Politics, History,' *Dialogues in Human Geography*. Vol 11 No 2, pp. 170–89.

Chapter 2

How the non-human turn challenges the social sciences

The case of environmental struggles at Notre-Dame-des-Landes, France

Sylvaine Bulle

Mid-twentieth-century territoriology first offered a specific vision of the possible collaboration between the social and the natural sciences; today, in current times of climate crisis, it offers new topics for research and knowledge, spurring innovative work (Brighenti and Kärrholm 2020). Recent literature has explored the interweavings of different forms of territorial life, understood not only in terms of life environments, but as 'acting' environments. Territoriology thus joins the trajectory of other sciences, all of which appear transformed in the age of Anthropocene and Capitalocene. In similar research approaches, non-humans appear to be key players, capable of challenging the separation between nature and culture. 'Nature defending itself,' animals, even shamanism and spirituality, are all part, not only of life environments, but of a theoretical space that has expanded its domain of enquiry beyond social and normative criticism. The so-called environmental humanities question anthropocentrism and criticise the Western idea of Nature. They resonate widely across human geography and urban planning, science history and the arts, as well as in the public discourse. In environmental struggles, for instance, multiple living collectives are evoked, such as forests and animals, who appear as agents or 'actants' in the environment, and even actors in a series of struggles. New theories and ethnographic methods emphasise participation in the modes of existence so as to create new alliances and new controversies.

By contrast, sociology, a classical science, has so far made limited use of the relation between humans and non-humans. Is this an oversight, or does it respond to a necessity to keep at a distance from a perhaps too enthusiastic relational ecology? Questions indeed arise about the robustness of the ontological turn: Are these neo-vitalist currents apt to gain a fuller scientific knowledge of the Anthropocene, where, after all, the human presence remains central?[1] In this chapter, I analyse the anthropological and philosophical limits of the new ontological approaches. In doing so, my central concern is that

1 On this, we concur with Brighenti and Kärrholm (2020): vitalism is, per se, not sufficient to renew territorial sciences – it is rather the modes in which different forms and materials come into relation that it is important to analyse.

DOI: 10.4324/9781003196365-3

these approaches, highlighting connections and non-social qualities, often result in polishing the world and erasing conflict from it. First, I look more closely at the ontological turn in terms of its epistemology, as it appears deployed both in the anthropological literature and in concrete political engagement. Next, I move to consider what this turn might mean for sociology and for local political mobilisations. On this point, I consider the example of the 'Zones to defend' (*Zad*) in France. In the third part, I set out to image a sociological model that could be in dialogue, but also in productive tension, with the emerging approaches mentioned above. I evoke a form of 'critical pragmatism,' capable of integrating human–natural relationships without erasing social conflict and the specificities of human social action.

The ontological turn in the environmental humanities

The Anthropocene provides plenty of opportunities for the social and territorial sciences to participate in the debate on the possibilities of inhabiting the earth. In this context, two main political and philosophical positions about the place of humans in the ecology can be outlined. The first position, widely shared by economists and environmentalists, asserts that a crucial difference between humans and non-humans is needed in order to better respond to the global climate emergency. This literature evokes a 'Capitalocene,' an age of ecocide perpetrated by large economic and state actors. The second position questions anthropocentrism, enlarging political participation to the whole community of the living, well beyond human beings alone. In this case, the objective is to deconstruct the traditional division between nature and culture, which is responsible for the loss of vital relationships between humans and other beings. The latter perspective rejects any dualism between nature and culture, as well as between living things and objects. In this vein, over the last three decades, scholars such as Philippe Descola (2005) and Bruno Latour (2012) have critically examined the modern Western episteme and the 'Great Cleavage' between Nature and Culture it has instituted. Around the Great Cleavage, a number of additional dichotomies – such as matter *vs* spirit, object *vs* subject, primitive *vs* modern, non-human *vs* human – have appeared. Modernity has thus been described as an ontological coup-de-force that has degraded, if not spoiled, the ways in which non-modern societies used to integrate non-humans into their way of functioning.

The environmental humanities, a new area of study across the human and the natural sciences, appear to have largely integrated a philosophy and an anthropology of non-humans, often relegating classical sociological and political-science approaches to the background. As put by Viveiros de Castro (2019), who are enthusiastic supporters of the new turn, in the Anthropocene 'we are all likely to be confronted, at one time or another, and in reality at each moment, with the choice of "becoming-Indian" – living on the margins, living on the edge … as opposed to remain in our strongholds.' Before examining how new relations to the environment can be built upon these assumptions, let us unpack more in depth some underlying epistemological foundations, which are best visible in anthropology. Here, one should keep in mind that anthropology is a discipline that even traditionally has never really endorsed the nature–culture dualism, unlike history and sociology. Being mainly concerned with non-modern societies, which did not consider themselves apart from nature, anthropology has subsequently been able to bring a unitary gaze onto Western societies. Another aspect to be kept in mind is the preponderance of cultural anthropology within the field, with its emphasis on language and symbolism, as opposed to the emphasis on institutional and statistical realities in sociology (Boltanski 2009). Central authors of the ontological turn, such as Haraway (2020) and Stengers (2020), propose to redefine relationships with other species (animals, plants, microbes and bacteria), so as to reconstitute a kinship, and forge new alliances. The anthropologist Viveiros de Castro (2009) lays emphasis on indigeneity as central to challenging our way of seeing the world. Similarly, Escobar (2018) emphasises how Amerindian shamans establish bridges across species, as they are capable to understand the point of view of other beings, of their different corporealities and affects. Another anthropologist, Kohn (2017), claims that today we must learn to live with an ever-increasing variety of life forms, including weeds, pests, pets, wild animals, as well as technoscientific mutants: this fact alone pushes us to regard the human being as part of a larger whole formed by other beings who think. This, in turn, invites us to develop modes of knowledge to fully join the political depth of the environment.

Such a perspectival epistemology mirrors Bruno Latour's 'symmetrical' epistemology. Earlier on, in *Science in Action* (1989), the French philosopher-sociologist argued that knowledge does not so much represent the unknown, it interacts with it. Accordingly, science in action is not about contemplating, reflecting or communicating, as it is about creating new environments. As Latour writes in a more recent essay entitled *Enquête sur les modes d'existence* (2012), it is a question of multiplying the agents and populating our world. On this account, a political or ecological experiment can dispense with practices, insofar as it is limited to asserting equivalences between an Indian, a virus, an activist, or a bird, all living together in a grove. Ontological pluralism becomes the key: it is a kind of scientific 'subversion' enabling us to take possession of hitherto unknown or unseen territories. What matters is the deployment of different relationships between beings, which are not based on hierarchy, and which allow us to develop a radical otherness (even aesthetically).

Subversion is not only epistemological, but also political, insofar as the exterior of societies and the relations they maintain with heteronomy are called into question. It is in this sense that the philosopher and anthropologist Pierre Clastres, a pioneer of political anthropology and an inspirer of anarchist currents, is regularly cited in current essays on indigenous peoples and emancipation. An ethnologist of the Amazonian Indians, in his *Society against the State* (1974), Clastres pointed out the existence of collectives who do not recognise any separation between nature and humans. In pre-state Amazonian societies, collective identification with non-human beings ties people to the earth and turns into a factor of solidarity and integration. Viveiros de Castro (2009; 2019) goes one step further: he postulates that the political and the cosmological non-separation of beings are parallel processes. If, in other words, collective life takes the form of a multiplicity of relationships between human and non-human actors, then the possibility of any transcendent political authority is reduced. We have already pointed out that this paradigm is now central in the anthropology of nature, and entails a shift away from a causal and social vision, focused on human responsibility and human institutions. Such a shift easily accommodates the – non-human, in-human – 'other' in a new metaphysics of knowledge which replaces traditional empirical approaches (Tsing 2015, 2020; Coccia 2020).

To sum up, the method of non-separation is the herald of a relational ecology; accordingly, it is not surprising to find it in the environmental sciences (Ferdinand 2019), the sciences of territory (Duperrex 2019; Ait-Touati and Coccia 2021) and the study of 'dwelling' (Ingold 2011). But the approach has also become common in architecture (Rahm 2020; Ait-Touati et al. 2019) and is spreading among activists and artists.

Becoming-animal, becoming-indigenous: tools and devices

Being a Forest, To Live as a Bird, On the Animal Track. The titles of some recent books evoke forest life (Vidalou 2017), terrestrial life (Latour 2017), animal life (Morizot 2017; Despret 2019) and indigenous life (Escobar 2018). How can these approaches be related to the social sciences? Perspectivist and symmetrical approaches, and more generally the ontological turn, propose to revisit not only the foundations of the human and social sciences, but also their relationship to normativity and the world. Indeed, the theorists of connectionism and perspectivism want to be the designers of new environments as well as mediators between beings. A vivid example is provided by Donna Haraway in *Staying with the Trouble* (2016) (Haraway 2020). Haraway's erudite and fascinating story is set in the Chthulucene and tells the story of an imaginary migratory people called the Children of Compost, who shape their own worlds through connections with other actors in order to heal the world and make it habitable again. Their reproduction is not biological, but symbiotic, and results in the birth of hybrid beings, half humans half animals, capable of saving endangered species (such as certain species of butterflies) as well as slipping into the folds of the Anthropocene traversing its migratory corridors.

While Haraway does not explain the mechanisms leading to the ecological catastrophe, her critique operates by conjuring up an imaginary way of living where the borders between biological creature and machine are blurred, and where the historical dimension of existence is erased. Haraway therefore invents semi-real, semi-fictitious characters, highlighting the entanglement of humans, non-humans and artefacts within a shared environment. Haraway's characters do not occupy any clearly recognisable economic or social position, as they are fully and simply 'natureculture' itself. Ultimately, Haraway's speculative approach evokes a universe populated by beings who overthrow human exceptionalism to make the earth habitable again. These fascinating silhouettes neutralise all social functions and traditional categories (people, nation, territory, state) and yet remain quite material, inscribed in recognisable environments such as, for instance, urban environments. Haraway's Chthulucene is cut across by territorial struggles – not by chance are the Children of Compost also called Camille, a generic name quite widespread in territorial struggles, suggesting that all indigenous and civilised lands must be freed from colonialism.

The new ethnography of nature in the Anthropocene: a blurred category?

To the anthropologist of 'natureculture' the world appears as a bundle of connections, intensifications and networks. Perspectivism and the ontological turn are not interested in the meaning of social activities. The stake lies elsewhere: their interest goes indeed towards the new agents or actants, such as nature, the shamans, etc., capable of defining new hybrid arrangements. The innovative works of Baptiste Morizot (2016), devoted to tracking wolves, offers an illustration; another one is Anna Tsing's (2020) exploration of the frictions of capitalism; still another is Emanuele Coccia's (2020) reflection on poetic pantheism. Just like Haraway, all these authors seek to upturn the modernist episteme, granting importance, not to practices, but to the new perspective of a gigantic web of interrelationships, which can be related to the Deleuzian rhizome and its becoming.

The critics of these approaches, such as Chandler and Reid (2020) and Holbraad and Pedersen (2016), have attacked the ontological turn, characterising it as a form of exoticism that runs the serious risk of consolidating the Western colonial stance, rather than challenging it. In this respect, the question we must address is whether the ontological turn may inadvertently end up devaluing the tools of the social sciences. Whereas sociology analyses the operations carried out by acting human collectives, the symmetrical anthropologies distribute beliefs to all beings, and may largely overestimate the possibilities for dialogue between them. In regard of this, it is also interesting to observe how the new approaches reconsider empirical objects that were traditionally tackled by sociology: for instance, patterns of dwelling, health crises, local political mobilisation, and the emergence of new political actors. Whereas the new terminology includes 'socio-hydraulic maps', 'extractionism' and 'animal diplomacy', substantively, such methods of enquiry seem quite close to descriptive sociology, whose aim is to explain the contexts and the reasons of the involved actors.

One clear shortcoming of the ontological turn, I suggest, is its disregard for the power of the social reality to shape the perceptions of the actors. The anthropologists of nature emphasise that the relations to non-human beings, too, can be symbolic: different beings are seen as communicating – through songs, rituals and dreams – with animals, plants and spirits. This way, relations which we used to regard as social, become symbolic: in the case of the Achuar tribe, notes Descola (2005), kinship extends to the hunter's prey as well as to the cultivated plants. Similarly, animism recovers some of its authority, notably through shamanism, which names the enemy to be hunted or, on the contrary, a creature that enables one's connection to further entities. Whereas the sociologist sees social properties and belonging, dispositions and reasons to act, the new notions of 'composition' or agency emphasise the connections that bodies and objects can establish. These new connections are as wide as 'Gaia' (Latour 2015). Here, practices are no longer simply social, but represent many starting points for revealing infinite interconnections. To build a different relation to the living thing, the new anthropologists are thus led to minimise social conflict and classic economic relations, in favour of larger 'frictions' between animals, territories and humans.

But, is this not a way of forgetting the specificities of human social relations? Attributing beliefs to all beings and establishing infinite possibilities for dialogue between them; isn't this approach overestimating the power of relationality? And, what remains of specifically human action, endowed with logos and faculty of judgment? What is the sociological meaning of such 'de-anthropisation of politics' (Plumwood 2001; De la Cadena 2015)? The question needs to be addressed in more detail.

Challenging the ontological turn. The case of a *Zone à défendre* (*Zad*)

To do so, we can consider an emblematic case: the *Zone à défendre* (*Zad*) of Notre-Dame-Des-Landes (NDDL), located in western France. In 2012, when the project for an airport to be built in the area encountered growing opposition from eco-activists, the *zone* was occupied by various groups. Local residents, environmental activists and local farmers who already lived there saw the arrival of new neighbours: anti-authoritarian and anarchist-revolutionary collectives. With the arrival of the latter, active resistance increased: farms were occupied, and the land started being cultivated. Geographically, the *Zad* covers an area of 200ha, with a few hundred occupants installed in houses or timber buildings. In 2018, after various cycles of police repression, support mobilisation, and extensive media coverage, the State abandoned the airport project. Since then, with the consent of the authorities, part of the area has remained occupied, and still is today, a precarious example of self-organisation and commons-oriented economy. In 2020, about 50 squatters remain in place, although the most radical elements have left in order to avoid having to negotiate with the State, who is the landowner.[2]

Rarely has a place produced so many stories about the role of nature in social struggles (Schaffner 2019, Lindgaard 2018). Scholars such as Descola, Latour, Starhawk, Shiva and novelists such as Alain Damasio all have contributed texts to celebrate the liveliness of the *Zad*. The 'Zadists' have become central figures of the new epistemology, with emphasis on their plural relationship to the world. In the stories about the *Zad*, multiple beings are summoned: 'We are Nature defending itself'; 'Be the territory': the forests, a pond, or a population of newts are recognised as characters invested with specific interests and values. Shamans speak with the occupants during dreams and hallucinatory trances.[3] All these creatures feature in the drawings, the stories and the songs of the *Zad*, not to mention the violent confrontations with law enforcement (Pignocchi 2019). Masks of newts and owls are used to express animism as a lifestyle, a way of being in the world, where everything is entangled on common soil. The questioning of the separation between nature and culture, between beliefs and realities, translates into stories in which the grove and its animals are credited with an interiority similar to that of humans, and are given the floor to freely express themselves.

A 'partition of the sensible' [*partage du sensible*] is, according to Rancière (2000), that division signalling an order of places and activities – but it can also be understood as the capacity of certain beings to upset the ways of perceiving, to modify the order of the visible and the invisible, to consolidate the common space of politics. This definition can be applied to the case of the *Zad*, whose mission is to rearrange the political order, so that all species can participate. To this effect, some have proposed to make the struggle 'autochtonous' (Glowczewski 2019). To peacefully manage coexistence on the same territory, the Zadists evoke the metaphor of diplomacy: getting to know the other and his/her/its perspective so as to communicate better. In the Zadists' stories, the newts become creatures who clash with the police and forge alliances with other beings. Similarly, the grove is endowed with intelligence and the capacity to understand human intentions. In this context, humans are neither superior

2 The analysis presented here is based on a case study conducted in NDDL from 2014 through 2018. The fieldwork explored the different political and ecological sensitivities of the occupants, and the ensuing internal antagonisms in the articulation of their project of political autonomy. The research's aim was to put the *Zad* back into a normative and political framework, taking into account the points of support (anarchism, political autonomy, anti-authoritarianism) of the actors beyond the mere register of vitalism and links with the land. The survey mentions the risks of generalisation or over-interpretation of the ecological 'fact' and the difficulties of objectifying social relations (history of the occupants, normative points of support) insofar as the actors themselves resist sociological objectification (Bulle 2020).

3 'For me, taking a substance that changes my state of consciousness, I felt like it changed the lives of everyone – that we had to go through this, that we rediscover an Indian thing that is essential for life, for it to go well. I felt it, powerfully.' (Interview with squatter, February 2016, transcribed by Pablo Carroyer, doctoral student in Political Sciences).

nor special.[4] Re-enchantment is key to produce artistic effects, but also to talk to anthropologists.[5] The *Zad* is presented as a sweet experiment, where different actors can make a new politics of nature together. The milieu becomes the central element in a community of struggle, around which all the other figures revolve.[6]

Bushes and swamps speak. But does this not lead to desocialisation and depoliticisation?

What is the deeper meaning of this movement? To understand it better, we must analyse the political implications of its theoretical tenets. Grignon and Passeron (1989) would certainly describe such tenets as a form of 'epistemological populism' that pushes for the rehabilitation of non-scholarly and native ways of thinking. For its part, sociology is attentive – even more than to objectification – to the conflictuality that shapes society. In this respect, the ontological turn neglects the fact that the relations between humans, and between humans and non-humans, are not the same. There is no chance that 'non-human spokespersons' can take a human point of view, since they have no 'logos' for joining politics. The invisible actors, the spirits, cannot account for the critical operations carried out by the social actors, nor for the various political sensitivities of the latter. Since sociological description must ban undue generalisations, in the case of NDDL the sociologist must first of all seek to clarify the peculiarly *political* character of the struggle. The ideology of the Zadists is grounded, first, in the critique of capitalism and the capitalist state (Polanyi 1983; Gorz 1975), second, in the critique of the transformation of nature into commodity (Jappe 2017). True, the Zadists aim to be less anthropocentric than other traditional struggles, but they cannot avoid issues of governance: their main concern is with political autonomy and the self-institution

4 'What I would also like to convey, besides knowing what to eat, is a certain way of walking on the earth. Slowly, patiently, carefully. This is not incompatible with guerrilla. On the contrary. We become more precise, we waste less, we destroy less.' (Tract on harvesting, quoted by Pablo Carroyer, *Tritons crêté-e-s contre béton armé. Du Maquis à la Forêt, des formes de cohabitations révolutionnaires sur la ZAD de Notre-Dame-des-Landes*. Master's thesis, Institut d'Études Politiques de Paris, 2015.)

5 See the film *Composer les Mondes d'Eliza Levy* (Amigo Icecream Productions, 2019) where Descola talks about the *Zad*, advancing a parallel between the Zadists and the Achuar people.

6 More information about the *Zad* can be found in *Notre-Dame-Des-Landes, ou le métier de vivre* (2018) by Patrick Bouchain and Christophe Laurens (Loco Éditions); *Habiter en Lutte* (2018) by Collectif Comm'un (Passager Clandestin); *Contrées* (2016) by Collectif Mauvais Troupe (Éditions de l'Éclat). Raoul Vaneigem, one of the co-founders of the Situationist International, wrote a text in support of the Zadists. (available at https://zad.nadir.org/spip.php?article5679). Films have also been shot in the *Zad*, such as *Le dernier continent* (2014) by Vincent Lapize, and *Les pieds sur terre* (2016) by Baptiste Combret and Bertrand Hagenmüller.

of society (Castoriadis 1975). Even when it evokes stateless peoples (Clastres 1974; Graeber 2014; Scott 2013), their ideology remains deeply political.

The blurred limits of 'subjectivism'

As a project of social transformation, the *Zad* is premised on an articulated critique of the social order and its institutions, challenging hegemony and domination with a set of grammars of autonomy (Castoriadis 1975). The Zadists are concerned with the inequalities produced by market capitalism, and do not cease to relate themselves to elements such as the law, eviction notes, company profits, etc. The squatters also employ various methods to counter the legal and institutional order, commissioning reports and appeals to their lawyers and economic consultants. At the same time, it also matters to them that such elements get translated and transfigured into mythopoietic narratives. The *Zad*'s political priority, however, remains opposition, resistance and self-organisation. The underlying model of political autonomy argues that societies and communities can redefine their own standards of existence and redesign themselves by appropriating their own times and spaces. As the squatters engage in local practices, divergences between groups also emerge. Some are more interested in social ecology, others in the revolutionary project. The question, for the sociologist, is how these different groups can hold together. Besides the biotic community, we encounter an irreducibly human world, with its inner political antagonisms and its various battle fronts. The ontological turn runs the risk of diluting and neglecting these aspects: far from being an undifferentiated immanent whole without, human societies have political characteristics that make them distinctive (see also Demeulenaere 2017).

A final question follows from the previous one: is the ontological turn compatible with political responsibility? Political ecology earlier on raised this issue, and the same question is interestingly also to be found at the heart of the *Zad* collectives as they reclaim for themselves neo-Marxist revolutionary roots, or more vague communitarian visions. Notably, the nature-society dualism is accepted by the political ideologies the Zadists appeal to. Marxism, anarchist socialism, and political ecology, all connect nature with the material conditions of its production (Bookchin 2014). As early as 1977, the New Left theorist André Gorz warned that the 'deification of nature' by some activists led them to overlook the criticism of commodities and industrial production. Similarly, today we have philosophies such as 'sobretism' (self-limitation) that reduce ecological concerns to individual ethical choices. A more robust criticism is made by revolutionary currents, such as Comité Invisible (2007), that plead for insurrection and the rejection of market capitalism. Other exit options range from impeachment to desertion, and are sometimes inspired by the notion of idleness (Agamben 2015).[7] The importance of these nuances within the *Zad* cannot be grasped by a simple concern for

7 In Agamben (2015), idleness is what makes it possible to put an end to 'the most miserable action that man can do: perform tasks.' In this sense, autonomist and neo-

ontology, but must be appreciated at the level of practical activities. Accordingly, in the next section we move on to examine how sociology could try to make sense of a territorial struggle by taking seriously the idea that human actors – rather than generalised actants – are the real movers of the process.

For a sociology of contentious milieus. Elements for analysis

How can sociology equip itself to grasp a complex plurality of collective modes of being-in-the-world, such as those present in the *Zad*, taking into account both the materiality of the events and the cognitive skills of the actors? What type of sociology is adequate to capture the political and social lines of force running through the *Zad* experience? Whether we consider situated, experiential, logical and discursive factors, a framework of analysis is needed that is capable of integrating affects and emotions as an intrinsic part of radical criticism. In the *Zad*, speech, emotions and bodily gestures become critical (signifying self-defense, appropriation of the land etc.), while also being the support of ordinary activities (such as agriculture, repair and maintenance work etc.).[8]

Pragmatic sociology at the time of the Anthropocene

The study of a territorial struggle raises two issues in the representation of social reality. The first is a meta-critique of institutions, such as the state. The force of the state, as we have seen, is present on the ground through its legal framework, but also more directly through police repression. The second is an ordinary critique of Zadists' commitments. The territorial defence they perform is grounded, as we have noticed, in common attachment and joint action. Activities including agriculture and mutual aid are proposed as gestures of self-defence and of resistance against institutional domination (police, justice, education). Since the squatting of the *Zad* proceeds through a mutual adjustment of perception and action, its living milieu can be investigated by pragmatic sociology (Boltanski and Thévenot 1991) as well as by critical pragmatism (Bulle 2020). Indeed, a struggling milieu such as a *Zad* is characterised by critical gestures meant to disengage themselves from the state, so as to emphasise

Marxist currents call for the suspension of all functions serving predetermined functions, and getting rid of all objects that maintain social reproduction. The aim is to drift away from all capitalist and control functions to affirm the ethical foundations of autonomous life.

8 We notice that, symmetrically, emotions are absorbed by the commodity and production system, and even by capitalist language. Emotions and affects are indeed increasingly present in the system of consumption, and in respect of this Eva Illouz (2019) speaks of 'emotional goods.' While the capitalist mobilisation of emotions criticism is impossible for ordinary consumers, the Zadists seek to initiate a critique of the world from ordinary gestures and emotions in deep connection to the environment.

local commonality. The pragmatic approach illuminates how the critique conducted by the actors does not stop at the production of narratives, nor at placing humans and non-humans on the same level – for indeed human action occupies a key place in the production of political subjectivities.

A few examples can support our claim. Let us consider the role of the territory, in its different dimensions. First, the territory facilitates the gathering of actors with the same sensitivity, attached to the land and its biodiversity. External supporters who come to the *Zad* for festive moments and major resistance events live territory in this way. But, for the anarchist squatters, the territory comes to coincide with an 'occupation-form' (Bulle 2018) designed to build new forms of life. The occupation-form encompasses cognitive and material levels. In the foreground, the main front of action mobilises to defend buildings the authorities want to evict; in the background, the resistance base is made of wild squatting, free-shops, canteens, food distribution points, anti-fascist meeting points, etc. In other words, the occupation-form engages with 'offensive withdrawal,' which seeks to part ways from capitalist society and the State through an active defence of the territory. In the second place, then, the territory becomes a living support where it becomes possible to build new milieus.

Objects in the struggle

Opacity is an important resource for this type of struggle (Bulle 2020): tactics of concealment and disguise are amply employed.[9] The use of objects is revealing: very few new items can be found in the *Zad*, as there is a clear preference for used, worn and marked out objects. Discarded and devalued objects here receive renewed appreciation. The Zadists stay clear of new objects as much as possible and, accordingly, learn new bodily skills with re-crafting stuff. A bottle can be used to mix the ingredients for a cake or a cocktail, or as a candle carrier; an empty gas tank can be made into a wood-fuelled cooker, or a dummy bomb to be displayed in the event of an eviction; cardboard can be used as a food tray, an old engine as a barricade, a garbage-can lid as a shield against the police; gardening tools can turn into weapons for barricade defence, just like tractors, pallets, tires and abandoned cars for roadblocks. All these objects become part of a strategy of invisibility. A reused object is put in circulation and opened up to new stories, new practices, new experiences. In a sense, objects also function as 'mediating devices,' as actor-network theory holds, joining humans to non-human artefacts. However, the emphasis here is on human intervention, not as a physical gesture but as a faculty of judgment which enables a change of use by breaking away from industrial society.

On the epistemological level, therefore, two aspects of knowledge are brought together: the first is pragmatic (situated experiential actions), the

9 See also Brighenti (2010), who distinguishes visibility from the visible, evoking social and relational qualities as recognised by specific actors.

second is critical (resignified, talked-about objects). Contrary to an indistinct sacralisation of nature, politicisation here passes through a precise human handling of objects: the more objects that are brought out of the consumerist orbit, the better.

Beyond ontology: multiple views of nature

Enacting multiple re-appropriations people become reflexive about their relationship to the industrial, commercial and institutional world. Squatters themselves are not univocal about this, and a simple 'diplomacy' of relations between different beings does not suffice to explain how a common world is practically attained and managed. As we have stressed, intentionality and deliberation, rather than spontaneity, are prerequisites for a politics of resistance. Of crucial importance is, in particular, the *gradation* of different commitments along a continuum from local resident, to farmer, to barricader. A political sociology of a milieu of resistance thus invites us to distinguish between various ways of embodying 'natureculture.' We must take care to identify the heterogeneity of actors and the terms of their commitment to the cause: for these may range from the reformists, who aim to slow capitalism down, to the radicals, who want to break free from it at once. Within the same occupy movement there are power struggles, points of disagreement and conflict, according to the different positions about how to relate to the outside world and to the collective project of emancipation. Three different and only partially overlapping sensibilities emerge: first, libertarian anti-authoritarianism with a specific 'primitivist' bent, second, ecological realist-utopians, third, insurrectionalists-revolutionaries. These three groups have distinct ways of practicing eco-activism: only some of them believe in an integral, self-determined environmental ethics, similar to the deep ecology approach (Næss 2009):

> There I take mushrooms. Well, it's my power-shamanic discovery … I take mushrooms with people at a party, and I start getting revelations. I see myself as an Indian, I have the impression of living with Indians, elves, fairies… I tell myself it's a crazy thing, that we are connected to the earth… And there I start to think that life, it must be beautiful and magical, beyond activism … People who based are in the West sector … we couldn't have enjoyed a psychotropic experience with them, they turn everything into a militant affair, without anything beyond that.[10]

10 Interview by Pablo Carroyer. The interviewee is an Eastern-Sector inhabitant (male, 30-year-old, with precarious job).

People based in the *Zad*'s Eastern sector,[11] in particular, have banned all petrol and electric devices:

> I want to be aware of what I use: you realize what you use, what 30l of water is like. In the water I drink there is the effort I made to get it, rather than the effort of people I don't know in an area I don't know have made to pump it, draw it, transport it … and with minerals it's even worse. So my choice goes towards reclaiming my energy use completely. Even if afterwards you can come back to mixed use, it is necessary for me to go through a total deconstruction, no longer having access to the button at all.[12]

Great attention is paid by them to the life of trees:

> I accept one chops wood only for really valid reasons. I criticized the sawmill workshop because they cut wood all too easily. Some projects seemed completely out of scale to me, large useless projects, you see. Do you really need that barn, all that space? Couldn't you cut half the trees? There's a bit of 'To prove that we're not just squatters who don't give a damn, we're doing this crazy thing.' That can be a fallacy.[13]

Such view is minoritarian, though, since the majority promotes a diversification of activities, including parties and celebrations open to the public. The latter type of events are denounced by the more intransigent as themselves polluting. In this respect, the subscribers to radical autonomy accept parties only if they facilitate the revolutionary project, which remains focused on land appropriation first.

Be the territory, or be productive? Ways of inhabiting the struggle

Slowdown, withdrawal or idleness, deep ecology: different relationships to environments become source of internal conflict in the NDDL *Zad*. Let us return, for example, to the area which was partially destroyed in 2018, the one which hosted the most anti-authoritarian and ecological fringe. In its origin, and its way of functioning, this sector embodied a perfectionist tendency: the collectives based here were not productive (neither farmers nor artisans), and avoided all technical and economic mediations. Maximising their separation from a destructive outside, they also avoided taking part in collective work, meetings, promotion etc. Their utmost

11 The Eastern sector was dismantled by the police in 2018. In contrast, other parts have been saved thanks to negotiations with the Prefecture (the local office of the central government).

12 Interview by Pablo Carroyer. The interviewee is an Eastern-Sector inhabitant (male, 25-year-old, former employee).

13 Ibidem. The average length of residence in the Eastern Sector varies between 2 and 4 years. The first squatters arrived in 2012.

authenticity was to be testified only by their own intimate experience with the vital elements of the environment. One notices here that the source of conflict lies in the qualification of the forms of life (Boltanski and Thévenot 1991). The lifestyles based on the appreciative 'valuation' (Dewey 2011) of scarcity do not depend on strategic interests, nor upon functions in a struggle, but on an overall preservation effort. Consider the conflict over the presence of visitors. The refusal of certain groups to see neighbours and onlookers come to the area is justified by the value accorded to the *Zad*'s enclosure and its creatures. While parties may help finance the struggle, they also cause a lot of damage: crowding, unrestrained behaviour, and a caricaturisation of autonomy. Accordingly, deep-ecology squatters consider parties as forms of an undesirable 'anarcho-tourism.' Similar examples abound: as said, the 'integrationists' reject the use of recycled materials, which they regard as a form of unwanted exchange value, while the protection of the grove has similarly led to numerous conflicts with traditional tenant farmers who cultivate the land with standard modern techniques and economically depend on the industrial system.

'Nourishing the struggle:' Opposing visions

We are now better positioned to see that, under the banner 'weaving alliances with the living world,' there hide diverging interests. Indeed, some collectives who prioritise political strategy have not completely broken with the industrial and commodity world: they travel by car and carry on revenue-generating activities to finance the struggle. Such is the 'Feed the fight' stance. Efficiency and realism are presented as political weapons by these groups. With reference to them, others raise the concern that running economic activities turns some occupants into de facto 'merchants with newt masks.' The latter, however, retort that the utter rejection of capitalist system's 'Babylon' leads the former but into a condition of objectively increased dependence. Since 2018, the cleavage between different collectives in the *Zad* has become apparent: endorsement vs rejection of productivity turned into a main issue for the Zadists. Choices were clearly guided by one's positioning within the front of the struggle: so, the same figure of the 'fighting newt' can convey different strategies, alliances and degrees of authenticity. Only subjects consciously fashioning a political culture can achieve this. Issues such as emancipation and attachment to the environment remain specific to human persons, as shown by the different conceptions of dwelling.

Just like the relationship to objects, different ways of living also evoke different imaginaries and plural worlds in their vision of autonomy. The most 'alternative' and strategic occupants have installed permanent buildings located in the centre of the settlement. Others, more isolated, live in movable huts, with no other project than that of establishing a direct relationship with the living world. These differences became particularly exacerbated in the second phase of the NDDL *Zad*, when the most anti-authoritarian and anti-productivist group explicitly dissociated from the others. But the groups who have pursued a strategy of normalisation and settlement are those who have lasted the longest. In 2021, with the arrival of some newcomers, the current occupants have agreed to be part of an agro-ecological project coordinated with the State. The new main objectives has become to make ecological choices as visible as possible: slowing down the use of land, employing manual methods, and pooling equipment. All these practices provide an ecologically governable space based on Do It Yourself philosophy. For the supporters of the formula, this proves that a realist ecological utopia is achievable. The other squatters have had to leave the premises. Their shacks have been razed by the police. This proves that the 'composition of a common world' is far from being a harmonious process. Here again, a sociological perspective, such as in particular the perspective of critical pragmatism, makes the nuances.

Towards interactional territories

'Becoming-native,' 'becoming-animal,' 'becoming-environment:' these formulas are at the pivot of current ecological upheavals, in a context where social movements reclaim the land for themselves, against its capitalist exploitations. Such an effervescence does not at all imply a de-politicisation nor, for that matter, a demise of social relations. Accordingly, the 'natureculture' turn should not lead us to obfuscate the specificities of the relations between humans. The construction of common worlds beyond the human being is not indifferent to economic determinations and societal arrangements, which collide or intermingle with beliefs and imagination. It is not enough to simply overlook the boundaries between body and mind, North and South etc., to push forward a territorial and environmental agenda. Since new relationships with non-humans are forged without dissolving the notion of humanity, neither the sole criticism of capitalism, nor the sole plea for the 'actor-network' seem sufficient to envision a more-than-human sociality.

In the context of global ecological crisis, concern for the environment offers vital avenues to the social and territorial sciences. These, however, cannot content themselves with a simple 'Gaia ontology.' Territorial science can successfully explore emerging arrangements and compositions in the new socio-ecological worlds only if it goes beyond the simple postulate of immanence. In this sense, a non-deterministic approach to 'animated lands' (Brighenti and Kärrholm 2020), just like a renewed 'terrestrial' approach (Latour 2017), interweave the notions of local and global, environment and system, crisis and regulation. The new earthly order calls for special attention to be paid to the transformation processes through which different visions are articulated, superimposed or confronted. This is evidenced by the processual nature of environments and social struggles, made of interactions and rhythms. An interactionist sociology is particularly suited to grasp this. Neither the local nor the terrestrial per se should be fetishised, any more than nature itself. In each case, we have to go back to the intersection between a history of ideas, the historical paths of actors, and the intimate as well as collective visions expressed locally or within a given environment, albeit in different temporalities.

Finally, we need a theoretical modelling of the 'critical takes' (Chateauraynaud 2011), namely, those processes of attention and enhancement of ecologically sensitive topics.

A renewed social science must proceed alongside the actors. This is also what the history of the NDDL *Zad* suggests. As we have seen, the Zadist front encompasses different currents, ranging from anarchism to wilderness, to real utopias. Philosophy and critical theory are needed to describe alienation and emancipation, but a context-sensitive sociology is helpful to capture how objects interact within specific social formats. It involves grasping political legacies, rules of life, and overcoming the classic oppositions between theory and empiricism, constructivism and realism, vitalism and determinism. A careful ethnographic observation of a social-territorial environment such as a *Zad* discourages hasty generalisations. Understanding the peculiarity of a lived political regime dos not necessarily lead to a 'sociologisation of politics' (Rancière 2005), but might rather lead to a case-based theory that is 'limit-aware' (Pellizzoni 2021).

This type of approach, we have pointed out, requires opting for sociological pragmatism. The latter can answer to two basic requirements. First, pragmatism excludes a predetermined knowledge of social categories: indeed, in contentious situations, the actors are ahead of the sociologists. To understand a world-in-the-making, we must go beyond the tools of objectification routinely mobilised by sociologists, attaining a more ambulatory and fragmentary work. Second, pragmatism avoids the naturalistic temptation and the flattening of levels and actors, as it happens for instance with the 'mother nature' metaphor. Far from opposing emotional-psychological and objective dimensions, pragmatism as a theory of action indeed allows two elements to be brought together: a critical process, and a cognitive apparatus which allows actors to orient themselves. This, in the case of *Zad* NDDL, is what we have described as 'offensive withdrawal' and 'critical capture.' Critical pragmatics makes it possible to articulate formats of criticism without ignoring the reflexivity of the actors. In the occupied milieu of the *Zad*, immanence constantly rubs shoulders with strategy, dialogues with tactics. To tackle these, a radical empiricism (James 2007) is recommended. This type of sociological exploration may also apply to other cases. A science of territories must now take into account new adventures, located on the threshold where one world can become another.

(translated from the French original by Andrea Mubi Brighenti)

References

Agamben G. (2015) *L'Usage des corps. Homo Sacer IV(2)*. Paris: Éditions du Seuil.

Ait-Touati F. and Coccia E. (2021) *Le cri de Gaïa. Penser la Terre avec Bruno Latour*. Paris: La Découverte.

Ait-Touati F., Arène, A. and Grégoire A. (2019) *Terra Forma. Manuel de cartographies potentielles*. Paris: Éditions B42.

Boltanski L. (2009) *De la critique. Précis de sociologie de l'émancipation*. Paris: Gallimard.

Boltanski L. and Thévenot L. (1991) *De la justification. Les économies de la grandeur*, Paris: Gallimard.
Bookchin M. (2014) *Pour une écologie sociale et radicale*. Neuvy-en-Champagne: Le Passager clandestin.
Brighenti A. M. (2010) *Visibility in Social Theory and Social Research*. Basingstoke: Palgrave Macmillan.
Brighenti A. M. and Kärrholm, M. (2020) *Animated Lands. Studies in Territoriology*. Lincoln: University of Nebraska Press.
Bulle S. (2018) 'Formes de vie, milieux de vie. La forme-occupation,' *Revue Multitudes*, 2:71, 168–175.
Bulle S. (2020) *Irréductibles. Enquête sur des milieux de vie autonomes*. Grenoble: UGA, Ecotopies.
Castoriadis C. (1975) *L'Institution imaginaire de la société*. Paris: Éditions du Seuil.
Chandler D. and Reid J. (2020) 'Becoming indigenous: the "speculative turn" in anthropology and the (re)colonisation of indigeneity.' *Postcolonial Studies*, 23:4, 485–504.
Chateauraynaud F. (2011) *Argumenter dans un champ de forces. Essai de balistique sociologique*. Paris: Éditions Pétra.
Clastres P. (1974) *La Société contre l'État*. Paris: Les Éditions de Minuit.
Coccia E. (2020) *Métamorphoses*. Paris: Bibliothèque Rivages.
omité invisible (2007) *L'insurrection qui vient*. Paris: La fabrique éditions.
De la Cadena M. (2015) *Earth Beings – Ecologies of Practice Across Andean Worlds*. Durham: Duke University Press.
Demeulenaere E. (2017) 'L'anthropologie au-delà de l'anthropos. Un récit par les marges de la discipline,' in G. Blanc, É. Demeulenaere and W. Feueurhahn (Eds), *Humanités environnementales. Enquêtes et contre-enquêtes*. Paris: Publications de la Sorbonne, Paris.
Descola P. (2005) *Par-delà nature et culture*. Paris: Gallimard.
Despret V. (2019) *Habiter en oiseau*. Arles: Actes sud.
Dewey J. (2011) *La Formation des valeurs*. Paris: Les Empêcheurs de tourner en rond.
Duperrex M. (2019) *Voyage en sol incertain*. Marseille: WildProject.
Escobar A. (2018) *Sentir-Penser avec la terre*. Paris: Éditions du Seuil.
Ferdinand M. (2019) *Une écologie décoloniale. Penser l'écologie depuis le monde caribéen*. Paris: Éditions du Seuil.
Glowczewski B. (2019) '*Se soigner en soignant la terre*,' *Multitudes* 4:77, 161–167.
Gorz A. (1975) *Écologie et politique*. Paris: Galilée.
Graeber D. (2014) *La Démocratie aux marges*. Lormont: Le Bord de l'eau.
Grignon C. and Passeron J.-C. (1989) *Le savant et le populaire. Misérabilsime et populisme en sociologie et en littérature*. Paris: Éditions du Seuil.
Haraway D. (2020) *Vivre avec le trouble*. Vaulx-en-Velin: Éditions des Mondes à Faire.
Holbraad M. and Pedersen M. A. (2016) *The Ontological Turn: An Anthropological Exposition*. Cambridge: Cambridge University Press.
Illouz E. (2019) *Les marchandises émotionnelles: l'authenticité au temps du capitalisme*. Paris: Premier Parallèle.
Ingold T. (2011) *Being Alive. Essays on Movement, Knowledge and Description*. London: Routledge.
James W. (2007) *Philosophie de l'expérience: Un univers pluraliste*. Paris: Les empêcheurs de penser en rond.

Jappe A. (2017) *La société autophage: Capitalisme, démesure et autodestruction*. Paris: La Découverte.
Kohn E. (2017) *Comment pensent les forêts: vers une anthropologie au-delà de l'humain*. Bruxelles: Zones sensibles éditions.
Latour B. (1989) *La Science en action*. Paris: La Découverte.
Latour B. (2012) *Enquête sur les modes d'existence. Une anthropologie des modernes*. Paris: La Découverte.
Latour B. (2015) *Face à Gaïa, Huit conférences sur le nouveau régime climatique*. Paris: La Découverte.
Latour B. (2017) *Où atterrir? Comment s'orienter en politique*. Paris: La Découverte.
Latour B. (2018) 'Esquisse d'un parlement des choses,' *Écologie & politique*, 1:56, 47–64.
Lindgaard J. (Ed.) (2018) *Éloge des mauvaises herbes. Ce que nous devons à la ZAD*. Paris: Les liens qui libèrent.
Morizot B. (2016) *Les diplomates*. Marseille: Wildproject.
Morizot B. (2017) 'Nouvelles alliances avec la terre. Une cohabitation diplomatique avec le vivant,' *Tracés. Revue de Sciences humaines*, 33. https://journals.openedition.org/traces/7001.
Morizot B. (2018) *Sur la piste animale*. Arles: Actes Sud.
Næss A. (2009) *Vers l'écologie profonde*. Marseille: Wildproject.
Pellizzoni L. (2021) 'Nature, limits and form-of-life,' *Environmental Politics*, 30, 1–2, 81–99.
Pignocchi A. (2019) *La Recomposition des mondes*. Paris: Éditions du Seuil.
Plumwood V. (2001) *Environmental Culture*. London: Routledge.
Polanyi K. (1983) *La Grande Transformation*. Paris: Gallimard.
Rahm P. (Ed.) (2020) *Histoire naturelle de l'architecture - Comment le climat, les épidémies et l'énergie ont façonné la ville et les bâtiments*. Paris: Pavillon de L'Arsenal.
Rancière J. (2000) *Le Partage du sensible*. Paris: La fabrique éditions.
Rancière J. (2005) *La Haine de la démocratie*. Paris: La fabrique éditions.
Schaffner M. (Ed.) (2019) *Un sol commun*. Marseille: Wildproject.
Scott J. C. (2013) *Zomia ou L'Art de ne pas être gouverné*. Paris: Éditions du Seuil.
Stengers I. (2020) *Réactiver le sens commun. Lecture de Whitehead en temps de débâcle*. Paris: Les Empêcheurs de tourner en rond.
Tsing A. (2015) *Le Champignon de la fin du monde. Sur les possibilités de vie dans les ruines du capitalisme*. Paris: La Découverte.
Tsing A. (2020) *Friction. Délires et faux-semblants de la globalité*. Paris: La Découverte.
Vidalou J.-B. (2017) *Être forêts. Habiter des territoires en lutte*. Paris: La Découverte.
Viveiros de Castro E. (2009) *Métaphysiques cannibales*. Paris: Presses universitaires de France.
Viveiros de Castro E. (2019) *Politique des multiplicités. Pierre Clastres face à l'État*. Arles: Editions Dehors.

Chapter 3

Commercial drones and the territorialisation of the air

Towards an aero-volumetric understanding of power and territory

Francisco Klauser

> If Ulysses and his companions manage to escape from Polyphemus' den, it is because the monster, devoid of his eyesight, inspects but 'superficially' the sheep that are leaving the cave. Without realising or wanting to, the cyclops experiences the 'map' simply as a surface. He does not inspect what lies 'beneath', and consequently remains unaware of the volume or sphere in which any society evolves. The map is but a metonymic apprehension of territory; the map is not territory itself. Consequently, the multidimensionality of territory that it represents remains inaccessible.
>
> (Raffestin 1999; my translation)

Scholarly accounts of territory have long remained locked in two-dimensional thought and language, mirroring the cyclops' speculative gesture over his beloved sheep's back, rather than learning from Ulysses' cunning use of depth. Concerned with all types of points, lines and planes, and derived graphic forms such as networks, rings and circles, close attention has been paid to the earth's skin. Yet in approaching territorial forms through mathematical metaphors – implying incorporeal linear connections and separations between punctual locations, across planar surfaces – conceptions of territory have failed to grasp, both theoretically and terminologically, the intrinsic volumetric complexities of the studied realities (Sloterdijk 2016: p.257; Morin 2009: p.67).

This has started to change recently. From different theoretical and empirical perspectives, three-dimensional thought has been introduced in politico-geographical literatures, channelled through notions such as 'vertical geopolitics' (Graham 2004; 2016; Graham and Hewitt 2013; Elden 2013), 'politics of verticality' (Weizman 2003; 2004) and 'voluminous states' (Billé 2020), amongst others.

This chapter contributes to this emerging literature. It does so through the discussion of how drones mediate novel ways of engaging with the air, both from the perspective of their users and from a societal viewpoint more generally. To give focus to this discussion, the chapter concentrates on professional drone usage by private companies (hereafter: commercial drone usage). Looking into how drones are used commercially, such is the chapter's basic assumption, tells us

DOI: 10.4324/9781003196365-3

a lot about the complexity and multidimensionality of the spaces of the air in which they fly, and about the conveyed processes and logics of territorialisation. Empirically speaking, this discussion draws upon selected results from a survey conducted in 2017 among professional drone users in Switzerland, in which 922 private businesses and public services took part (Klauser et al. 2017). On these grounds, the chapter pursues three interrelated conceptual objectives. These further pursue a series of previous engagements with the topic (Klauser 2021a; 2021b; Klauser and Pauschinger 2021).

First, the drone example serves as an entry point for the discussion of the aerial realm as a socially produced and managed, i.e. territorialised and socio-political, reality (Deleuze and Guattari 1981; Raffestin 2012). This highlights the need to conceptualise territory as a volume, rather than as a planar surface. Thus the volumetrics of territory are approached here from a specific aerial viewpoint.

Second, the drone problematic is taken as a prism through which to advance novel understandings of the simultaneously elemental and affective, sensory, cognitive and practical dimensions of the territorialised aero-spatial volumes within, through and upon which drones act. Thinking about how these dimensions are bound together offers a route for a volumetric conceptualisation of territory across differing ontological realms (McCormack 2008; 2018).

Third, the chapter adds a specific power sensitivity to its aero-territorial curiosity. Referring to contemporary drone usage, the air is being portrayed as a contested realm on which and through which power is being exercised in highly unequal ways, leading to a wider discussion of the role of the aerial dimension in the exercise of power within, on and across territory.

Accounting for the volume

In the pursuit of these objectives, the chapter connects with three lines of research that have in recent years sharpened our understanding of the volumetric complexities of territory and power. A first body of literature, much of which has adopted an urban focus, revolves around the material dimensions of territory both above and below the ground (Graham 2016). There has been a growing engagement with the lived vertical dimensions of urban morphology, as seen in Brighenti and Pavoni's analysis of urban climbing as a way of 'inhabiting verticality' (2017) and in Bachelard's phenomenological account of the house as an imagined and experienced vertical being. As Bachelard puts it, 'it [the house] rises upward. It differentiates itself in terms of its verticality. It is one of the appeals to our consciousness of verticality. [...] Verticality is ensured by the polarity of cellar and attic' (Bachelard 1969: p.17). As regards the power issues inbuilt in the verticalities of urban settings, we owe a lot to Graham and Hewitt's (2013: p.8, p.9) critique of the trends of 'secession by ascension' and 'vertical capsularisation' inherent in today's 'skyscraper geographies' (McNeill 2005). There is also a fascinating body of work that focuses on the relationship between urban policing and verticality. As Adey puts it, 'securing the megacity is a battle of dimensions' (Adey 2010b: p.53).

Regarding the subterranean dimensions of cities, repeated attention has been paid to the power issues related to urban infrastructures (McFarlane 2008) and to the historic development of subterranean cities more broadly (Pike 2005). Moving beyond cities, scholars have also focused on the volumetric practices and politics conveyed by bunkers (Bennett 2011), tunnels (Cullen Dunn 2020) and mining (Bridge 2013) and on the governance of the geological underground more generally (Braun 2000). This chapter distils from these literatures a particular interest for the complex and manifold ways in which the air is bound up with the (inherently volumetric) material and practical realities on the ground.

A second body of literature addresses the volumetrics of territory from an aerial viewpoint. It invites a reflection on the aerial realm as a geopolitical space that is lived and socio-politically produced in highly unequal ways (Adey 2014b; 2015), whilst also pointing at the ways in which the air is bound up with and mediates action on the ground (Adey 2010a; Elden, 2013). Regarding the latter, consider Graham's work on the USA's aerial bombing of Baghdad (Graham, 2016) and Adey et al.'s analysis of the dynamics of distance and reach implied by aero-mediated remote control systems, which change both the conception of and action on the terrestrial 'air target' (Adey et al. 2011: p.174). These investigations of the air as simultaneously an object, a stake and a perspective of techno-mediated practices of control and power are pushed yet further in Dodge and Kitchin's study of the aerial logics of software, relating to air travel (Dodge and Kitchin 2004). The aerial realm is implicitly depicted here as an 'electrosphere' (Weibel 2012), i.e. as an orbital environment of circulating data that is linked intrinsically to informational infrastructures on the ground.

This chapter's focus on drones connects neatly with these literatures. In particular, the arguments advanced take inspiration from Williams' study of military drone operations in Britain (Williams 2007, 2011a; 2011b, 2013). Showing that drone-related strategies of aerial control and defence are as much about looking up from below as they are about looking down from above, Williams highlights that the drone-mediated, aero-visual 'power projections' (Williams 2011b: p.254) must be approached not merely as a vertical, but as a multi-directional, indeed volumetric, geopolitics. Furthermore, Williams underlines the extent to which the practices and knowledge relating to military drones are both shaped by and, in turn, affect the legal and political dimensions of the airspace in which they unfold. This portrays the airspace as both the product and producer of specific ways of exercising power, i.e. as a carefully managed socio-political reality in a Lefebvrian sense (Lefebvre 1991).

This chapter takes up this relational and power-sensitive problematic of the air, but pushes it beyond Williams' focus on the military and legal-political realms, focusing instead on more mundane and trivial engagements with the air by private companies. Pursuing Adey's plea 'to expand our knowledge of airspaces and the social relations they enhance and make possible' (Adey 2010a: p.15), the chapter affords insight into how commercial drones transform the ways in which the air is encountered and inhabited as a contested space of risks, opportunities and power in daily life. This allows a conceptualisation of the techno-mediated knowledge practices that bring the airspace into being not only as a problem of governance or state security, but as a lived, everyday reality.

Conceptually speaking, this means that the volumetrics of territory are not set here in relation to the state exclusively, but to power in a Foucauldian sense more broadly. This approach is rooted in Claude Raffestin's understanding of territory as socially appropriated, territorialised space which is both the dynamic outcome and the mediator of reciprocal relationships with and within society. As shown elsewhere in more detail (Klauser 2012), Raffestin's relational and processual understanding of territory testifies to his proximity to Lefebvre's conceptualisation of 'social space' (Lefebvre 1991; Raffestin 2012; Murphy 2012). In turn, Raffestin's insistence on the processes of territorialisation, deterritorialisation and reterritorialisation as a way into the concept draws heavily upon Deleuze and Guattari's terminology (Deleuze and Guattari 1981; Raffestin 1984; 2012). As Raffestin states, space is constantly territorialised, de- and re-territorialised, within socio-spatial relations that are mediated by concrete and abstract means (instruments, systems of thought and systems of signs). Thus mediated processes and relationships, rather than space itself, are at the conceptual core of territory (Brighenti 2006: p.65; 2010). A theory of territory, for Raffestin, is also a theory of territorialisation, and, consequently, a theory of mediation, thus resonating with other mediation-centred socio-spatial theory, spanning from Deleuze's (1990) writings on mediation to Latour's actor-network theory (Latour 2005). Analytically speaking, this approach to territory offers a conceptual frame for the investigation of the role played by digital technologies in the orchestration and organisation of the spaces of the everyday (Graham 2005; Kitchin and Dodge 2011; Klauser 2017). In its focus on commercial drone usage, the present chapter adds a volumetric dimension to this problematic.

Yet this chapter is interested not merely in the air as a stake of individually or collectively motivated forms of territorialisation, but also in the elemental (meteorological) and affective dimensions of the aero-spatial volumes within, through and upon which drones act. In this endeavour, the chapter draws upon a third body of literature, which has in recent years started to approach the air in its simultaneous meteorological and affective dimensions (Ingold 2006; Adey et al. 2013). Of particular importance here is McCormack's seminal analysis of the hot air balloon as a mediator that renders the air explicit as a meteorological, but also as a socially relevant, political, techno-scientific and affectively loaded, reality (McCormack 2008; 2018). A similar, if more generalist, reflection can be found in Sloterdijk's work on situations where air becomes 'explicit' as an object, perspective and mediator of power (Sloterdijk 2016).

Connecting with these literatures, the chapter's interest in the elemental and affective dimensions of the air follows in particular the path outlined by Adey's search for an 'elemental geography of air' (Adey 2015: p.71). As Adey puts it, 'airspaces are uneven, distributed, vertical and horizontal. They are domains and doings, performing different shapes and geometries of insides and outsides. Furthermore, they are particularly environmental, vital and immersive' (Adey 2010a: p.207). 'The air is more than just air but constitutive of the material affective relations that animate the experience of the city in a way which we might say is atmospheric' (Adey 2013: p.293). Thus Adey asks for an account of the air that foregrounds the materialities, imaginations, knowledges and sensations through which the air becomes sensible as a volume, i.e. in which people are affectively immersed. In what follows below, this is also how the drone-mediated 'aerial geographies' (Adey 2010a: p.11) will be approached, describing the air, for example, as a space of fear as well as of commercial hope. Leading back to the question of territory as a volume, this also invites a broader reflection on a possible conceptualisation of territory that cuts across diverse – affective, elemental, practical and political – realms. Addressing this problematic, and bringing the aforementioned literatures together, the analysis that follows is structured into four main parts. Subsequently, these explore the air as (1) an economic, (2) a social, (3) a materio-elemental and (4) a legal-political reality, that is invested with all kinds of interests, imaginaries, values and affects, and is bound up with the ground in complex and reciprocal ways.

The air as an economic reality

The 2017 survey stated that 79% of the commercial participants would not 'use the air' without a drone. Three quarters think that drones help their company save money, while for 95%, drones allow the development of new business activities. For 75% of companies that use drones, the technology has become indispensable. This means that for a large majority of commercial drone users, the technology has generated a new relationship with the air, which has since perpetuated itself. There are three main points to highlight with regard to the unfolding commercialisation of the air.

First, commercial drone usage implies that the air is being invested increasingly with monetary value and made explicit through logics of capital investment and return (Andrejevic 2016). More than one third (36%) of commercial drone users earn up to 10,000 Swiss francs a year (about 9,100 Euros at the time of writing) with their drone. Another 31% claim to earn up to 100,000 francs a year. Of the companies surveyed, 38% use their drone at least once a week, and another 35% at least once a month. This indicates that the economic benefits generated by drones relate to relatively small revenues and relatively sporadic missions. Drones have transformed the air into an object of commercial interest and hope, but this has opened up a complementary, rather than exclusive, business plan for the companies concerned. Yet 90% of commercial drone users expect their deployment of drones to be more frequent in the future, and 91% expect their drone to be replaced by a more sophisticated model. Thus the business-driven use of the air is expected to develop further in both quantity and quality, in search for increased profitability.

Second, commercial drone usage inscribes the air in a dynamic of economic specialisation and professionalisation. Services are delivered to peer companies by 47% of companies that use drones, 71% deliver services to other private companies, 68% to public institutions and 61% to private individuals. Thus using the air becomes a matter of practical and technical expertise.

An in-depth case study of a Swiss start-up company that specialises in the construction and use of spray drones in viticulture allows further elaboration on this (Klauser and Pauschinger forthcoming). The study exemplifies how companies today position themselves as 'experts of the air,' marketing and selling their technical expertise and practical skills in an attempt to establish themselves as 'obligatory passage points' (Latour 1987) in the organisational settings and coalitions of authority that shape the instrumentalisation of the air for entrepreneurial purposes.

Third, commercial drone usage also implies novel ways of territorialising the ground, due to the drone's imaging and/or transporting capabilities. With the exception of one survey participant, all commercial drone users said that they deployed at least one type of visual sensor with their drone, spanning from ordinary photo and video cameras (with and/or without live stream) to thermal and infrared cameras. As remote 'vision machines' (Virilio 2000), drones enable specific ways of watching the ground from and through the air, combining various geographical scales and spatially articulated logics of IT-mediated vision and visualisation from above and afar, depending on their flight altitude, reach and autonomy, on their mobility or fixity in the air, and on the cameras' technical features (camera type, zoom, angle of vision, verticality or angularity, etc.). There is a practical dimension to this visual form of territorialisation whenever drones support activities in the field, whether in real time or in providing image records for later use.

Resonating with Parks' work on 'vertical mediation' (Parks 2016: p.232), the air is discovered not only as a context in which to fly and as a stake of entrepreneurial interests, intentions and actions, but also as a perspective and mediator of vision onto and action on the ground, combining different spatial and temporal logics. As aero-visual 'techniques of power' in a Foucauldian sense – i.e. as chains of entities that mediate action on other actions (Foucault 1982; Latour 1999: p.210) – drones establish the air as a three-dimensional 'conveyor of things' (Adey 2014a: p.37). Think of agricultural drones for crop-spraying, of drones used to optimise the organisation of construction sites, or of drones in policing missions. In all these cases, what happens on the ground also depends on what happens in the air. Put differently, drones enable action in and on particular places insofar as these are approached as aerial volumes, thus underscoring – as discussed above – the need to understand territory not as a planar surface, but in its volumetric dimensions.

Interestingly, the drone-mediated territorialisation of the ground can go so far as to affect the very organisation of the latter. Consider the quote that follows, taken from the aforementioned case study of spray drones in viticulture.

> You have to accept some cultivation changes if you want to operate by drone. Doing things like we've always done, with a light thinning of the leaves, will be complicated. For me, operating by drone implies a much heavier leaf thinning.
>
> (Interview with pilot from AgroDrone who is responsible for the vineyards in the city of Lausanne, 24 March 2019)

Here, using the air requires an adaptation of the cultivation practices on the ground. Thus specific knowledge and practices in relation to the air also produce specific knowledge and practices in relation to the ground. Our interviewee continues:

> It's organic and it's ultra-precise. … These are things that are very positive, which also produce a more dynamic, modern and interesting image. I think there's a possibility here to favour the promotion and commercialisation of our wines, if we put more emphasis on these kinds of new technologies. We are losing the youth amongst the wine consumers. They drink beer, no more wine. And here, we may have something to interest them, to prove that it's something modern.
>
> (Interview with pilot from AgroDrone who is responsible for the vineyards in the city of Lausanne, 24 March 2019)

This quotation implies that sprayer drones affect agriculture not only in a practical sense, in that they change existing farming practices and force adaptations to be made to the crops and fields that need spraying, but also symbolically, in that they bring particular values and imaginaries into the farming sector. Of course, a much more detailed study of how agricultural drones are perceived by the population would be necessary in order to differentiate the advanced vision of the potential offered by the technology for the promotion and marketing of wines. Here, this comment is merely taken as an indication of the link between the symbolics and the visibility of drones, and the symbolics and societal visibility of farming. More generally speaking, this then raises the question of how commercial drone usage might affect the very perception and understanding of the professional fields in which a novel relation with the air is being established.

The air as a social reality

Commercial drone usage has developed exponentially over the last ten years. Only 6% of the commercial survey participants started using drones before 2010 (Klauser et al. 2017). Fifty-seven percent expect the number of drones to multiply between two and ten-fold over the next ten years, and 24% predict that there will be 10 to 20 times more drones in ten years' time. The survey also revealed that 78% think that peer companies will start using drones in the future. This underscores the recent proliferation, current momentum and future potential of commercial drone usage, and hints at the increased competition to come, coupled with economically motivated struggles over the air.

Yet this is not to say that the drone-mediated territorialisation of the air spans equally across all economic sectors, or across society as a whole. Rather, drone technology has been appropriated selectively. More than one quarter (28%) of the commercial survey participants specialise in aerial photography, 23% in land surveying or cartography and 16% in the cinematographic industry. From a societal viewpoint, a similarly unequal appropriation of the technology can be observed, as shown by a public opinion poll conducted in 2015 in the Swiss canton of Neuchâtel (604 participants) (Klauser and Pedrozo 2017). Both age and gender are important factors of differentiation. Whilst 17% of the respondents between 20 and 34 years have previous experience of flying a drone, this decreases to 11, 6.5 and 3.5% for the older age categories (35–49, 50–64, and 65–79 years). In addition, while 16% of the male respondents have previous experience of piloting unmanned aircraft, this is true of only 1.8% of the female participants. Drones are 'toys for the boys,' as Salter puts it (Salter 2014). Airspace remains a highly segregated space, as has been the case across its long history (Spain 1992; Millward 1998). What has changed is that the use of the air for purposes of aerial imagery is no longer the exclusive privilege of a few elderly rulers or experts (cartographers, statesmen, etc.) (O Tuathail 1996), but open to (some) businesses and technophile young men. This raises questions regarding the economic, gendered and intergenerational power relations that today underpin the socio-political production of airspace as a lived, perceived and conceived space in a Lefebvrian sense (Lefebvre 1991). With the unequal appropriation of the technology, the exercise of 'power through the air' becomes a social and a political issue in new ways (Williams 2011a, 2011b; Adey, Whitehead and Williams 2013). What Graham and Hewitt call 'secession by ascension' (2013: p.8, p.9) can also be seen from an aerial viewpoint. Territory, in its volumetrics, is shaped by all kinds of power relations.

A majority of the population is critical of this commercial occupation and instrumentalisation of the air. Whilst most respondents of the aforementioned public opinion poll are supportive of the use of unarmed military and police drones (65% and 72% respectively), approval decreases to 23% when it comes to commercial drones (Klauser and Pedrozo 2017; see also Thompson and Bracken-Roche 2015). Hereby, the public not only rejects commercial drone usage for purposes of aerial photography and filming, but also for postal services. What is at stake is not just the commercialisation of the aerial gaze, but the commercialisation of the air more generally. Privacy worries were reported by 60%, while 57% fear accidents in connection with commercial drones. Thus the entrepreneurial territorialisation of the air also raises societal concern and fear, especially amongst the elder generations (Klauser and Pedrozo 2017). Interestingly, this societal unease is also felt by commercial drone users themselves: 54% of survey participants think that there is a low acceptance rate of their activities among the public, and that this limits the scope of commercial drone usage. As Klauser and Pedrozo conclude,

> whilst it may be said that drones have redefined the aerial sovereignty and supremacy of the state, this does not go without inner-societal tensions and contestations. Put differently, drones make airspace more explicit and more available for social reflection and action, but it is also this very novel potential of societal co-production that makes airspace today an increasingly contested space in which, and through which, power is exercised in unequal ways.
>
> (Klauser and Pedrozo 2017: p.237)

In this light, the air appears not only as an economically coveted, but also as a socially contested, realm, which is being invested with societal feelings of suspicion, mistrust and anxiety. As Adey puts it, 'the air is more than just air but constitutive of the material affective relations that animate the experience of the city in a way which we might say is atmospheric' (Adey 2013: p.293). Territory as a volume must also be approached as an affectively laden reality, oscillating, in the case of commercial drones, between economic hope and societal fear.

The air as a materio-elemental reality

When asked to choose (from a list of twelve options) the three factors that most limit commercial drone usage, weather conditions were selected most commonly (by 74% of the commercial drone users). Almost half (49%) perceived that weather conditions were also the most important safety issue. Practically speaking, drone users thus encounter the air as a set of elemental processes, such as wind and rain, which become economically relevant in new ways. The air is thus being discovered 'because of what it does' (Adey 2014a: p.16), as a more or less agitated 'field of moving materiality' (Ingold 2006) in which drone users find themselves immersed, and which they cannot fully control. This underscores the need to approach the volumetrics of territory from a material, and indeed elemental, viewpoint.

Yet the experiences of the air masses in which drones fly do not only depend on the 'animate agency' (McCormack 2008: p.415) of the air's atmospheric infill. The 'envelopes of atmospheric experience' (McCormack 2018: p.10) of the pilots are also affected by the material and practical realities on the ground. Think of obstacles such as power lines and buildings, walls and trees, which raise both practical challenges and legal issues, connected with the legal obligation to keep the drone in the line of sight. Again, the example of agricultural drones is particularly interesting. As prescribed in the Swiss legal framework, flat field crops (salads, cabbages, etc.) require a minimal flight altitude of 20 metres for spraying pesticides by drones, to keep spray drift at the level of ground-based equipment for the application of pesticides. In contrast, vertical crops, such as those in vineyards and timber plantations, can be flown over at whatever height the pilot sees fit. Thus the crop's height defines the drone's height, and the vertical organisation of the ground is therefore bound up with the vertical organisation of the air. The air is regulated as a situated volume, and as such is linked intrinsically to the 'grounded fixities of landscape' (Ingold 2006: p.17). In this respect, it is also telling that 98% of commercial drone users consider the very fact that drones can be operated from the ground to be an important advantage of the technology. The very functioning of drones combines and connects entities in the air and on the ground. Analogous to Adey's study of air travel, drone flight 'is both constituted by and expressed in a set of geographies, infrastructures, relations and processes that connect both land and air' (Adey 2010a: p.8). Drones bring the air and the ground together into novel relations of 'vertical reciprocity' (Adey 2010a: p.3), and the spaces created and territorialised through drone usage must therefore be understood in their complex compositions of both aerial and terrestrial realms.

Pushing this reflection one step further, it appears that the qualities, shape and reach of drone users' volumetric spheres of action also depend on the pilots' earthbound location and corporal position. As confirmed by extensive observational research, drone pilots usually adopt a corporal position in which the head is bent backwards with the eyes fixed upwards on the flying engine, which Simonsen calls an 'aviation neck' (2011). Frequently, pilots also change location on the ground in order to keep the drone within visual line of sight (Klauser 2021a). Drone pilots thus also find themselves immersed in a bodily sense within the air's 'force field' (Stewart, in Gandy 2017: p.360). Drones instil their users not only with an airbound mind, but also with an 'air-minded body' (Adey 2010a: p.33). An investigation of how drones mediate their users' relationship with the air must look not only at how the air is engaged in specific practices, perceptions and imaginations, but also at how it is embodied as a 'persistent material or meteorological presence, either real or imagined, which envelops or unsettles the human subject [here: commercial drone users]' (Gandy 2017: p.355).

The air as a legal-political reality

In many ways, the width and height of the volumes created by the drones' aerial trajectories are also conditioned by legal regulations and limitations. The example given above of the prescribed height of spray drones has already hinted at this. Moving beyond the field of agriculture, Swiss drone legislation defines how high drones can be flown (flights over 300 metres' altitude require special authorisation) and where and how far drones can be flown (drones have to remain within visual line of sight and cannot overfly protected eco-reserves, risk sites or gatherings of people, which applies to most inner-city zones).

This vertical and horizontal legal-political ordering of the air creates an unevenly lived aerial geography of drone usage: commercial drone operations take place mostly in rural and peripheral urban areas (Pauschinger and Klauser 2020). A clear majority of the commercial survey participants, 83%, 78% and 61%, indicate that they never overfly high-risk sites, gatherings of people and protected eco-zones respectively. Almost all, 89%, always fly below 300m. Although these numbers should be interpreted cautiously, they underscore the 'uneven skies' (Adey 2010a: p.74) in which drone users find themselves. Furthermore, they exemplify that myriad individuals and organisations, agendas, laws and regulations, etc. intervene in pilots' relationship with the air. These must also be considered if we are to understand the 'complex geography of airspace management' (Adey 2010a: p.14) that regulates and affects territory in its aero-volumetric dimensions.

In this, the technical specificities of the deployed drones themselves also play an important role. In agriculture, for example, spray drones are only allowed if capable of autonomous flight. Also, the height, distance, duration, speed and stability of drone flight depend on the battery's autonomy, additional software applications, GPS sensors, and so on. What emerges is a complex 'socio-technical assemblage' of the air, in a Latourian sense, i.e. as a reality composed of combined and co-constituted technical and social elements (Latour, 1993, p. 62).

Thus, as with any mediator, drones have their own scope and limits, and as such condition their users' relationship with the air and environmental immersion. Depending on their technical specificities, drones cause their users to live the air as a more or less stretched volume, streaked with internal barriers and external contours. This provides drone users with a sense of immersion within a complex volumetric geometry that makes them think about all kinds of things, such as how far and how high to fly, what obstacles to avoid, how to position themselves, how to equip their drone, etc., which in turn affects their 'ongoing process of imagining and re-imagining' the air (Millward 1998: p.18).

Conclusions

In sum, the aero-spatial volumes of drone flight must be understood simultaneously in their elemental, economic, social and legal-political qualities, in their place-related and drone-related shapes and limits, and in their reciprocal relationships with the realities on the ground. They are being territorialised as the object of all kinds of intentions and practices, cognitive meanings and affective values (of fear or of hope, for example), imaginaries, practical considerations and strategic choices, and as such performed (named, imagined), experienced (as immersive environments) and embodied by drone users, whilst also being connected to other actors (e.g. policy makers, competing companies) and mediated by the technical specificities of the deployed drone system. Thus this chapter also sheds light on the complex relational configurations of material and immaterial realms, practices, affects and imaginations, from a wide range of actors, that co-produce and result from the present-day encounter of commercial drones and the air.

Regarding the conceptualisation of territory as a volume, this underlines that the aerial realm is not neutral, but the product and producer of all kinds of power relations in a Foucauldian sense. Drones mediate novel logics of striation of the air, to use Deleuze and Guattari's term (Deleuze and Guattari 1988), i.e.

they convey novel ways of ordering the air, both vertically and horizontally, and they produce legally, practically and materially defined geometries, internal structures and contours of the air. These geometries of the air are lived, experienced and socio-politically produced in highly unequal ways. Differing ways of accessing and using the air require differing tools, skills and legal authorisations. Furthermore, the air is not equally appropriated across society as a whole. The geometries of the drone-populated air remain inherently pluralistic, and as such fundamentally secessionary and conflictual. Indeed, from a societal viewpoint, the increased occupation of the air for professional purposes is not seen as legitimate in all contexts, or for all purposes. Rather, the air is becoming a focal point of societal concern and judgement, competition and dispute. In addition, this chapter has depicted the air as a volumetric territory that mediates the exercise of power in differing ways and on many levels. Drones engage the air in variable spatial and temporal logics of watching and acting, and imply novel ways of organising the ground. In sum, the drone-populated air appears not only as a locus and object, but also as a tool and perspective of power.

From this derives a wider agenda for future reflection and theorisation, in order to gain a more elaborate understanding of the plurality and pluridimensionality of the volumetric spaces in which, on which and through which power is being exercised, including by commercial drone users. In turn, this also invites further theoretical reflection on (a) the scope and basic vocabulary of a properly aero-volumetric way of thinking about power and territory and (b) the very possibility of a three-dimensional type of political geography.

Acknowledgements

This chapter brings together several previously published pieces of work, relating to the specificities of commercial drone usage (Klauser et al. 2017), police drones and the air (Klauser 2021a; 2021b), drones in the agricultural sector (Klauser and Pauschinger, forthcoming) and the societal perception of drones (Klauser and Pedrozo 2017). I thank my collaborators, Dennis Pauschinger and Silvana Pedrozo, with whom the fieldwork of these studies was conducted, before being further developed here with a view to a fuller theorisation of the aero-volumetric dimensions of territory.

References

Adey, P. (2010a) *Aerial Life*. Oxford, Wiley Blackwell.

Adey, P. (2010b) Vertical security in the megacity: Legibility, mobility and aerial politics. *Theory, Culture and Society*. 27(6), 51–67.

Adey, P. (2013) Air/atmospheres of the megacity. *Theory, Culture & Society*. 30 (7–8), 291–308.

Adey, P. (2014a) *Air*. London, Reaktion Books.
Adey, P. (2014b) Security atmospheres or the crystallisation of worlds. *Environment and Planning D: Society and Space*. 32(5), 834–851.
Adey, P. (2015) Air's affinities: Geopolitics, chemical affect and the force of the elemental. *Dialogues in Human Geography*. 5(1), 54–75.
Adey, P., Brayer, L., Masson, D., Murphy, P., Simpson, P. and Tixier, N. (2013) Pour votre tranquilité: Ambiance, atmosphere, and surveillance. *Geoforum*. 49, 299–309.
Adey, P., Whitehead, M. and Williams, A. J. (2011) Air-target: Distance, reach and the politics of verticality. *Theory, Culture & Society*. 28(7–8), 173–187.
Andrejevic, M. (2016) Theorizing drones and droning theory. In: Završnik, A. (ed.) *Drones and Unmanned Aerial Systems: Legal and Social Implications for Security and Surveillance*. Cham, Springer, pp. 21–43.
Bachelard, G. (1969) *The Poetics of Space*. Boston, Beacon Press.
Bennett, L. (2011) Bunkerology: A case study in the theory and practice of urban exploration. *Environment and Planning D: Society and Space*. 29(3), 421–434.
Billé, F. (2020) *Voluminous States: Sovereignty, Materiality, and the Territorial Imagination*. Durham, Duke University Press.
Braun, B. (2000) Producing vertical territory: Geology and governmentality in late Victorian Canada. *Cultural Geographies*. 7(1), 7–46.
Bridge, G. (2013) Territory, now in 3D! *Political Geography*. 34, 55–57.
Brighenti, A. M. (2006) On territory as relationship and law as territory. *Canadian Journal of Law and Society*. 21(2), 65–86.
Brighenti, A. M. (2010) On territorology, towards a general science of territory. *Theory, Culture & Society*. 27(1), 52–72.
Brighenti, A. M. and Pavoni, A. (2017) Climbing the city: Inhabiting verticality outside of comfort bubbles. *Journal of Urbanism International Research on Placemaking and Urban Sustainability*. 11(2), 1–18.
Cullen Dunn, E. (2020) Tunnel striating and militarizing subterranean space in the republic of Georgia. In: Billé, F. (ed.) *Voluminous States*. Durham, Duke University Press, pp. 52–63.
Deleuze, G. and Guattari, F. (1981) Rhizome. *Ideology and Consciousness*. 8, 49–71.
Deleuze, G. and Guattari, F. (1988) *A Thousand Plateaus: Capitalism and Schizophrenia*. London, Athlone.
Deleuze, G. (1990) *Mediators*. In: *Negotiations*. New York, Columbia University Press, pp. 121–134.
Dodge, M. and Kitchin, R. (2004) Flying through code/space: The real virtuality of air travel. *Environment and Planning A*. 36(2), 195–211.
Elden, S. (2013) Secure the volume: Vertical geopolitics and the depth of power. *Political Geography*. 34, 35–51.
Foucault, M. (1982) The subject and power. *Critical Inquiry*. 8(4), 777–795.
Gandy, M. (2017) Urban atmospheres. *Cultural Geographies*. 24(3), 353–374.
Graham, S. (2004) Vertical geopolitics: Baghdad and after. *Antipode*. 36(1), 12–23.
Graham, S. (2005) Software-sorted geographies. *Progress in Human Geography*. 29, 562–580.
Graham, S. and Hewitt, L. (2013) Getting off the ground: On the politics of urban verticality. *Progress in Human Geography*. 37, 72–92.
Graham, S. (2016) *Vertical*. London, Verso.
Ingold, T. (2006) Rethinking the animate, re-animating thought. *Ethnos*. 71(1), 9–20.

Kitchin, R. and Dodge, M. (2011) *Code/Space: Software and Everyday Life*. Cambridge, MIT Press.

Klauser, F. (2012) Thinking through territoriality: Introducing Claude Raffestin to Anglophone sociospatial theory. *Environment and Planning D: Society and Space*. 30(1), 106–121.

Klauser, F. (2017) *Surveillance and Space*. London, Sage.

Klauser, F. (2021a) Policing with the drone: Towards an aerial geopolitics of security. *Security Dialogue*. Online early view.

Klauser, F. (2021b) Police drones and the air: Towards a volumetric geopolitics of security. *Swiss Political Science Review*. Online early view.

Klauser, F. and Pauschinger, D. (2021) Entrepreneurs of the air: sprayer drones as mediators of volumetric agriculture. *Journal of Rural Studies*. Online early view.

Klauser, F., Pauschinger, D., Pedrozo, S., Stuber, L. and Placi, R. (2017) Professional drone usage in Switzerland: Results of a quantatative survey of public and private drone users, Working Paper, 2–2017/E, Neuchâtel University. Available from: https://www.unine.ch/files/live/sites/maps/files/shared/documents/wp/WP-2_2017_FK_et_al.pdf [Accessed 12 February 2021].

Klauser, F. and Pedrozo, S. (2017) Big data from the sky: Popular perceptions of private drones in Switzerland. *Geographica Helvetica*. 72, 231–239.

Latour, B. (1987) *Science in Action*. Cambridge, Harvard University Press.

Latour, B. (1999) *Pandora's Hope*. Cambridge, Harvard University Press.

Latour, B. (2005) *Reassembling the Social: An Introduction to Actor-Network-Theory*. New York, Oxford University Press.

Lefebvre, H. (1991) *The Production of Space*. Oxford, Blackwell.

McCormack, D. (2008) Engineering affective atmospheres on the moving geographies of the 1897 Andrée expedition. *Cultural Geographies*. 15(4), 413–430.

McCormack, D. (2018) *Atmospheric Things: On the Allure of Elemental Envelopment*. Durham, Duke University Press.

McFarlane, C. (2008) Governing the contaminated city: Infrastructure and sanitation in colonial and post-colonial Bombay. *International Journal of Urban and Regional Research*. 32(2), 415–435.

McNeill, D. (2005) Skyscraper geography. *Progress in Human Geography*. 29(1), 41–55.

Millward, L. (1998) The 'aerial eye': Gender and the colonization of airspace. *Michigan Feminist Studies*. 13, 1–18.

Morin, M.-E. (2009) Cohabitating in the globalised world: Peter Sloterdijk's global foams and Bruno Latour's cosmopolitics. *Environment and Planning D: Society and Space*. 27, 58–72.

Murphy, A. (2012) Entente territorial: Sack and Raffestin on territoriality. *Environment and Planning D: Society and Space*. 30(1), 159–172.

O Tuathail, G. (1996) *Critical Geopolitics*. London, Routledge.

Parks, L. (2016) Drones, vertical mediation, and the targeted class. *Feminist Studies*. 42 (1), 227–235.

Pauschinger, D. and Klauser, F. (2020) Aerial politics of visibility: Actors, spaces and drivers of professional drone usage in Switzerland. *Surveillance and Society*. 18(4), 443–466.

Pike, D. L. (2005) *Subterranean Cities: The World Beneath Paris and London, 1800–1945*. Ithaca, Cornell University Press.

Raffestin, C. (1984) La territorialité: miroir des discordances entre tradition et modernité. *Revue de l'Institut de Sociologie de l'Université de Bruxelles*. 3–4, 437–447.

Raffestin, C. (1999) *Du plan à la sphère ou le dialogue entre urbanisme et sciences humaines.* Unpublished manuscript.

Raffestin, C. (2012) Space, territory, and territoriality. *Environment and Planning D: Society and Space.* 30(1), 121–141.

Salter, M. (2014) Toys for the boys? Drones, pleasure and popular culture in the militarisation of policing. *Critical Criminology.* 22, 163–177.

Simonsen, D. G. (2011) *The aviation neck: Techno-choreographies of early flight.* Talk given at the conference Up in the Air: early flight and 'air-mindedness'. London, Westminster University.

Sloterdijk, P. (2016) *Foams. Spheres Volume III: Plural Spherology.* Cambridge, MIT Press.

Spain, D. (1992) *Gendered Spaces.* Chapel Hill, University of North Carolina Press.

Thompson, S. and Bracken-Roche, C. (2015) Understanding public opinion of UAVs in Canada: A 2014 analysis of survey data and its policy implications. *Journal of Unmanned Vehicle Systems.* 3, 156–175.

Virilio, P. (2000) *The Information Bomb.* London, Verso.

Weibel, P. (2012) Elektrosphären. In: Heibach, C. (ed.) *Atmosphären. Dimensionen eines diffusen Phänomens.* Munich, Wilhelm Fink, pp. 155–170.

Weizman, E. (2003) The politics of verticality: The West Bank as an architectural construction. In: Biesenbach, K. (ed.) *Territories: Islands, Camps, and Other States of Utopia.* Walther König, Köln, pp. 64–118.

Weizman, E. (2004) Strategic points, flexible lines, tense surfaces, and political volumes. In: Graham, S. (ed.) *Cities, War and Terrorism: Towards and Urban Geopolitics.* Wiley-Blackwell, Oxford, pp. 172–191.

Williams, A. J. (2007) Hakumat al Tayarrat: The role of air power in the enforcement of Iraq's boundaries. *Geopolitics.* 12(3), 505–528.

Williams, A. J. (2011a) Enabling persistent presence? Perfoming the embodied geopolitics of the unmanned aerial vehicle assemblage. *Political Geography.* 30(7), 381–390.

Williams, A. J. (2011b) Reconceptualising spaces of the air: Performing the multiple spatialities of UK military airspaces. *Transactions of the Institute of British Geographers.* 36(2), 253–267.

Williams, A. J. (2013) Re-orientating vertical geopolitics. *Geopolitics.* 18(1), 225–246.

Chapter 4

Inhabiting Together

Manure Contracts and Other Territorial Compositions Between Pastoralism and Agriculture in Western Burkina Faso

Alexis Gonin

Introduction

How to inhabit together with other living beings? Two global trends clearly show the new relevance of this issue: on the one hand, the increase in inequalities and the difficulty of equitably sharing resources is a sign of the distension of human collectives; on the other hand, the rapid erosion of biodiversity shows our difficulties in sharing ecosystems with beings other than humans. The global upheavals of the Anthropocene can also be read as a crisis of inhabiting with others on the same planet (Latour and Chakrabarty 2020). Inhabiting means adapting oneself to the place where we live, and, at the same time, making it fit for us. This involves stabilizing relations with others: one always shares a place with others, inhabiting is always inhabiting together. It is not simply a matter of leading parallel lives, but a recognition of our interdependencies with others, and at the same time an effort to adjust these interdependencies, if possible making them mutually beneficial.

Territory is a possible answer to the question of inhabiting together. Territory shows how the world is made inhabitable by living beings. We will argue that territories result from a process of stabilizing the interrelations they depend upon. The territory of the 'Moderns' (Latour 1993) was designed to control and dominate populations, and secure access to resources. It is a territory of power, which gave the illusion of erasing all other forms of territoriality. But modern territoriality has been overtaken of other territorial forms (Antheaume and Giraut 2005). Territories result from the activity of a great diversity of actors. They care for the interdependencies that bind them to the multitude of those with whom they inhabit. This chapter, participating in its own way in the collective effort of this book, aims to enrich the notion of territory to address the challenges of the Anthropocene. It proposes an interpretation of territory based on a dialogue between research approaches that most often ignore each other. Their fruitful crossover could be further explored.

The adjustment of our relationships with others is at the heart of the question of inhabiting together. Territories are produced by relationships (Brighenti 2010). However, what is a relationship? Through what processes, in what ways

DOI: 10.4324/9781003196365-4

do relationships produce territories? These questions have been addressed by geographers who, in the 1990s and 2000s, used actor-network theory (ANT) to lay the foundations of a relational geography (Massey 2005, Thrift 2006), drawing on a vast relational turn in the humanities and social sciences. In this movement, it is above all the notion of space that has been reassessed (Law 1992, Murdoch 1998, Malpas 2012). The notion of territory has been largely let aside, even though some analyses have paved the road to a reassessment of territory according to a relational approach (Murdoch 2005, Kärrholm 2007, Jones 2009, Brighenti 2010, Müller 2015). This apparent neglect may be explained by the fact that, at the time, territory still appeared first and foremost as the space of power, and as such a leading notion in political geography (Agnew 2013). On its turn, ANT was charged by its critics of diluting intentionality, a postulate at the basis of power games, and, consequently, of depoliticizing phenomena (Latour 2005). In this chapter, I attempt to go beyond these alleged shortcomings to further explore the fruitful intersection between ANT and territorial science.

The chapter is also consistent with a trend, of which Claude Raffestin (2012) may be the precursor, which explores the links between space and territory. The chapter is structured around the articulation of the two concepts. The space/territory couple is the keystone of the first movement of the chapter, from part 1 to part 2. The shift from space to territory is seen as a form of stabilization (Kärrholm 2007, Brighenti and Kärrholm 2020), a process of making the world inhabitable. The second movement, part 2 to 3, is based on the passage from intra-territorial relations to inter-territorial relations. In conclusion, I will sketch out a third movement, from part 3 to part 1, to close the cycle, and suggest that the process of territorialization can be undone, and that fragments of territories can be mobilized in new spaces.

This interpretation of the notion of territory is mobilized to examine the nature of pastoral territories and their relationship with agricultural territories. In particular, we refer to pastoralism in the Sudanian savannas of West Africa, a bioclimatic area where annual rainfalls range from 400 to 1200 mm. Fieldwork was conducted there between 2007 and 2017. Herders, farmers, village leaders, administrators, politicians and experts were interviewed. Pastoralism has been practiced in Western Burkina Faso since the 1970s. Previously, the region was almost exclusively agricultural, and the bush was sparsely anthropized. Agriculture still dominates land use today. More and more farmers practice animal husbandry, while almost all herders also practice agriculture. They must therefore inhabit together in the territories of pastoralism and agriculture.

The Spatial Dimension of Territories

One way to understand territory is to address its spatial dimension, in the sense that territory 'derives' from space (Raffestin 2012). Relationships constitute the framework of space. Understanding first the dynamic nature of spatial relationships will then help us to better understand territorial relationships.

Relationships and Spatial Dynamics

Far from the Euclidean version of space as an absolute container of the objects and phenomena it houses, in the social sciences space is widely regarded as a fundamentally relational construct (Law 2000). The relational structure of space can be better understood if attention is focused on spatial dynamics: spatial relationships and dynamics are mutually generated. For example, what makes a pastureland a space? Rain falls, water infiltrates the soil, which retains moisture, grasses rise, herds come to graze, selecting certain plant species whose growth is stopped in favor of those of others, animals deposit their excrement which brings organic matter to the soil and nutrients for the plant species… This temporal sequence shows how change flows through the spatial relations between entities, how action is 'dislocated' (Latour 2005). One change leads to another, connections are made. Relationships are established that allow movement to flow through space, as well as to constitute it. The space extends as far as the movement continues. It ends when the movement ends, or when a connection is interrupted, so relationships are no longer established. A pastureland stops when it stops raining; or when the nature of the soil changes and the grass no longer grows; or when a field is cleared and growing grass is removed by a farmer. Relationships allow movement to continue and expand space. Space is fundamentally both relationships and dynamics.

The FulBe pastoralists, an ethnic group that speaks Fufulde language, and who are the main transhumant herders in the Sahelo-Sudanian savannas throughout West Africa, regard pastures as spatial dynamics. They are able to identify different grazing ecosystems as so many spatio-temporal processes endowed with their own seasonal dynamics. The FulBe use spatio-temporal categories that allow herds to be led according to three key variables, which change with the seasons and the weather: fodder availability, water availability and the risk of crop damage (the risk of herds entering cultivated fields during grazing movement). These categories (see Figure 4.1) first described by Eric

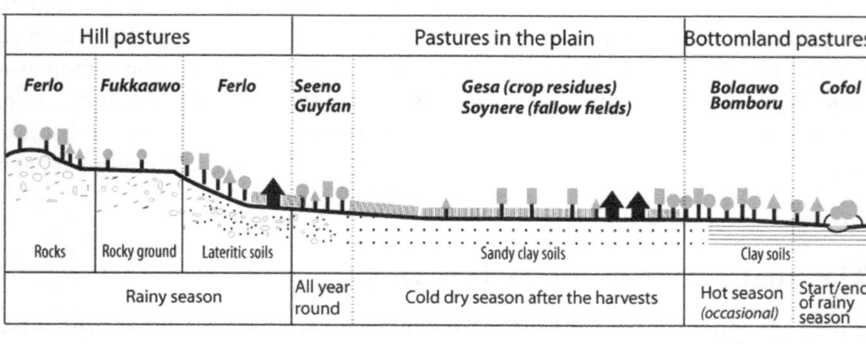

Figure 4.1 Spatio-temporal categories used by FulBe to characterize pastures in Western Burkina Faso (based on figure in Vall and Diallo 2009: 129).

Vall and Mohamadoun A. Diallo (2009) were confirmed in my interviews with herders during fieldwork.

In the early rainy season (called *gataaje* by FulBe herders in Western Burkina Faso) pasturelands primarily expand in the lowlands (*cofol*), where the grass grows earlier and the first ponds of the season appear. They also expand on the slopes, through areas that will then be cultivated (*soynere* and *gesa*, see Figure 4.3). Rainy season (*ndungu*) pasturelands form in the fallows (*soynere*) between cultivated fields, and on the hills (*ferlo, fukkaawo*), where the grass grows and which have the advantage of being away from the fields that are being cultivated. At the beginning of the dry season (dry and cold season, *dabbude*), the agricultural areas (*gesa*) on the slopes gradually become pastoral as they are harvested. Crop residues become the main fodder (*nyayle*). During the second half of the dry season (dry and hot season, *ceedu*), the pastoral areas retract. It is a difficult season for the herds, the largest of which go southward on transhumance, towards areas where first rains come sooner. Traditional ecological knowledge underlying herding decisions of pastoralists (Tamou et al. 2018) shows the FulBe view landscapes in terms of spatial dynamics. Each of the categories of pasturelands inseparably links the spatial and temporal dimensions. For example, a *cofol* (lowland pasture) exists as a pastureland when the first rains green up herbaceous fodder in these places and allow

Figure 4.2 A shepherd trying to keep zebu away from a cultivated field (photograph by author).

Figure 4.3 *Gesa*, a field before its cultivation, during early rainy season (photograph by author).

the animals to water. In the rainy season, it loses its value (watering ponds and better quality fodder are available elsewhere, on the hills, *ferlo and fukkaawo*, and fallow land, *soynere*). In the dry season, when there are neither ponds nor fodder, *cofol* no longer exists as a space from a pastoral point of view. A space exists in a place, at a time. When the connecting movement that gave birth to it stops, the space disappears.

Spatial dynamics thus arise from the process of establishing relationships. Movement is relayed through spatial relationships. The notion of agency, as understood by ANT (Latour 2005), is helpful to describe dynamics unleashed by the creation of relationships. Connected entities are enrolled in a spatial dynamic that overwhelms and modifies them. Consequently 'agent' names entities that can be enrolled in a movement, and which relay action because they are connected to each other. Agents do not act alone or on their own, agency is always distributed. Agency exists through relationships, and thus it flows through space and constitutes it. It is spatial, in the sense that the relations through which the action flows are spatial: the reciprocal situations of entities mobilized by the action, the topographical or topological distance, the material properties in which these relations are embodied, give agency its spatial dimension. In other words, space acts as a mediator of the relations. Moreover, each agent which participates in the action extends itself through space *via* its relations with others. The metabolism of the zebu and its nutritional needs sets the scale of the pastures it needs, and participates in the dynamics of these pastures. There is a continuity between individuals or groups and their space. Agencies flow through relationships and are the vectors through which space is assembled. How are they assembled to compose a particular space?

Spaces as Trajectories of Assembled Agencies

I draw on the notion of *affordance* defined by James J. Gibson (1977) as 'what [the environment] offers the animal, what it *provides* or *furnishes*, either for good or ill.' The notion helps to understand the way in which agencies are associated with each other. The agencies offer several grasps, they are available for different interpretations, representations, uses, which are not mutually exclusive. Moreover, the possible grasps give rise to interpretations, representations and uses that do not precede them, which are invented at the moment they are grasped. The idea of a resource implies that agents meet needs expressed by actors, after having been redirected, in a one-way relationship. By contrast, an affordance implies a subtle and nuanced dialogue between the one who grasps and the one who is grasped.

From this point of view, a pastoral space proceeds from a trajectory that assembles afforded agencies, inflecting them in a certain way. The trajectory of a herder and his herd follow successive grazing ecosystems that are interpreted as pastures; ponds used as watering places; fields seen as risky places to be bypassed to avoid crop damage and conflict with farmers; and other agencies that are interpreted in a pastoral way. Until the 1970s and the beginning of the great pastoral migrations from the Sahel, the Sudanian bush in Western Burkina Faso was hardly ever visited by herders (Bassett and Turner 2007). Their ecosystems could be considered as objects in a fluid space (Mol and Law 1994) or agents in a 'plasma' (Latour 2005: 244). They were not yet assembled in a pastoral space (even though they could be considered agricultural territories). Pastoral spaces were assembled when the pastoralists arrived, based on a pastoral interpretation of the affordances offered by agencies present in the Sudanian bush.

Grazing movements are a good illustration of affordance grasps and the assemblage process that leads to the composition of spaces. A grazing movement is a seasonal composition of pasturelands. The herd is led according to a spatio-temporal sequence composed according to its nutritional needs. A transhumance is a regional seasonal movement over periods of several weeks to several months that assembles at least three essential but geographically distant types of pasture: the Sahelo-Sudanian grazing lands in the north, with their excellent fodder species in the rainy season; crop residues in the fields harvested when the herds move south at the beginning of the dry season; and the Sudano-Guinean grazing lands in the south, where the rains arrive earlier in the year, thus shortening the difficult dry season and its shortage of fodder and water for the animals. A pastoral space can also be read in its meanders, and the agency that its trajectory avoids. Sudanian pastures are abandoned as soon as the rainy season sets in because parasites proliferate there. Likewise, during the rainy season, cultivated fields are no-go zones to be avoided by the herds. I followed a transhumance herd of about 300 zebu led by six shepherds and managed by two herders (the sons of the animals' owner) on its way back from the southern Sudano-Guinean to the northern Sahelo-Sudanian pasturelands. I interviewed the herders about their daily choices, and observed the composition of the herd's trajectory through the landscape, the behavior of the herd, the interactions with the farmers met along the way. The data collected allowed me to understand better their herding choices. The corridors from Sudano-Guinean to Sahelo-Sudanian pasturelands are followed by a large number of herds; they give the general south–north direction. But within each corridor, each herder composes his own route: 'There is a recognized path, but in the bush you can move, change direction' (BO, a transhumant herder). The aim of transhumance is not only to move the herds from rainy season to dry season pasturelands. Herders are reluctant to speed up during the north–south grazing movements at the beginning of dry season. Grazing movements are also intended to feed and water the animals, to provide frequent rest stops, and to avoid damage to the fields. It is by trying to conciliate as much as possible all these objectives that herders make daily choices in the conduct of the herd, and thus compose the pastoral space of the transhumance.

On the way back north at the beginning of rainy season, the choices are strongly constrained by the agricultural season that starts at the same time. The fields are being sown, and therefore cannot be crossed. The herds sometimes find themselves trapped in the middle of vast cultivated spaces that they can neither cross nor bypass. In order to create a viable pastoral space in this predominantly agricultural area, the shepherds target the hills (*ferlo* and *fukkaawo*). They are not cultivated, and although they still offer few fodder resources at the beginning of the rainy season, they mainly allow the herds to rest for the night. Herders lead the animals from one hill to the next, using between them fields that are not yet cultivated (*gesa*, Figure 4.3) fallow land (*soynere*), and lowlands (*cofol*). These pastures allow the herd to move forward, to feed and to water at the same time. When these are not available, the herds use remnants of bush between fields (*guyfan*, see Figure 4.4) or laterite tracks built for vehicle traffic, but these paths do not provide any forage, they only allow the herd to move forward. The two herders on bicycles went ahead of the herd each day to check that the key passages were not obstructed by fields. Through their choices, the herders adjust to the affordances and risks presented by the agencies to assemble a pastoral space that lasts the time of the transhumance. The grazing movement links pastures and connects spatial dynamics. This space is composed following the needs of the herd during transhumance (to move, to graze, to water, to rest).

This example shows that the spatial assemblage can be read as a trajectory that connects agencies in order to support livelihoods, or a way of inhabiting the world. The mobility of herds constitutes the initial trajectory upon which the composition of pastoral spaces is based. The movements of herders, their families and animals

Figure 4.4 Zebu crossing a *guyfan* (remnant patch of bush between fields) (photograph by author).

respond to a multitude of information about the various agencies: rainfall; the availability of fodder (the greening of pastures and whether or not they are often frequented by other herds); the availability and quality of water; the presence of diseases; the good or bad reception given to herders by local villagers. The trajectory drawn by the herds thus intersects with other trajectories: that of the vegetative cycles in the savannah, the monsoon clouds and the rainfall they bring or not, the cycle of the agricultural calendar… Without being the result of chance, this trajectory, and the space it draws, are contingent, insofar as it could have passed through other agencies, or grasped the same agencies in a different way. Here is a trajectory; it could have been different: space circulates in the wide range of possibilities offered by agencies and their multiple affordances. The composition of space lies on encounters, intersecting trajectories: what Denis Retaillé and Olivier Walther (2011) call "mobile space", and which can be related in certain aspects to the fluid space characterized by Annemarie Mol and John Law (1994).

Fragile and Uninhabitable Spaces?

However, spaces thus composed are still very fragile. The trajectories on which they rely are movements that can be interrupted. Assemblages are always 'temporarily achieved' (Anderson et al. 2012). They are built from agencies, each of which retains its own dynamic and can therefore leave the trajectory. Moreover, each agency is open to other possible trajectories, which would grasp it from another side. When an agency is mobilized in another trajectory, and therefore in another space, it is modified, oriented in another direction, altered. An exclusive grasp could make it unsuitable for the other spaces in which it participated. For example, since the 1970s, the *seeno* pastures on the slopes of the talwegs in Western Burkina Faso have been more and more mobilized for their soils in agricultural spaces. The fallow land on which herds could graze used to last for 20 to 30 years until the 80s, when land pressure was low; now they are much shorter or even disappearing. Savannah ecosystems are now much more widely cleared, ploughed and cultivated during the rainy season. 'The bush is over' as the saying goes in Western Burkina Faso. Thus, the pastoral affordance of the *seeno* is becoming increasingly difficult to grasp during the agricultural season:

> There are problems feeding the cattle because all the exit doors are closed, in the rainy season the cattle can no longer get out. This is the main problem. This is where there is the most damage to the crops.
> (Interview with SB, herder in the village of Samarogouan)

Another element of fragility: trajectories pass through agencies that are themselves in relationship, caught in networks that can extend very far. They can be affected by multiple changes occurring at a given point in the network. For example, the irregularity of rainfall, the main source of uncertainty in pastoral areas, is further accentuated by global warming. Yet pastoralists obviously have no control over this global change, nor over the factors of climate forcing. Pasturelands are affected by connections that extend beyond the reach of herders. The fragility of pastoral spaces then comes from the instability of their framework. The trajectories pass through agencies, connect them, assemble them. But grasping an affordance, assembling agencies does not equate with controlling them. The chains of relations between agencies relay their movement and influence their dynamics: they act as mediators (Latour 2005). If intermediaries are reliable relays in causal relationships, mediators feed the uncertainties and instability of spaces. They make space uninhabitable if it is not taken over by territories.

Building Territories: Stabilizing Spaces to Make them Inhabitable

While space is fundamentally unstable, building a territory is an attempt to stabilize networks, a way to ensure the sustainability of relationships to the things on which one relies.

From Space to Territory: Consolidate Assemblages to Secure Livelihoods

Spaces and territories have the same network structure; but the nature of the relationships they are made of differentiates them. The shift from space to territory (what we call 'territorialization' after Gilles Deleuze and Felix Guattari (1987) and Claude Raffestin (2012)) can occur through a change in the nature of the relations which aims to keep assemblages together. The goal of territorialization is to bind other actors in one's network by making them interested in participating to a common territory. By consolidating spatial relations into territorial bonds, one can expect a greater reliance of the agencies on which one depends, and make them less sensitive to the changes that occur through other connections. Territorial bonds offer a way to maintain the dynamics in which the agencies have been grasped. In this way, territorialization is an attempt to 'institutionalize' (Brighenti and Kärrholm 2020) a certain way of grasping the affordances of space. It is, with Bruno Latour (2005), a question of moving from a wide and fluctuating range of possibilities to the anchoring of a specific trajectory. A trajectory that puts into a certain order agencies and that institutionalizes, for a moment, one space among many others into a territory.

Pastoral spaces are composed from unstable agencies. For the first herders who arrived in Western Burkina Faso in the 1970s from Sahelian savannas, further north of Burkina and Mali, territorializing spaces of mobility was a way to secure their livelihoods. How then have they built territories from pastoral spaces? Until the arrival of pastoralists in the Sudanian bush of Western Burkina Faso in the 1970s, the affordances of the bush, water points and fields were not grasped along pastoral trajectories. These new pastoral grasps of affordances that were previously apprehended in different directions (especially agricultural ones), remained fragile. The establishment of camps for herders on the outskirts of villages or in the surrounding bush could not be perpetuated without the agreement of local customary leaders. Frequent damages to crops caused by a lack of animal surveillance could quickly degenerate into violent conflicts with farmers, deteriorate social climate, and make it impossible to graze in the surrounding bush. It was also impossible to subsist in the areas of transhumance without trading, buying supplies and caring for the animals. It was therefore necessary for herders to establish diplomatic relations with local farmers, otherwise the newly invested space would have collapsed. Trajectories taken were based on space agencies that were too unstable.

In order to secure their pastoral grasps of affordances, pastoralists gradually wove networks of inter-knowledge with villagers, notably by exchanging milk for grain produced by farmers. They also established special relationships with a number of hosts (*djatigui* in dyula language), often merchants, who could mediate between them and the villagers in case of problems. A *djatigui* in the village of Djigoué, explains his role:

> What happens when the transhuman herds cause crop damage? If the guy comes to say so, you support him, otherwise you give up. If he comes, I gather the old FulBe who are around, and we go and talk to the natives [the descendants of the village founders, who are the land managers]. The natives usually chase the animals to the pound [a fenced area managed by the prefecture where animals are kept while awaiting payment of a fine for roaming]. We try to intercept the animals before they get to the pound, negotiate that FulBe give something [financial compensation]. But the case seldom goes to the prefecture.
>
> (Interview with SA)

During the transhumance movement, herders do not establish relationships with *djatigui* in every village they pass through:

> *Do you have a* djatigui *in Logoniégué?* No, we don't have a *djatigui* because we settle in the bush, so we don't need one. But sometimes when we arrive in the villages we try to get in touch with the chief of the village and inform him that we are settled in his area.
>
> (Interview with BM, herder from Bama met during its transhumance in Logoniégué)

When a transhumant herd causes damage to crops and the herder has no *djatigui*, he is in trouble. Sometimes he chooses to flee before the farmer can find him. If he is caught, he may be demanded by the farmer, backed by the village leaders, to pay very large amounts of compensation. A herder who has established territorial bonds to consolidate the spatial assemblages he depends upon is thus more secured than a herder who is simply moving through a space.

Adjusting Relationships of Interdependence into Common Territorial Issues

To involve the spatial actors on whom one depends in one's issue, or to operate a process of translation (Callon 1984), leads to consolidated relations by forming *de facto* alliances. By promoting relationships of interdependence, more permanent attachments are formed that give birth to a territory. This way pastoralists have been able to reduce uncertainties about livestock mobility. They have transformed uncertain agencies (mediators) into much more reliable agencies that participate, in their own way, in pastoral territories. Pastoral territories belong not only to pastoralists, but also to all human and non-human agents interested in the same (now territorial) issue, and not simply passed through by a (spatial) trajectory. Their agencies have been oriented in the direction of a common territory. For instance, herders sometimes enter into manure contracts with local farmers. The farmers allow the herders to graze their animals in their fields once the harvest is done. Farmers benefit from the manure naturally deposited by the herds grazing in their fields, which increases their fertility. In this case, relations become territorial bonds when they become reciprocal relations of interest.

The agents who enter into a relationship of interdependence participate in a common territorial issue. They adjust themselves in relation to each other, and are transformed accordingly. For example, pastoralists historically bred *seenooji* cattle, a type of zebu with large horns and prominent hump, in the Sahelian areas. However, this breed has proven to be very susceptible to new parasites (mainly ticks and tsetse fly) that are found in greater numbers in Sudanian pastures. If nothing had been done, the spatial relationship between the zebu and the Sudanian pastures could have been broken by the parasites, and the zebu could have moved out of the trajectory specific to the pastoral space. The *seenooji* cattle were then hybridized with the local parasite-resistant *mereeji* breed. The result, known as *worsooji*, proved to be both more resistant to parasites and at the same time endowed with the build-up of a walker, a highly valued characteristic (Bassett and Turner 2007). To sum up, two agents, the zebu and its parasites, were spatially related. But their relationship was unstable: the hybridization of animals represented an adjustment to build a stronger relationship, a territorial one. The nature of the relationship changed, as did the zebu and their parasites, who became territorialized as they adjusted to the other.

Boundaries and Territoriality Hold the Territory

Even if the relations of territorial interdependency are more stable than spatial trajectories, and even if the actors who integrate a territory have adjusted to each other, the territory is not uniform. The actors involved remain disparate. So what unites a territory?

First, in comparison with space, which, from link to link, has an indefinite extension, the territory is bounded, if not delineated. For example, pastoralists manage to attach harvested fields to the pastoral territory by consolidating the relationship that binds them to the cultivator through a manure contract. But they have no power over the other relationships that bind a field, which is still a multi-territorialized agent. They cannot, for example, influence the choice of crop rotation to favor those whose residues are most palatable to their animals (maize and millet rather than cotton for example). This dimension of the agency of a field is beyond the control of pastoralists because it is rather integrated into an agricultural territory (crop rotation depends on agronomic succession, possibilities of commercialization of harvests into value chains, farmers' needs of food and cash, etc.). Fields are land markers for the boundaries of pastoral territories, and therefore, as such, places of interactions between pastoral territories and other ones (Brighenti and Kärrholm 2020). A boundary separates, on one side, the insiders of a territory, interdependent from each other and who participate in the same problem; and on the other side, a number of independent outsiders (but who are probably interdependent, moreover, with other actors in other networks). A territory thus extends along the ramifications of a network of spatial agents until the mutual adjustments stop, until the power of the coalition of actors to interest outside agents in their own problems fails. The boundary draws the outline of a highly integrated network fragment, within which bonds are strong. It holds the territory and thus participates in its unity.

Second, unity is found in the manner of assembling agencies and consolidating relationships to compose a territory. This specific manner can also be defined as a territoriality. It recalls what Andrea M. Brighenti and Mattias Kärrholm (2020) name the 'constitution' of a territory (not necessarily a legal one). It depends on a spatial trajectory, the needs and dependencies it satisfies, a way of grasping the affordances of agencies, dispositions of these agencies in relation to each other, and the mutual adjustments that accompany the consolidation of interdependent relationships. At the heart of the manner in which pastoralists build relationships of interdependence is the need to secure the mobility of their herds. The relationships that constitute a pastoral territory must be both flexible enough to allow for fluid mobility, and at the same time secure enough to ensure access to a vast array of resources, even far from the pastoralists' place of residence (Fernandez-Gimenez 2002). This double imperative of flexibility and security of mobility is at the root of pastoral territoriality. In the Sudanian savannas of Western Burkina Faso, this double requirement is generally achieved through a regime of open access (Gonin et al. 2019). Each herder has a 'liberty of access' (Hohfeld 1913) to pastures and surface watering points during transhumance. This means that no other users of these bushes have the right to prevent him from grasping in a pastoral sense the affordances offered by grassland ecosystems and surface water. 'Liberty of access' is a legal relationship distinct from the right of access defined in the strict sense as a claim-right (Hohfeld 1913): it allows a herder, while not being the owner of a pasture, to graze his animals on it. It does not entail ownership, as a right can.

> 'Does a FulBe herder have a place that he owns?' wonders a herder.
> (Interview with DY, herder in the village of Niambrigo)

'Liberty of access' is the privileged manner of integrating pastures into a pastoral territory, and is therefore at the heart of the fluid and flexible nature of pastoral territorialities. In contrast, agricultural territoriality is sedentary, exclusive, topographic. Farmers are looking for land security that allows them, year after year, to improve the fertility of their fields and, in the long term, to be able to transmit their land to their children. To achieve this, they negotiate land rights that compel others to respect the investments made in terms of labor and fertilization. A farmer-herder in the village of Diarakorosso explains the difference in the customary ceremonies that ground the rights to live, to farm or to graze:

> [When we arrived here in Diarakorosso] we gave a chicken and a goat. When you settle down but you don't want to farm, you give a chicken. When you want to farm, you give a chicken and a goat. [The herders]

> who come on transhumance to Diarakorosso give nothing, neither chicken nor goat, they are not settled.
>
> (Interview with LH)

Customary rules with locally legitimate land managers allow for the recognition of rights to cultivate the land, and, by reciprocity, the duty of others (farmers, herders…) to respect the cultivation of such space, i.e. the duty to respect the integrity of the agricultural territory thus constituted. The rights to cultivate plots of land are the basis of agricultural territoriality. Conversely, no sacrifice founds a proper right to graze. Grazing is based on liberty of access, which constitutes the essence of pastoral territoriality.

Territoriality is the logic that holds a territory together despite the heterogeneity of the spatial agencies that make it up. It impregnates an identical manner of grasping the affordances of different agencies. This particular grasping can be found all over the territory. It makes it possible to distinguish one territory from another by contrasting the manner in which they are built. It reveals a specific manner of inhabiting the world, a specific manner of building relationships to ensure one's livelihoods.

Territory as a Collective Effort

Territory is fundamentally a collective of agents interested in a common issue (Brighenti and Kärrholm 2020). Territorialization, which aims to stabilize relations in order to make the space habitable, by means of mutual interest and adjustment, is a process that is essentially collective. Even if a group of actors can be at the origin of its trajectory (the pastoralists for example), it is necessarily a work in concert with others. It is only in relation with others that a habitable territory for everyone can be created. It is with others that interdependent relationships can be negotiated, whenever possible, so that no territory belongs to one group alone. For example, farmers eventually participate in pastoral territories (which are not herders' territories) in many ways: their fields are integrated into it, fertilized by the manure of the livestock; the income from cash crops allows them to buy animals that graze on pastoral territories; and so on. The territoriality of the Moderns, defined by Robert D. Sack (1986: 259) as 'the attempt by an individual or group to influence, affect, or control objects, people, and relationships by delimiting and asserting control over a geographic area,' is an exception. It is a univocal territoriality, which implies very unequal relationships. A pastoral territory is not dominated, controlled, mastered by herders, but negotiated between herders, farmers, zebu, tsetse flies, rains, herbaceous species in the bush… which adjust to each other in an effort of reciprocal interest in the same issue. Territories result from compromise, reciprocal agreement and interdependent relationships. They are held by disparate actors. We have seen this with the manure contract: farmers and herders recognize and value the mutual benefits of their agreement (crop residues as fodder/ fertilization of the fields by livestock). Both herders and farmers will take care of the relationship by which they participate to a common territory. In short, they will take care of the territorial collective. Here again, the territories managed by a single actor, such as the State for 'its' national territory, are rather an exception that reflects a modernizing, univocal and exclusive vision of territories.

The inherently collective nature of the territory is also a guarantee of its permanence. For territorialization is an unfinished process, always started over again: one tends towards the territory, in an effort to stabilize it, but the territory is never definitively established. This effort is facilitated when it is taken up again, supported by several coalesced agents who have interests in the same territory, rather than when it is the result of the effort of a single actor, however powerful it may be (such as a State).

Inter-territorial Relations: Territories Stand Together

In the search for the stabilization of relationships, it is not enough to consolidate the internal relationships that constitute a territory. It is still necessary for a territory to stand with others in order for cohabitation to be fully resolved. No territory stands by itself. However, no territory is exclusive, and conversely, no actor participates exclusively in a single territory. This shows that each territory maintains multiple relationships with the others, which make it last.

The Proliferation of Territories Raises the Question of their Coexistence

The (re-)discovery of territorial complexity went hand in hand with the renunciation of a monolithic vision of territory, based on a single standard, the delimited space of state sovereignty (Antheaume and Giraut 2005). The geometric grid of Westphalian territories has turned out to be an epistemic fiction, overwhelmed by the proliferation of territories of all kinds: administrative territories at all levels, territories of life, of project…

Far from the idea that the world is partitioned by a territorial grid, there is a tangle of territories that overlap one another. How can territories coexist when the issues that underlie them could be antagonistic? How are 'polyphonic assemblages' (Tsing 2015) of territories composed? Moreover, agents are themselves multi-territorialized: caught in a web of relationships that link them to several different territories. How can they participate in two distinct territorial issues at the same time, without betraying one or the other?

Adjusting Territorialities to One Another

A territory maintains itself if it is adjusted to others. Adjustments take place where several territories coexist: in multi-territorialized agents, situated on territorial boundaries, which work as an interface (Brighenti and Kärrholm 2020). In these places, different logics clash, exclude or reinforce each other. However, in order to cohabit, it is not enough to negotiate the sharing of an agency as if the agent in question shared access to a resource, with each agent's share depending on the balance of power. Neither is it a question of combining spatial trajectories according to clever configurations that allow them to go along side by side, each one keeping its integrity. In short, cohabitation is not only a matter of arranging territories, but also of translating between territorialities. Territorial construction cannot be built upon the sheer attempt to understand the other: what is needed is an understanding of the way another territory is constructed, its 'constitution' (Brighenti and Kärrholm 2020), to accommodate different manners of making territory (i.e. two territorialities) wherever they meet.

Pastoral territoriality is ultimately the expression of mobility, whereas agricultural territoriality is the expression of sedentary life. The first aims both to secure and facilitate grazing movements, the second essentially focuses on the relationships that secure access to land and its fertility. The 'manure contract' offers the example of a composition between these two territorialities: it is not a simple sharing of a resource (crop residues), rather, it encompasses and mutually reinforces both territorialities, the pastoral one (by offering essential fodder to the herds at this time of the year), and the agricultural one (the natural amendment maintains the fertility of the fields, keystones of sedentarity). Two different ways of grasping the field's affordances are adjusted. The essential for each territory is preserved: herds do not pass through the field when it is cultivated; farmers do not collect or destroy the fodder resource (crop residues). Potential competition between the two territories is defused here. Diplomacy lies in understanding what others depend on to subsist; where they must absolutely go through; and which is therefore non-negotiable (Morizot 2016): distinguishing the essential from the contingent, in order to be able to establish relations by changing the contingent if necessary, and preserving the essential for each one. The two territories are interwoven: they support each other in their respective existence.

Similar compositions of territorialities also concern other relations between agricultural and pastoral territories: milk for cereals exchanges, pastoralists' guarding of farmers' cattle, harnessed cultivation and draft cattle rearing, saving income from cash crops by investing in livestock. Spatial actors can participate in both territories, and mutually reinforce them. Each one needs the others to subsist (Tsing 2015), or, in Latour's terms (2013), each agent must pass through other entities and other networks. This is the case here: beyond simple coexistence, when two territorialities are aligned they can sustain one another, each existing thanks to the other.

Territorial Antagonisms

However, the composition between territories or between their territorialities does not always take the form of diplomatic adjustments leading to mutually beneficial relationships. The relations of interdependency can also break down.

In some villages, for example, there is a tendency to grab crop residues for the exclusive benefit of the farmer's few animals, as this farmer from the village of Diarakorosso does: 'May other herds come into your bean and groundnut residues? No, it is my animals that graze first' (interview with SO).

Two or more territorialities can be antagonistic and a mutual adjustment may prove impossible. Two grasps of the affordances of the same agency may be mutually exclusive. For example, a cleared and cultivated bush can no longer be grazed during the agricultural season. The antagonism bursts when animals still enter the field and damage the crops (Figure 4.2). The antagonism is most often resolved peacefully by compensations of the farmer by the owner of the animals, but sometimes it leads to conflict. The damage of animals in the field is an example of direct competition between two territories, in their contradictory grasp of the affordances of the same agency.

The antagonisms can also stem from the intrinsic logic of territorialities, which are sometimes contradictory. In the savannas of Western Burkina Faso, while land pressure is increasing sharply and in some areas bush is almost entirely cleared and cultivated, agricultural territorialities take precedence over pastoral territorialities. We have seen that pastoralists, in order to graze their animals, go through tacit agreements with other pastoralists, farmers, land managers in villages, which give them a 'liberty of access' to the bush not cleared for agricultural use (Gonin et al. 2019). This liberty of access' facilitates mobility and is at the heart of pastoral territorialities. But 'liberty' is not a right that would legally protect access to bush, because farmers do not have a reciprocal duty to respect the pastoral grasp of bush affordances. When they want to extend their fields, they negotiate customary rights with the lineage leaders to clear and cultivate the grazed bush. These are then full rights: when the fields are cultivated, the pastoralists who used to take their animals to these areas now are forbidden to go there. Thus, the very manner of relating in agricultural territories (rights that involve duties for third parties), leads to the disintegration of the relationships that sustain pastoral territories (simple liberty of access that does not involve reciprocal duties for third parties). In a context of land pressure and multiplication of agencies shared between pastoralism and agriculture, pastoral territorialities dissolve into agricultural territorialities.

Adjusting Territories: A Process to Make all Living Beings Inhabit Together

Inhabiting the world is about making sure that the assemblages of agencies on which livelihoods depend are reliable. This requires a process of territorialization, which changes the spatial connections between agencies into binds that enshrine interdependencies. All the agents who participate in a same territory are interested in a common issue. They relay a same flow of agencies. Territory thus holds agencies together better than space. This process of territorialization is collective in essence, as it concerns assemblages whose connections must be ensured. Territories are multiple and overlapping, it is therefore necessary to compose the different manners of building territories, i.e. of inhabiting the world. The construction of territories thus shows that to inhabit is already, always, to inhabit together: both inhabiting with those who participate in a common territorial issue, and inhabiting with those who participate in other territorial issues.

This construction based on the relationships between agencies is dynamic by essence. It makes the space very unstable, and the territory always in movement. In this sense, territories represent an ever unfinished effort of stabilization, caught in a cycle of territorialization–deterritorialization–reterritorialization (Deleuze and Guattari 1987). Temporarily institutionalized territories, or fragments of their networks, are crossed by new spatial trajectories. In order to last, they must be stabilized in new territorializations, which they can substitute into, recompose or juxtapose themselves to existing territories. This proliferation invites us to answer, from a dynamic perspective, the question of inhabiting together. Territory thus appears as a notion that can meet the challenges of inhabiting together in a complex and changing world. The postmodern approach has made it possible to broaden the notion of territory beyond the sole state actors (Antheaume and Giraut 2005). At a time when all forms of modernism and postmodernism are being called into question (Latour 1993), a new broadening and deepening of the territory seems necessary in order to inhabit with living beings other than humans. Integrating ethological insights into a larger framework for the study of territories (Brighenti and Kärrholm 2020) would make it possible to take into account all the 'ways of being alive' (Morizot 2020). This common framework could at the same time allow us to recognize the importance of interdependencies, and to adjust our interrelationships with all living beings with whom we inhabit the planet.

Bibliography

Agnew, J. A., 2013. Territory, politics, governance. *Territory, Politics, Governance*, 1 (1), 1–4.

Anderson, B., Kearnes, M., McFarlane, C., and Swanton, D., 2012. On assemblages and geography. *Dialogues in Human Geography*, 2 (2), 171–189.

Antheaume, B. and Giraut, F., 2005. *Le territoire est mort, vive les territoires! Une (re) fabrication au nom du développement*. Paris: IRD éditions.

Bassett, T. J. and Turner, M. D., 2007. Sudden shift or migratory drift? Fulbe herd movements to the Sudano-Guinean region of West Africa. *Human Ecology*, 1 (35), 33–49.

Brighenti, A.M., 2010. On territorology: towards a general science of territory. *Theory, Culture & Society*, 27 (1), 52–72.

Brighenti, A. M. and Kärrholm, M., 2020. *Animated Lands: Studies in Territoriology*. Lincoln: University of Nebraska Press.

Callon, M., 1984. Some elements of a sociology of translation: domestication of the scallops and the fishermen of St Brieuc Bay. *The Sociological Review*, 32 (1 suppl), 196–233.

Deleuze, G. and Guattari, F., 1987. *Capitalism and Schizophrenia: A Thousand Plateaus*. London: Bloomsbury.

Fernandez-Gimenez, M. E., 2002. Spatial and social boundaries and the paradox of pastoral land tenure: a case study from postsocialist Mongolia. *Human Ecology*, 30 (1), 49–78.
Gibson, J. J., 1977. The theory of affordances. *Hilldale, USA*, 1 (2), 67–82.
Gonin, A., Filoche, G., and Delville, P. L., 2019. Dynamics of access to pastoral resources in a farming area (Western Burkina Faso): unveiling rights in open access regimes. *International Journal of the Commons*, 13 (2), 1049–1061.
Hohfeld, W. N., 1913. Some fundamental legal conceptions as applied in judicial reasoning. *Yale Law Journal*, 23 (1), 16–59.
Jones, M., 2009. Phase space: geography, relational thinking, and beyond. *Progress in Human Geography*, 33 (4), 487–506.
Kärrholm, M., 2007. The materiality of territorial production: a conceptual discussion of territoriality, materiality, and the everyday life of public space. *Space and Culture*, 10 (4), 437–453.
Latour, B., 1993. *We have never been Modern*. Simon and Schuster.
Latour, B., 2005. *Reassembling the Social: An Introduction to Actor-Network-Theory*. Oxford: Oxford University Press.
Latour, B., 2013. *An Inquiry into Modes of Existence*. London: Harvard University Press.
Latour, B. and Chakrabarty, D., 2020. Conflicts of planetary proportions - a conversation. *Journal of the Philosophy of History*, 14 (3).
Law, J., 1992. Notes on the theory of the actor-network: ordering, strategy and heterogeneity. *Systems Practice*, 5 (4), 379–393.
Law, J., 2000. *Objects, Spaces and Others*. Lancaster, UK: Center for Science Studies, Lancaster University.
Malpas, J., 2012. Putting space in place: philosophical topography and relational geography. *Environment and Planning D: Society and Space*, 30 (2), 226–242.
Massey, D., 2005. *For Space*. London: Sage.
Mol, A. and Law, J., 1994. Regions, networks and fluids: anaemia and social topology. *Social Studies of Science*, 24 (4), 641–671.
Morizot, B., 2016. *Les diplomates. Cohabiter avec les loups sur une autre carte du vivant*. Paris: Wildproject.
Morizot, B., 2020. *Manières d'être vivant: enquêtes sur la vie à travers nous*. Éditions Actes Sud.
Müller, M., 2015. Assemblages and actor-networks: rethinking socio-material power, politics and space. *Geography Compass*, 9 (1), 27–41.
Murdoch, J., 1998. The spaces of actor-network theory. *Geoforum*, 29 (4), 357–374.
Murdoch, J., 2005. *Post-structuralist Geography: A Guide to Relational Space*. London: Sage.
Raffestin, C., 2012. Space, territory, and territoriality. *Environment and Planning-Part D*, 30 (1), 121.
Retaillé, D. and Walther, O., 2011. Spaces of uncertainty: a model of mobile space in the Sahel. *Singapore Journal of Tropical Geography*, 32 (1), 85–101.
Sack, R.D., 1986. *Human Territoriality: Its Theory and History*. Cambridge University Press.
Tamou, C., De Boer, I. J. M., Ripoll-Bosch, R., and Oosting, S. J., 2018. Traditional ecological knowledge underlying herding decisions of pastoralists. *Animal*, 12 (4), 831–843.
Thrift, N., 2006. Space. *Theory, Culture & Society*, 23 (2–3), 139–146.
Tsing, A. L., 2015. *The Mushroom at the End of the World: On the Possibility of Life in Capitalist Ruins*. Princeton University Press.
Vall, É. and Diallo, M.A., 2009. Savoirs techniques locaux et pratiques: la conduite des troupeaux aux pâturages (Ouest du Burkina Faso). *Natures Sciences Sociétés*, 17 (2), 122–135.

Chapter 5

Territory Glimpsed Through Lache Eyes

A Tale of Non-Euclidean and Symbolically Authentic Excursions in Liminal Space

Les Roberts

'Space, vast space, is the friend of being.'

(Gaston Bachelard 1994: 208)

Sketch of a spatial anthropology of early lockdown

The form of this essay, much like the ideas and content it seeks to unpack, is fraught with confusion and general disorientation. Hopefully not *too* fraught, but for introductory purposes it is important to point out the origins of these ideas and the psychosocial and intellectual cross-currents that have informed their development. First and foremost, the disorientation of which I speak is spatial. This refers not so much to being lost somewhere *in* space, as if having wandered too far from a familiar path and discovered that there are no longer any navigable waymarks to assist one's ongoing passage through that space. The sense of spatial disorientation that I am referring to reflects more ontological and existential concerns. It is as if the very fabric of space has become warped or frayed in such a way as to render the embodiment of space uncertain. Indeed, since March or April 2020, it has sometimes felt like the elemental *beingness* of space has been dislodged or recalibrated in ways that haven't always – or yet – made a great deal of sense. Due to the geographical and somatic constraints imposed by the coronavirus lockdown, the interiority of psychosocial space and the exteriority of sociomaterial space have become intermeshed in a manner which feels both unprecedented (to use a word that very quickly became something of a lockdown cliché) and *uncharted*.

The use of this latter term lends a territorial inflection to what are very particular dialectics of space (Lefebvre 1991) that the global pandemic has brought into play. The role and spaciousness (or lack of) of the imagination seems a particularly key element in this commingling and intermeshing of different spatial registers. The paradox of imagination under lockdown is that it can feel simultaneously both stretched, as if melded to the unfettered digital byways of the internet, and violently curtailed. As my own experience attests, when entanglements with virtual spaces are momentarily arrested, and the gaze, as mine is doing now, is cast beyond

DOI: 10.4324/9781003196365-5

the rectangular screen, it is another rectangular frame, that which surrounds the fragment of world that can be glimpsed through my office window, that I am more prosaically confronted with, and with it, the snap realisation that my spatial horizons begin and end there. In both cases, it is the chronotope (Bahktin 1981) of the *frame* that provides the organisational template whereby space and time are marshalled into a sufficiently adaptable resource that can be put to work in fashioning the quotidian architectures of my lockdown day. When the call of exercise becomes too insistent to ignore, it is another frame, that surrounding the front door of my house, that mediates my relationship with the world 'out there.' But my embodied encounters with the frame of the door are qualitatively different from those of screen or window. That there is a physical threshold that requires crossing is not without significance. The door, as Simmel points out, 'speaks' (1994: 7) insofar as it is able to play host to a (potentially) agentive form of 'spatial play' operative between horizons and frontiers (Marin 1984, 1993):

> The finitude into which we have entered somehow always borders somewhere on the infinitude of physical or metaphysical being. Thus the door becomes the image of the boundary point at which human beings actually always stand or can stand.
>
> (Simmel 1994: 7)

The daily exercise, and my desire to see and feel the phenomenologically proximate territory I am granted access to through 'Lache Eyes' (a term and toponym I will explain shortly), is thereby invested with meaning and affectivity beyond those merely limited to the need to 'stretch my legs.' That I am almost immediately confronted with a sign displayed in the front bedroom window of a house a few doors down that says 'if you can read this, go home,' serves as an unwelcome reminder that, in the eyes of some, my daily walk is seen as a territorial transgression (wrongly, I might add, as the lockdown guidelines introduced in March 2020 by the UK Prime Minister and first ministers of Scotland and Wales, as with those issued subsequently, permitted the taking of exercise as long as this was restricted to one's local area).

As I will go on to explore later in this essay, there were other territorial barriers that I had to negotiate when attempting to beat the bounds of public rights of way that came to define the localised mise-en-scène of my early lockdown excursions. But before that, it is necessary to pay heed to my neighbour's rather un-neighbourly injunction to go home, and to explore the more fine-grained territory of interior space. We will do this via the short fiction of J.G. Ballard and by attempting some brief and tentative forays into the perplexing world of 'pataphysics.' This is principally limited to René Daumal's unfinished pataphysical novel *Mount Analogue: A Tale of Non-Euclidean and Symbolically Authentic Mountaineering Adventures*, which was published posthumously in 1952 (and which provides the inspiration for the title of this essay). It is the non-Euclidean properties of the interior or inner spaces of home that these works directly or indirectly engage with that has drawn me to them. More particularly, it is the question of what these literary ruminations on the intimacy and fragility of inner spaces might offer phenomenological reflections that have as their starting point the enforced (legally, morally, experientially) adjustment to ideas and practices of home under lockdown. In this regard, J.G. Ballard's short story 'The Enormous Space' (adapted for television by the BBC in 2003 and renamed *Home*) serves as a particularly insightful catalyst for the re-imaginings of territory, where attention to the liminalities, intimacies and interiority of spatial proximity enables the charting of frontiers that stretch beyond the affective geometries of everyday living.

As the foregoing discussion suggests, a key point of departure and axis of orientation in these ruminations is my own embodied experience. As an assemblage of ideas and reflexive observations, what follows is thus in part autoethnographic (a process whereby the focus of attention under lockdown has inexorably shifted towards the reflective immanence of self and body), and part psychogeographic (a slightly delirious project of wayfinding whereby the phantasmagoric spaces that have come to shape the everyday geographies of lockdown are allowed to collapse, dissolve and become re-animated through processes of critical-creative intervention). There is of course a wide body of literature that we could reach out to here that engages with both autoethnography as a method of socio-spatial analysis and psychogeography as a rather undisciplined set of spatial practices that are variously mobilised around political, creative, aesthetic, literary, archival and archaeological engagements with landscapes, spaces and environments. For my own purposes, however, it is the interdisciplinary terrain loosely delineated by the terms *deep mapping* and *spatial anthropology* that I am principally proceeding from (e.g. Roberts 2016a, 2018; Pearson and Shanks 2001; Bodenhamer et al. 2015). These interdisciplinary dispositions and approaches will be fleshed out in more detail below. But what any sketch of a spatial anthropology of lockdown will sooner or later arrive at, or find itself confronted with, is the question of how to navigate the everyday entanglements with virtual spaces as these have manifested themselves in direct response to the confinements and transfigured intimacies of lockdown.

It seems almost superfluous to observe that one of the issues the experience of lockdown has brought into sharper relief is the nature of our relationship with the digital tools and technologies that have become an indispensible part of everyday life in networked societies. Confined to our homes, umbilically attached to a profusion of devices and digital communication hubs, the need to adapt to virtual modes of living, socialising and working has ceded an ever-faster proliferation of hybrid spaces: spaces that are 'coextensively' embodied (Saker and Frith 2020) in ways that blur or smooth the boundaries between virtual environments and those that bear the more solid and material attributes of physical space. In *The Poetics of Space*, written in the late 1950s, Gaston Bachelard combs through the fine-grained dialectics of intimacy and immensity that are phenomenologically encountered in interior spaces of the home.

'When human solitude deepens,' he writes,

> then the two immensities [the space of intimacy and world space] touch and become identical… In this coexistentialism every object invested with intimate space becomes the centre of all space. For each object, distance is the present, the horizon exists as much as the centre.
>
> (1994: 203)

This sense of interiority/intimacy as both gateway and barrier to the immensity/spaciousness of the world dovetails seamlessly with a post-lockdown experience of space and time in which the mediatisation and virtualisation of the everyday world supplements that world as a space of dwelling while simultaneously denuding it of flesh, warmth and embodied sociality. Glimpsed through the disorienting prism of COVID-19, the digital world offers at best a simulacrum of spaciousness or the capacity to 'roam.' The existential interiority that feeds the desire for more immersive – or, indeed, immense – forms of embodied spatial practice remains bound to the mast of the digital apparatus that renders them virtually possible. In Jorge Luis Borges's short story, the titular 'Aleph' – a heterotopic portal to worlds beyond and 'one of the points in space that contains all other points' (1973: 17; Soja 1996: 54–59; Roberts 2018: 189–190) – for all its wonders, is in the end only navigable via the dusty confines of the residential basement in which it is housed. Such are the spatialities of the digital world under lockdown, with video conferencing, and the now-customary mosaic of atomised interiors and domestic backdrops that are constellated daily by Zoom or Microsoft Teams applications, reinforcing participants' sedentariness through the virtual mechanics of its amelioration.

I am certainly not the first to wonder what the writer J.G. Ballard, were he alive today, would have made of the global pandemic and the reconfiguration and reimagining of the idea of home that it has brought in its wake (O'Connell 2020; Sterling 2020; Self 2020). Accordingly, it is the Ballardian and pataphysical properties of Home (the capital letter here is intended to signify a space that has become something other than a routine locus of domesticity) to which we now turn.

Sketch of a pataphysics of Home (an enormous space)

world no longer turning
like it did when fire
rained down from the sky
and cars stacked up along
dynamic hard shoulders
bound for cities that are
smarter than smart
like everything else
under the spiralling sun

I reach out but you are not there
or here or wherever it is we are

behind doors that remain closed
we breathe the lilac perfume of our thoughts
as if the contagion were only physical
to purge is to be human
is what I tell myself
when the desire to reboot
outpaces the need to remain
in the flesh of your suffering

during snatches of outside
when running the gauntlet of applause
that is not mine
things fall out of range
and are no longer syncing
I tumble like Doug and Tony
the faint line of my ghosting
passes unnoticed through lache eyes
and I slip outside of this time

One of my initial attempts to process and work through the disorientations of early lockdown was by making sketches in poetic form, and then, over time, shaping these sketches into what felt like a sufficiently complete poem, 'Lache Eyes'. As a toponym, Lache Eyes refers to a small area of reclaimed marshland situated on the English side of the England–Wales border in Saltney, a small town which straddles the boundary between the county of Flintshire in North Wales and Cheshire in England. The name 'Lache' is derived from an Old English word for pond, pool, or swamp (which in turn stems from the Latin *lacus*, meaning lake, pond, tank, or reservoir) and hence alludes to the area's former topographic status (Wright 1905: 495). As a poem, 'Lache Eyes' can in part be understood as an inductive method designed to open up a space of critical-creative reflection – a space both geographical and figurative – that ostensibly serves a heuristic purpose. The poem is in two parts, the first of which speaks to the subject matter being explored in the current section. The second part relates to questions and critical spatial interventions which we'll go on to explore in the next section.

It is worth noting that the poem also serves a mnemonic function insofar as it documents certain fragments of experience that have subsequently become inscribed on the map of memory with which I retrace some of the impressions, itineraries, emotions and serendipitous encounters that shaped my early lockdown experiences. The weekly 'Clap for Carers' event (eight o'clock every Thursday evening), for example, that saw householders lining up in their front gardens or porches in order to clap (or clatter pots and pans) in a show of appreciation for frontline National Health Service (NHS) and other key workers became fused with recollections of my walking to the local supermarket around the same time and feeling a little uneasy having to pass by those faithfully observing the ritual, who, perhaps, were wondering why I wasn't (like many, I had my reasons for not joining in what had started to become an empty and tokenistic gesture that played its part in cementing the fiction that 'we are all in it together' (Leslie 2020)). The otherwise mundane streetscapes that I strolled through almost on a daily basis suddenly took on the properties of a territory that I had a less obvious right to enter or lay claim to than I had previously. My habitus of place and belonging had been temporarily disrupted, and it is for this reason I suspect the memory has lingered. Similarly, sitting in the garden with my family on a different Thursday at 8pm and listening to the Mexican wave of handclapping and clanging saucepans as it rippled around the neighbourhood felt ever so slightly subversive or dissident, as if the unsolicited cognisance of the fact that we weren't joining in had somehow affirmed our otherness. Our back garden had become a heterotopia in ways it hadn't before (Foucault 1986; Hetherington 1997).

Another confluence of early lockdown memory, this time cultural, came in the form of the 1960s American science fiction series *The Time Tunnel*. I have fond memories of watching this as a child growing up in the 1970s. The series was being repeated on a horror and science fiction genre television channel that I infrequently tuned into. It was the first time I had seen the programme in over 40 years. Each week the two main protagonists, Doug and Tony, are deposited in a point in time – invariably in the past and quite often at a significant moment in the near recent history of the United States – which, by the end of the episode, they find themselves having to extricate themselves from once more. Throughout this seemingly unbroken cascade through different historical times (they never seem to require any sleep), Doug and Tony are watched over by a team of scientists stationed in present time in an Arizona-based government complex situated deep underground, and which houses the titular time travelling machine. Watching *The Time Tunnel* again after such a long passage of time inevitably stirred memories of or from my childhood. These quickly became braided with the disjointed spaces and curious concertina of time that were conspicuous features of enforced home lockdown, where, confined to our homes, time, for many, was spent travelling down the vertiginous wormholes of the internet. The images that bookend each episode of *The Time Tunnel*, which show Doug and Tony tumbling through a spiralling vortex of time, became therefore – for me at least – an iconic marker of a unique point in time in which the challenge of *escaping* the slow and relentless onslaught of time, or of at least finding a way of coming to better terms with it, was such an indelible part of early lockdown experience.

But perhaps the most forceful shunting of cultural memory that I found myself responding to in March and April 2020, was back to the early 2000s and the broadcast of a BBC television adaptation of J.G. Ballard's short story, 'The

Enormous Space.' I remember watching the dramatisation (which was called *Home*) when originally shown on the BBC in 2003, but had not seen any trace of it since. To the best of my knowledge, *Home* has been repeated just once on the BBC (in 2009), but has never been released in DVD or blu-ray format, nor is it, at the time of writing, available to watch on the BBC's streaming service, BBC iPlayer. My interest in the drama having been triggered by questions prompted by the experience of lockdown, I was pleased to discover that someone had uploaded a VHS recording of it to YouTube.

Home is reasonably faithful to the short story that it is adapted from. 'The Enormous Space' was first published in 1990 in the collection *War Fever* (Ballard 1990). The story revolves around a relatively simple premise: a man, Geoffrey Ballantyne (renamed Gerald in the BBC production), one day makes the decision to never again leave his house. Unlike the dinner party guests in Luis Bunuel's 1962 film, *The Exterminating Angel*, who inexplicably find themselves unable to exit the host's mansion when the party is over, Ballard's bourgeois anti-hero finds himself housebound as the result of conscious intent. Hatching a darkly surreal project in suburban self-sufficiency (if you could imagine what the classic 1970s sitcom *The Good Life* (BBC 1975–78) might have looked like had David Lynch or David Cronenberg directed it, then *Home* wouldn't be too wide of the mark), Ballantyne embarks on an adventure in inner space. Resolving that henceforth he would depend on the outside world for nothing, and that he would eat only whatever food he could find within the house (which includes the snaring and consumption of his neighbour's pets), when food supplies had finally run out, Ballantyne's longer-term plan was to 'rely on time and space' to sustain him (Ballard 2014: 698). By then, he figures, 'I will have long since moved into a different… far richer realm formed from the elements of light, time and space' (ibid: 699, 700).

As his project progresses over the ensuing weeks and months (and as his descent into mental breakdown becomes ever more consuming), Ballantyne's relationship with the domestic interiors of his home is steadily transformed. The uniformity and mundanity of the architectural space that was formerly his suburban home had dissolved into something else entirely, although what, exactly, is never fully determined. Melded with Ballantyne's equally disintegrating inner world, the dimensions of the interior zones of the house become amorphous and, potentially, limitless. It is as if the house is breathing in rhythmic and arrhythmic unison with the increasingly frenetic disposition of its inhabitant. 'I have embarked on a long internal migration,' Ballantyne observes, 'following a route partly inscribed within my head and partly within this house, which is a far more complex structure than I realised. I have a sense that there are more rooms than there appear to be at first sight' (ibid: 702). This realisation brings with it a resolved sense of purpose and a push towards re-evaluating what has become a thoroughly defamiliarised locus of habitation; a space that not only demands new skills in interior navigation but also sets in train a renewed vigour for territorialisation. Ballantyne adjusts to these challenges as any would-be pioneer might: by taking on the mantle of explorer, surveyor and cartographer. He is gripped by a powerful conviction that he is on the verge of a unique discovery, 'the equal perhaps of Columbus's discovery of the new world' (ibid: 707). In *Home*, a sequence shows Ballantyne securing climbing ropes to the ground floor stair newel post, then making his way upstairs as if a mountaineer or polar explorer, cautiously advancing into hitherto uncharted territories. He records the ascent with a video camera (Figure 5.1). We next see him lying down in one of the upstairs rooms, taking measurements which he jots down in a note book or expedition journal. The elements of light, time and space referred to in the short story are here rendered into images. Wearing sunglasses to protect his eyes from the glare, Ballantyne ventures into the 'almost planetary vastness' (ibid: 708) of the space that awaits him in the upper regions of the house. However, despite the evident embracing of his métier as new world adventurer and explorer of inner space, Ballantyne is unable to completely shake off the possibility that it is all just a product of his increasingly fevered imagination. Towards the end of 'The Enormous Space,' he considers whether, by shutting out the world, '[his] mind may have drifted into a realm without yardsticks or sense of scale' (ibid: 709).

As I have discovered in some of my previous interventions in spatial anthropology, the work of J.G. Ballard has a habit of nudging its way into my ruminations and reflections, almost as if by accident rather than design (see, for example, Roberts 2014, 2015). The experience of early lockdown proved no exception. Although I wouldn't have been able to clearly articulate it at the time, the compulsion to revisit *Home* was in part driven by the need to filter the mutating space-times of Home under lockdown through a Ballardian lens. I am not sure whether my doing so had any therapeutic impact in terms of the psychological adjustments that I, and indeed we, needed to make in these early months of the coronavirus pandemic. But, without question, a Ballardian-infused response offered a means by which to conceptually process the experiential geographies of lockdown in ways that seemed to make perfect sense. In my

Figure 5.1 Stills from *Home* (BBC TV, 2003).

mind, the observation, made in April 2020, that 'This is the ultimate coronavirus lockdown film,' which was one of the comments accompanying the video of *Home* uploaded to YouTube (see link for BBC TV 2003), only served to reinforce a nascent structure of feeling that Ballard's typically prescient writing had helped pull into shape.

As well as being prompted to reacquaint myself with the ideas of J.G. Ballard, what I also found myself reaching for around this time was the copy of René Daumal's novella *Mount Analogue* that had been gathering dust somewhere in my house (for me, the self-sufficiency Ballantyne goes in search of had become a necessity when it came to library resources; access to materials not available in electronic formats meant having to rely on one's own collection of books, or resorting to online purchases of items that ended up becoming part of that ever-growing collection). Although, if pressed, I would have struggled to delineate obvious links between *Mount Analogue* and Ballard's 'The Enormous Space,' there nevertheless did seem to be elements specific to each that spoke to the shared cultural and phenomenological particularities of pandemic-induced home confinement and the expansion of interior space (or the need for) that that experience has brought more sharply into relief. Having since dug a little deeper, I now know that it is the concept of 'pataphysics' where any attempt to map points of connection between Daumal and Ballard would need to start from. More indirectly, it is the writers' respective affiliations with, or interest in, surrealism that provide suggestive, if indistinct, lines of confluence. Daumal's encounters with surrealism were, in the first instance, through the 'proto-surrealist' writings of the French symbolist, and inventor of the absurdist philosophy or 'science' of pataphysics, Alfred Jarry (1873–1907) (Pecotic 2014: 371). Daumal was also briefly connected with the Surrealist movement, having been invited to join the group of artists and writers in 1926 by none other than André Breton. The dalliance would prove to be short-lived, however, not least on account of Breton's distaste for the perceived spiritualist leanings of Daumal's writing (Rosenblatt 1999: 64). For an uncompromising atheist like Breton, the slightest hint of religious or spiritualist sensibilities infiltrating the avant-garde ranks of Surrealism would have been stamped out without a moment's equivocation. It was indeed the case that some of Daumal's inspiration as a writer came from sources that would have otherwise struggled to gain a foothold in the artistic and intellectual circles that Surrealist luminaries such as Breton frequented. Whether this be the Vedic literature of Hinduism, or the teachings of the Russian philosopher and esoterist George Gurdjieff (Pecotic 2014; Rosenblatt 1999), Daumal's idiosyncratic blend of Jarryesque pataphysics and Gurdjieffian metaphysics would attain its fullest realisation in the allegorical narrative that became the work he is most closely associated with.

The explorers and adventurers whose story we follow in *Mount Analogue: A Tale of Non-Euclidean and Symbolically Authentic Mountaineering Adventures* are by no means housebound in the way Ballantyne in *Home* or 'The Enormous Space' is (a chronotopically necessary conceit, as we have already discussed). They do, however, embark on an expedition which has as its territorial imperative a destination that can only ever be conquered if those embarking on such an adventure accept the need to part company with, or strive to reach beyond, conventional Euclidean topologies of space. According to the narrator of *Mount Analogue*, the mountain in question must have the following properties: '*its summit must be inaccessible, but its base accessible* to human beings as nature has made them. It must be *unique* and it must *exist geographically*. The gateway to the invisible must be visible' (Daumal 2004: 32, emphasis in original). The mountain can only ever be scaled if one possesses the vision to see what others don't see; without such a vision, the mountain is simply not there and thus represents a space that cannot be entered. As Rosenblatt suggests in her introduction to the 2004 translation of *Mount Analogue*, this idea (embodied in the titular mountain) and the science that underpins it (which is explained by Father Sogol, the expedition leader), serves as a 'scientifically embellished metaphor for Gurdjieff's explanation of how esoteric knowledge is not truly hidden but simply imperceptible to those who are not seeking it' (2004: 13). The stipulation that Mount Analogue 'must exist geographically' is followed through with calculations that locate it southeast of Tasmania and southwest of New Zealand (Daumal 2004: 57). But it is Sogol's insistence that 'The territory in question must be able to exist *in any region* on the surface of the globe' (ibid: 52, emphasis in original) that invites comparisons with the pataphysical journey Ballantyne embarks on in 'The Enormous Space.' Sogol goes on to observe that 'it might be possible, *theoretically*, for it to exist *in the middle of this table* without our having the slightest inkling' (ibid, emphasis in original).

Even a minimally satisfactory unpacking of the philosophy or science of pataphysics would require a lengthy foray into subject matter that risks tipping the discussion beyond the parameters of what is strictly necessary for the purposes of this chapter. As a starting point, we could attempt to nail down some rudimentary definitions, but even that is far from straightforward, or even possible. As Hugill (2012: 3) suggests, to attempt to do so would itself be considered unpataphysical. Bök makes a similar point when describing pataphysics as a 'capricious philosophy,' and an 'oneiric science aware of its own status as a dream' (2002: 4). But these important caveats aside, it is certainly instructive to cite Alfred Jarry's own loosely prescriptive definition, which holds that '*Pataphysics is the science of imaginary solutions, which symbolically attributes the properties of objects, described by their virtuality, to their lineaments*' (in Hugill 2012: 3, emphasis in original). When this is mapped on to the ideas that Daumal sets out in *Mount Analogue*, as well as those that Ballard is surrealistically playing with in 'The Enormous Space,' this definition does perhaps make better sense than it would if considered without the illustrative benefit of creative pataphysical application. The realigned geometric lineaments that Ballantyne finds himself 'discovering' – the phantasmic projection of his imagination onto the architectural dimensions of his suburban home – are not too out of kilter with those that Father Sogol schematically outlines on a blackboard when briefing the soon-to-be expeditionary team in the second chapter of *Mount Analogue* (Figure 5.2). Hugill's analytical pairing of pataphysics alongside the principles of conventional physics is also useful when weighing up the pataphysical attributes of the literary works under discussion:

> It is essential to pataphysics that the basis of empirical physics, the repeatable experiment which produces an outcome that may be generalized into a law or axiom, is challenged by the *science of the particular*. Each experimental occurrence is, in pataphysical terms, a *unique event that follows its own singular laws*.
>
> (2012: 8, emphasis added)

It is the task of establishing a potentially liberatory gateway to the particular – a science of territory that doesn't so much challenge the conventions of quotidian spatial practices as circumvent them entirely – that Ballantyne, in his own unique way, and Sogol's expeditionary party, in another, are principally engaged with. Ballard's contention (or provocation) that the role of the writer in late modernity has shifted to that of a scientist '[who is] faced with an unknown terrain' (in Cord 2017: 8) is given poetic expression in the image of Ballantyne valiantly embarking

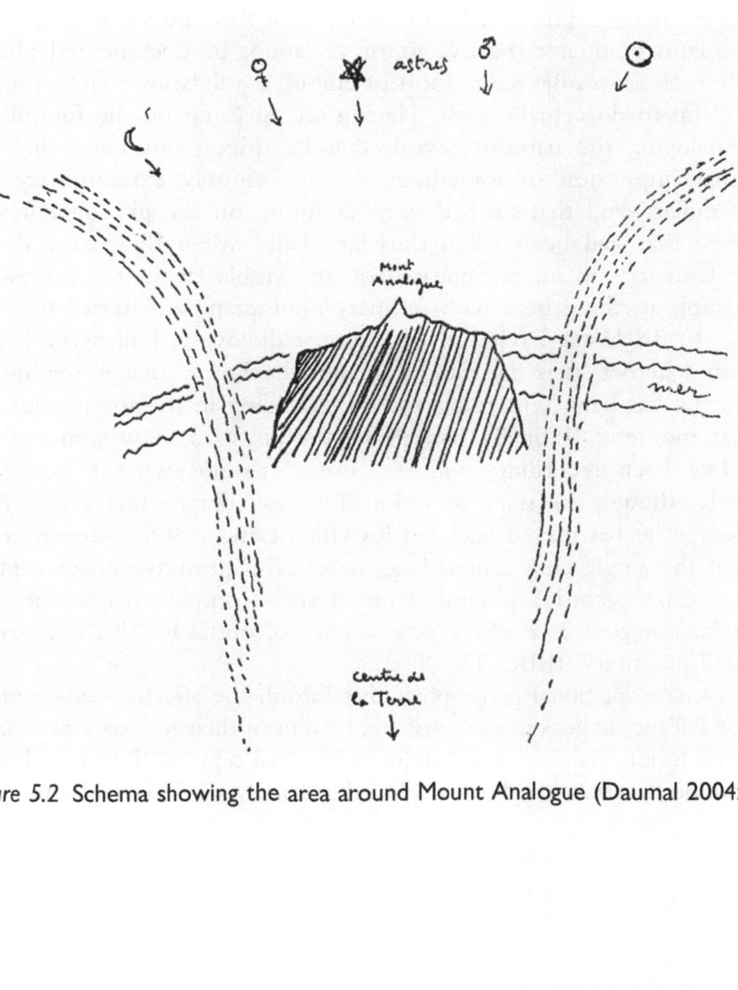

Figure 5.2 Schema showing the area around Mount Analogue (Daumal 2004: 54).

on a creative rite of passage that leads into the unknown; a liminal journey that carries with it the possibility of never finding one's way back from wherever it is the journey ends. Home, in this sense, is radically defamiliarised terrain, the cognisance and acceptance of which 'makes space' for new and renegotiated encounters with everyday geographies. And if, by this reckoning, it is appropriate to think of Ballard (or Ballantyne as his alter-ego) as a scientist, then, as Cord suggests, 'it can only be as a pataphysician' (ibid). However, while it is the case that Ballard did draw inspiration from 'Jarry's cod-philosophical creation' (Self 2010), it is arguably on account of pataphysics's proto-surrealist credentials, rather than any influence that pataphysics may have had on its own uniquely irrational terms, that would explain Ballard as a sometime alumnus of the pataphysical school that Jarry founded. As Garcia notes (2015: 4), it is the influence of Surrealism upon Ballard's construction of territory that is more broadly representative of critical perspectives that scholars have routinely brought to bear on ideas of expressly 'Ballardian' urban geographies and, in particular, the Augé-esque non-places which crop up in many of Ballard's fictional worlds (Augé 1995; Roberts 2014).

Before moving on from – or out of – the inner spaces of Home, one final thematic consideration that straddles the expeditionary narratives of both 'The Enormous Space' and *Mount Analogue* relates to the pataphysical/surrealistic mechanics of image capture. It becomes apparent that the vision that is the driving impetus of their respective journeys cannot be documented photographically such as to offer some form of empirical validation that the spaces they lay claim to do actually exist. Having set up camp on the foothills of Mount Analogue, the narrator reveals that he '[does] not know how to capture that impression of something at once entirely extraordinary and entirely familiar,' and that he had been counting on the photographs and film footage that had been taken thus far. '[B]ut when they were developed,' he laments, 'no image appeared on the visible layer. It is impossible to photograph anything here with ordinary photographic material' (Daumal 2004: 77, 78). In *Home*, having made a similar discovery, Ballantyne begins to question whether 'it is my mind, and not the house' that is responsible for all that he has been witnessing and experiencing in the months leading up to that moment: 'I finally had the opportunity to view some of the material I've been recording, and it's, um… it's not what I expected.' Immediately, though, he starts to rationalise away the routine ordinariness of the footage he has played back on his video camera: 'Of course it could just be that this single chip camera,' he muses, 'this primitive image capture system just can't record a phenomenon of such complex magnitude, and perhaps what's needed is a whole new science of optics for this new world of exploded geometry' (BBC TV 2003).

The non-representational geographies that furnish the affective sensorium of Home that Ballantyne goes in search of are, by dint of their necessary *psycho*geographic constitution, resistant to technologies of visual capture. If, that is, there is the expectation that these might be deployed to harness or document some kind of empirically demonstrable reality. If one of the key principles of Jarry's pataphysics is that the virtuality of objects is a pre-given in the sense of being written in to the experiential dynamics of 'imaginary solutions' as they are realised in practice (and in real time), then the means by which this inherent virtuality is itself 'made virtual' – in this case, by capturing on videotape – is such that it can only ever be doomed to failure. It would indeed require a 'new science of optics,', and it is perhaps for this very reason that one of the disenchantments of the spatialities of lockdown is that the virtualities of all that is within the immediate purview of experience are already virtual insofar as they are transacted in the immaterial spaces of online worlds. It is little wonder, then, that the urge to spread one's wings and take flight from the embodied confinement of these very particular 'interior spaces' should prove so compelling. The lure of the outside, to avail oneself of spaces that are felt to have a depth, texture, and intensity that the rectangular frame of a computer screen so obviously lacks, puts into play an altogether different science of territory.

In search of the slow ways of deep territory

where Boundary Lane curves
into the sandy shallows of a homeland
we've pledged to find
when the water table rises
the border ploughs on
across fields and drains
into a pool of softly spoken rushes

tall tales

smugglers and pilgrims
ferrying night's cargo
between stations of the locked-down day
from isolation to solitude stolen
weighing the murmur of the slumberous dead

the leech coil of spring
pulls limbs from the causeway
we share an embrace that straddles the ages
like groundwater passing through rock
or the alveoli of chanced-upon clearings
where voices come and go in the suspect wind

I can breath
I can breath

expressway traffic has thinned to nothing
birdsong spans the air like a cathedral arch

and prayers take flight in the spaces left empty
all the world is contained herein
we chart a passage through to Balderton
then buffer in the slipstream
of our rebooted lives

Clearly, the spatial disorientation and collective sense of stasis that the rapid tilt into early lockdown had instilled demanded some degree of processing, whatever form this might have taken from an individual perspective. For me, as mentioned earlier, the process of sketching poetic 'maps' of the real-and-imaginary worlds I was inhabiting certainly enabled me to chart pathways, however ill-defined, through the unheimlich spaces that were unfolding and mutating around me. By far the more potent psychosocial medicine, however, was the ability to embrace precisely those opportunities that Ballantyne's project purposely prohibited: stepping outside the front door and seeking to access and entangle oneself within the hyper-local territories that lay beyond. To these ends, what I found myself doing far more enthusiastically than I ever had in pre-pandemic days was establishing the routes of local pathways and public rights of way. The area of marshland known as the Lache Eyes was already known to me, both in terms of enjoyable walks that could be taken near to where I lived at the time (I have since moved, which is alluded to in the reference to a 'homeland' my wife and I had 'pledged to find' further beyond the boundary into Wales), and as part of long-standing research into the cultural geography of the wider Dee Estuary, of which Lache Eyes and the town of Saltney, where I lived, are a part (see Roberts 2012, 2016b, 2018). But I was also keen to explore what the open spaces of the Lache Eyes could link up to by way of walks that followed a more expansive route across scrubland and farmland that stretched for miles along the England–Wales border.

What lent these hyper-local excursions a greater sense of occasion, or which contributed to their memorableness, was an awareness of others doing the same or similar in their own localities and neighbourhoods. The otherwise unremarkable act of beating pathways through local parks, fields, green spaces, edgelands, and any other open stretch of land that the lockdown-weary found themselves drawn to became notably less unremarkable when re-imagined as a form of collective spatial practice. This collective groundswell of Home evacuees is partly reflected in initiatives such as the Slow Ways network, a project set up in response to the coronavirus restrictions, the aim of which is to create a network of walking routes (using and, where necessary, re-establishing existing footpaths) linking villages, towns and cities across the UK. On the project website (slowways.uk), the catalysing role of the pandemic in the formation of the initiative is made clear: 'During lockdown 700 volunteers from across the country collaborated to produce a first draft of the Slow Ways network, creating a stunning Slow Ways map in the process… While COVID-19 has forced millions of us to stay at home and indoors, that hasn't stopped us from being collaborative, imaginative, creative and productive' (Slow Ways 2021).

Slow Ways was developed from an idea proposed by the self-styled 'guerrilla geographer' Dan Raven-Ellison (https://ravenellison.com/). Described as 'an approach to place-based education that compels learners to interact with the landscape through meaningful and playful actions' (Larsen et al. 2021: 5), the suggestion that forms of geographical intervention might constitute 'guerrilla' activity brings with it the possibility of that action breaching territorial boundaries and conventions, or of harbouring transgressive intentions designed to uproot or deterritorialise established spatial orthodoxies (Askins and Raven-Ellison 2012: 164). In this respect, some of the underpinning motives of guerrilla geography invite comparisons with the ludic and subversive motivations that can be attributed to Situationist-inspired psychogeography (Sadler 1998; Richardson 2015) or any number of similar, re-branded modes of critical-creative spatial intervention, including those that fall within the purview of deep mapping and spatial anthropology.

The phenomenological and non-representational orientations that are evident in many of these methods and disciplines are less concerned with the immediacies of 'capture,' if by this is meant the territorial disciplining that is incumbent on the cartographer, surveyor, documentarian, and so forth, to produce as an outcome of their time spent in the field. As with *Mount Analogue* and *Home*, attempts to project these imaginary or playful geographies onto film or a digital screen are almost certainly destined to end in disappointment, perhaps even sowing the corrosive seeds of doubt as to the validity or veracity of the experience itself. That said, a wholly speculative stab in the dark might hold that, outside of recorded Zoom or Microsoft Teams meetings, the visual (photographic or videographic) documentation of early lockdown, were it possible to review or provide a totalising inventory of such a thing, would reveal a visual culture predisposed towards the Outside (as opposed to the interior spaces of Home). From this, we could venture that the desire for mimesis – what André Bazin describes as 'the creation of an ideal world in the likeness of the real, with its own temporal destiny' (1967: 10) – is more fully realised when the body-subject (Merleau-Ponty 2014) is immersed in the warmth and fleshiness of the world as it is lived. While not discounting the possibility that the virtual spaces of representation which play host to animated and affectively-charged interactions online can be considered 'lived spaces' in the terms that Lefebvre (1991) adumbrates, their capacity for visceral, embodied, and kinaesthetic entanglements with the world are not, I would suggest, even remotely on par with those that can be found in the 'slow ways' of landscapes such as Lache Eyes (Figure 5.3).

For a start, an infusive sense of *spaciousness* is undoubtedly one of the foremost psychosocially restorative affects that being in the flat, wide open spaces of the Lache Eyes brought immediately into play. The view towards recognisable landmarks that could be attained by simply standing or rotating oneself as if in panoramic tribute to all that could be gathered through the act of seeing what was there to be seen, created a means by which a degree of orientation –

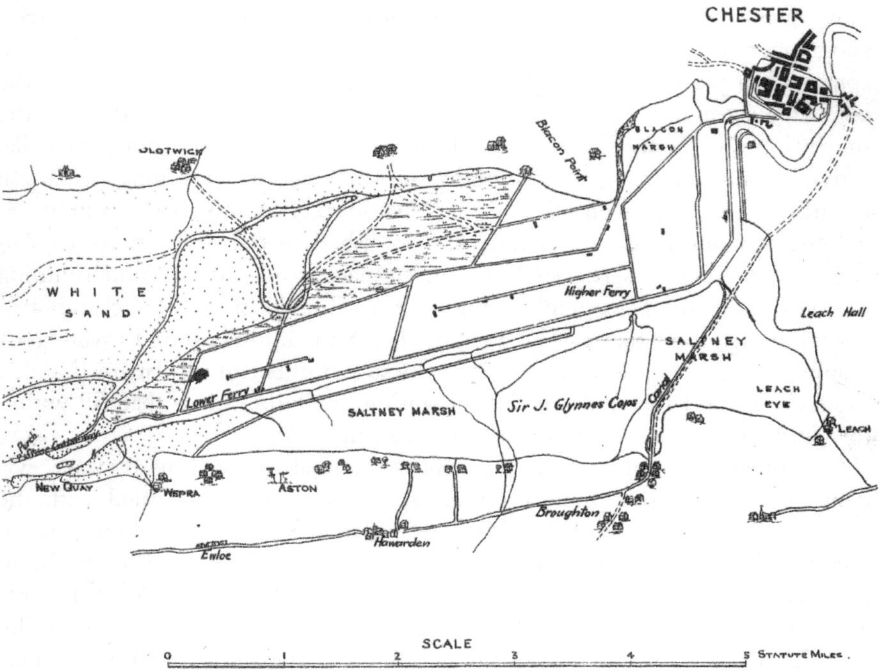

Figure 5.3 Detail of reproduction of Thomas Boydell map 1770–1771 showing Saltney Marsh south of the newly canalised stretch of the River Dee. Lache Eyes (referred to as 'Leach Eyes' on the map) appears on the bottom right (Courtesy of Canalmaps Archive).

geographically, yes, but also emotionally and psychologically – could be reclaimed. Equally, the soundscapes that began to unfold – as if in concert with the visual sweep of the landscape – brought with them an almost elemental lightness of being. The tussle of wind on face and hair, carrying with it snatches of sound – the whirring of a lawn mower or motorcycle engine, the excited babble of children playing, or the cathedral of birdsong that the lockdown seemingly unleashed (Lovatt 2021), as if being heard for the very first time – served as a welcome reminder of a world that exists outside of or beyond the rectangular frame of the computer and television screens that I was otherwise in thrall to. The sensation of the wind, as R. Murray Schafer observes (1994: 22), is both tactile and aural. It can touch the body in ways that buffet the wayfarer towards accretions of affect and memory that reveal themselves in topographic pockets of '*ideal earthen matter*... capable of *receiving* and *maintaining* any form' (Bachelard 2002: 60, emphasis in original), shimmering with all they struggle to contain. Drifting through Lache Eyes in spring 2020, the sense of being able to *breath*, a spatial and kinaesthetic affordance as much as a respiratory or somatic one, served in part as an empathetic reminder of all those who, at the time, were struggling to breathe, whether these be the early casualties of the COVID-19 virus or, come May, George Floyd, the unarmed American black man whose death at the hands of a white Minneapolis police officer – by 'asphyxiation by sustained pressure,' to cite the autopsy report (The Guardian 2020) – sparked anti-racism protests around the world.

The wind, Schafer writes, 'possesses an infinite number of vocal variations' (1994: 22). To be open to the possibility of the wind being a carrier of voices is not just to allow one's attention to shift towards the shape and timbre of the soundscape as a phenomenological locus of aurality. It is also to be accepting of the multi-layered 'soundings' (Roberts 2018) that the embodied spaciousness of landscapes such as Lache Eyes help invoke, salvage, or pull back into being. The voices which these soundings permitted access to are the 'simultaneity of stories-so-far' (Massey 2005: 9) that confer on Lache Eyes the attributes of spatio-temporal depth. Re-envisioning landscape in this way needn't necessarily require the adoption of a conscious strategy or method, it can simply be a readjustment to a habitus of place suffused with the sonority of deep time. Walking becomes the means by which an archaeology of the imagination is woven into practice. In the introduction to their book, *Ways of Walking: Ethnography and Practice on Foot*, Ingold and Vergunst remark that 'treading in predecessors' footprints, so that they might mingle with one's own, is enough to establish a relationship of co-presence' (2008: 7). To imagine the landscape as a locus of deep time and a simultaneity of spatial stories is 'to enter into correspondence with it' (Ingold 2012: 14; 2021).

As someone who has maintained ongoing correspondence with the landscapes and territories of the Dee Estuary for over a decade, the hyper-locality of the Lache Eyes, and the experience of lockdown that precipitated my reacquaintance with it, brought my own practices of mobility into dialogue with those of earlier wayfarers who had trod these same fields and byways long before the large-scale reclamation of the estuarine marshland in the 1700s brought into existence the town of Saltney (named after the marsh that preceded it). As common land, the Lache Eyes is territory that historically has been put to use for the purposes of grazing cattle and has remained a public right of way linking English-Welsh Saltney and the villages of Balderton and Dodleston in England (Barnwell and Carpenter 2017: 7). 'Drifting purposefully' (Sinclair 2003: 4) into the territory with the knowledge that the Lache Eyes, prior to the reclamation of this stretch of the tidal estuary, offered a less hazardous pathway across the marshland was to drift into a space where historical time is unfixed, coiling itself around the detritus and organic materiality of the present-day landscape.

It is springtime as I write this, as it was a year ago when first encountering the surrealist geographies of lockdown. The 'limbs' of roots and branches being pulled from the causeway became entwined with those of the dead rising as if from their slumber. The spectral voices the wind carries aloft are not those of the Romans for whom the marshes – known in Welsh as *Morfa Caer Leon*, or 'marsh fort of the legions' (Owen 1994: 125) – presented an unnavigable and impenetrable barrier in their attempts to push westward into Wales. For the powerful and imperial, Saltney Marshes, including the area of estuarine wetlands that is the Lache Eyes (Barnwell and Carpenter 2017: 11), were literally uncharted territory. In her short story, *Morfa*, Gee Williams describes the marshes as 'two thousand acres of legion-defying swamp' (2008: 186; Mason 1987: 153). In these liminal landscapes, the murmur and susurration of the wind tells the spatial story of those whose power, such as it is, lies in the deterritorialised knowledge that can be gleaned from the habitual and routinized geographies of everyday life. These are the absentees of history; the ragged caravan of the voiceless and marginal who eke out their existence in the folds and furrows of landscapes that they strive to make their own, despite all that is pitched against them, whether by natural or human agency. With a degree of effort, these everyday gleaners can themselves be gleaned from the fragile folds of history as was the case with those I enlisted into the 'Cestrian Book of the Dead,' a deep map of geo-referenced sites of drownings (c.1500–1820) extracted from Chester Quarter Sessions Coroners' Inquest records (Roberts 2016b, 2018). As an exercise in necrogeography, the project of mapping estuarine deaths by drowning was not solely driven by curiosity as to the circumstances and geographies of people's untimely deaths on the River Dee; necrogeography was a means to an end rather than an end in itself. The aim was to explore what such mapping 'might tell us about the symbolic worlds and spatial stories that populate the everyday landscapes of the living' (Roberts 2018: 189). Accordingly, necrogeography was only of value to the extent it could productively contribute to a wider project of spatial anthropology; a project that this essay provides a further contribution towards insofar as, geographically, it falls squarely within the same research 'catchment area'.

The inherent performativity that deep mapping and spatial anthropology brought to what were otherwise leisurely strolls across an open green space on the England–Wales border, played an important part in helping shape what became a disruptively imaginative science of territory. The reflexive enactment of this science is to 'make space' for the anthro-historical *depth* of the Lache Eyes to be both acknowledged (an important starting point) and performatively filtered through sedimentary layers of time such that the voices embalmed within might be brought into correspondence with a traveller passing through these same territories today. The discovery that one's rightful access to a territory has been denied, a common occurrence in my attempts to navigate the wider network of pathways that criss-cross the fields and open spaces around Saltney, is itself a reminder of the striated nature of social space, a reassertion and entrenchment of socio-spatial divisions that is hardly peculiar to the 2020s, lockdown or no lockdown (Figure 5.4).

Figure 5.4 Signpost near to the town of Saltney in Flintshire indicating the route of a public footpath obscured to disguise or inhibit access (photograph taken by author, April 2020).

The territoriological science of imaginary solutions

In their book *Theatre/Archaeology*, Mike Pearson and Michael Shanks exhort us to pay closer attention to 'the grain and patina of place' by performatively embracing the 'juxtapositions and interpenetrations of the historical and contemporary, the political and the poetic, the factual and the fictional, the discursive and the sensual' (2001: 64). As a method and critical-creative mode of spatial enquiry, what Pearson and Shanks set out here maps seamlessly on to the subject matter, and the means by which this has been unpacked, that is the focus of the present discussion. The starting point has been to consider how, from one very localised corner of the world and the embodied and experiential dispositions that define the particularities of my own place within that corner of the world, we might go about navigating some of the spatial disorientations of lockdown. From this starting point came the preliminary sketching of a route map that has served as a guide, of sorts, into the innate surreality of place and space as experienced in the early period of the coronavirus pandemic in the UK. In the first instance, this route map/sketch came together in poetic form, eventually spawning a finished poem called 'Lache Eyes.' As a non-representational method of enquiry (referring to the poetising/mapping rather than the finished poem/map), the process of entangling and disentangling the threads of affect, emotion, observation, dwelling, immersion, and so on, that was the poem's principle function, led, in turn, to the collision of ideas and the accrual of intellectual and creative capital from which this essay has emerged. Conceived of as a method, poetry permits the opening of a space and imbues that space with liminality and possibility. In her essay, 'Writing and the Threshold Life,' the poet Jane Hirshfield suggests that '[w]ithin the separateness of liminality, connectedness itself is remade' (1998: 204). Reinforcing this observation, Hirshfield goes on to cite a stanza from Czeslaw Milosz's poem 'Ars Poetica:' 'The purpose of poetry is to remind us / how difficult it is to remain just one person, / for our house is open, there are no keys in the doors, / and invisible guests come in and out at will' (in Hirshfield 1998: 205).

Physically confined to our homes, as unwitting Ballantynes one of the challenges of lockdown has been finding ways of keeping our houses open and thresholds traversed. It has been knowing how to maintain – or remake – connectedness with the world without at the same time shrinking ever further from that world. Ballantyne was in equal parts both pioneer and pilgrim, yet his journey ended in utter isolation. No one can claim that any of this has been easy. As I write these closing lines, one year to the day from the start of the first UK lockdown, the UK once again finds itself in lockdown. If we are looking to delineate a science of territory under lockdown then perhaps it is the science of imaginary solutions where we need to be directing our attention.

References

Askins, K. and Raven-Ellison, D. (2012), 'Mission: Explore Food,' *Geography*, 97 (3), 163–166.

Augé, M. (1995), *Non-Places: Introduction to an Anthropology of Supermodernity*. London: Verso.

Bachelard, G. (1994), *The Poetics of Space*. Boston: Beacon Press.

Bachelard, G. (2002), *Earth and the Reveries of Will: An Essay on the Imagination of Matter*. Dallas: The Dallas Institute Publications.

Bakhtin, M.M. (1981), *The Dialogic Imagination: Four Essays*. Austin: University of Texas Press.

Ballard, J.G. (1990), *War Fever*. London: Collins.

Ballard, J.G. (2014), 'The Enormous Space,' in *The Complete Short Stories*, Volume 2. London: Fourth Estate, 697–709.

Barnwell, C.E. and Carpenter, R.J. (2017), *Archaeological Desktop Study: Wrexham Road Development Area*. Chester: Chapel Archaeology CIC.

Bazin, A. (1967), *What is Cinema?* Volume 1. London: University of California Press.

BBC TV (2003), *Home*. Directed by Richard Curson Smith. First broadcast 6 October 2003. Accessed on YouTube: https://youtu.be/Kce94adFCMc (accessed 3 March 2021).

Bodenhamer, D.J., Corrigan, J. and Harris, T.M. (eds) (2015), *Deep Maps and Spatial Narratives*. Bloomington: Indiana University Press.

Bök, C. (2002), *Pataphysics: The Poetics of an Imaginary Science*. Evanston, Illinois: Northwestern University Press.

Borges, J.L. (1973), *The Aleph and Other Stories 1933–1969*. London: Picador.

Cord, F. (2017), *J.G. Ballard's Politics: Late Capitalism, Power, and the Pataphysics of Resistance*. Berlin: De Gruyter.

Daumal, R. (2004), *Mount Analogue: A Tale of Non-Euclidean and Symbolically Authentic Mountaineering Adventures*. Trans. C. Cosman. New York: The Overlook Press.

Foucault, M. (1986), 'Of Other Spaces,' *Diacritics*, 16 (1), 22–27.

Garcia, P. (2015), 'J.G. Ballard's One-Man Worlds,'*Reflexiones marginales*, August–September 2015, 1–28.

Guardian, The (2020), 'George Floyd: Medical Examiner Says Death was a Homicide,' 2 June 2020: https://www.theguardian.com/us-news/2020/jun/01/george-floyd-death-homicide-police-brutality (accessed 12 March 2021).

Hetherington, K. (1997), *The Badlands of Modernity: Heterotopia and Social Ordering*. London: Routledge.

Hirshfield, J. (1998), *Nine Gates: Entering the Mind of Poetry*. New York: Harper Perennial.

Hugill, A. (2012), *Pataphysics: A Useless Guide*. Cambridge, Mass: MIT Press.

Ingold, T. (2012), 'Introduction,' in Janowski, M. and Ingold. T. (eds), *Imagining Landscapes: Past, Present and Future*. Farnham: Ashgate, 1–18.

Ingold, T. (2021), *Correspondences*. Cambridge: Polity.

Ingold, T. and Vergunst, J.L. (2008), 'Introduction,' in Ingold, T. and Vergunst, J.L. (eds), *Ways of Walking: Ethnography and Practice on Foot*. Farnham: Ashgate, 1–19.

Larsen, T., Tabor, L. and Smith, P. (2021), 'End of the Field? Hacking Online and Hybrid Environments for Field-Based Learning in Geography Education,' *Journal of Geography*, 120 (1), 3–11.

Lefebvre, H. (1991), *The Production of Space*. Oxford: Blackwell.

Leslie, E. (2020), 'Are we Really All in this Together?' *Culture Matters*, 4 June 2020: https://www.culturematters.org.uk/index.php/culture/tv/item/3393-are-we-really-all-in-this-together (accessed 18 March 2021).

Lovatt, S. (2021), *Birdsong in a Time of Silence*. London: Penguin.

Marin, L. (1984), *Utopics: The Semiological Play of Textual Spaces*. Atlantic Highlands, NJ: Humanities Press International.

Marin, L. (1993), 'Frontiers of Utopia: Past and Present,' *Critical Inquiry*, 19 (3), 397–420.

Mason, D.J.P. (1987), 'Chester: The Canabae Legionis,' *Britannia*, 18, 143–168.

Massey, D. (2005), *For Space*. London: SAGE.

Merleau-Ponty, M. (2014), *Phenomenology of Perception*. Trans. D.A. Landes. Abingdon: Routledge.

O'Connell, M. (2020), 'Why We are Living in J.G. Ballard's world,' https://www.newstatesman.com/2020/04/why-we-are-living-jg-ballard-s-world (accessed 18 February 2021).

Owen, H.W. (1994), *The Place Names of East Flintshire*. Cardiff: University of Wales Press.

Pearson, M. and Shanks, M. (2001), *Theatre/Archaeology*. London: Routledge.

Pecotic, D. (2014), 'Mountains Analogous? The Academic Urban Legend of Alejandro Jodorowsky's Cult Film Adaptation of René Daumal's Esoteric Novel,' *Australian Religion Studies Review*, 27 (3), 367–387.

Richardson, T. (ed.) (2015), *Walking Inside Out: Contemporary British Psychogeography*. London: Rowman and Littlefield.

Roberts, L. (2012), 'The Sands of Dee: Estuarine Excursions in Liminal Space', in Andrews, H. and Roberts, L. (eds), *Liminal Landscapes: Travel, Experience and Spaces In-between*. London: Routledge, 103–117.

Roberts, L. (2014), 'The Violence of Non Places,' in Andrews, H. (ed.), *Tourism and Violence*. London: Ashgate, 13–31.

Roberts, L. (2015), 'The Rhythm of Non-places: Marooning the Embodied Self in Depthless Space', in Roberts, L. (ed.), Special Issue on 'Deep Mapping', *Humanities*, 4 (4), 569–599.

Roberts, L. (2016a), 'Deep Mapping and Spatial Anthropology', in Roberts, L. (ed.), 'Deep Mapping', Special Issue on 'Deep Mapping', *Humanities*, 4 and 5 (2015–2016), 1–7.

Roberts, L. (2016b), 'The Cestrian Book of the Dead: A Necrogeographic Survey of the Dee Estuary,' in Cooper, D., Donaldson, C, and Murrieta-Flores, P. (eds), *Literary Mapping in the Digital Age*. Abingdon: Routledge, 182–204.

Roberts, L. (2018), *Spatial Anthropology: Excursions in Liminal Space*. London: Rowman and Littlefield.

Rosenblatt, K.F. (1999), *René Daumal: The Life and Work of a Mystic Guide*. Albany: State University of New York.

Rosenblatt, K.F. (2004), 'Introduction,' in Daumal, R. *Mount Analogue: A Tale of Non-Euclidean and Symbolically Authentic Mountaineering Adventures*. Trans. C. Cosman. New York: The Overlook Press, 5–25.

Sadler, S. (1998), *The Situationist City*. Cambridge, Mass: MIT Press.

Saker, M. and Frith, J. (2020), 'Coextensive space: virtual reality and the developing relationship between the body, the digital and physical space,' *Media, Culture and Society*, 42 (7–8), 1427–1442.

Schafer, R.M. (1994), *The Soundscape: Our Sonic Environment and the Tuning of the World*. Rochester, Vermont: Destiny Books.

Self, W. (2010), 'Crash: Homage to J.G. Ballard,' in https://will-self.com/2010/04/19/crash-homage-to-jg-ballard/ (accessed 5 March 2021).

Self, W. (2020), 'Zooming through the looking glass,' https://www.prospectmagazine.co.uk/magazine/zooming-through-the-looking-glass (accessed 18 February 2021).

Simmel, G. (1994), 'Bridge and door,' *Theory, Culture and Society*, 11 (1), 5–10.

Sinclair, I. (2003), *Lights Out for the Territory*. London: Penguin.

Slow Ways (2021), https://slowways.uk/ (accessed 11 March 2021).

Soja, E.W. (1996), *Thirdspace: Journeys to Los Angeles and Other Real-and-Imagined Places*. Oxford: Blackwell Publishers.

Sterling, B. (2020), 'The continuing relevance of J.G. Ballard,' https://www.wired.com/beyond-the-beyond/2020/04/continuing-relevance-j-g-ballard/ (accessed 18 February 2021).

Williams, G. (2008), 'Morfa,' in *Blood, etc.* Cardigan: Parthian.

Wright, J. (1905), *The English Dialect Dictionary, Volume 3, H-L*. Oxford: Henry Frowde.

Chapter 6

Affirmatively reading deterritorialisation in urban space

An Aotearoa/New Zealand perspective

Manfredo Manfredini

Introduction

My territoriological approach to urbanism focuses on the growing creative, emancipatory and egalitarian potentials of disruptive processes that influence material, functional and organisational elements of the city. It considers progressive mediatisation and financialisation crucial distinctive phenomena of our age in which territories are increasingly mobilised and mobilities territorialised (Brighenti 2014). Aiming to combine the ecological and phenomenological approaches to understand territorial becoming (Brighenti and Kärrholm 2020), I engage with the issue of reception of three key references in the contemporary discussion in urban studies: the not aligned and idiosyncratic critical theories of space and relationality of Henri Lefebvre, Gilles Deleuze and Félix Guattari, and Jacques Rancière. These lines of inquiry have been interpreted in a way that needs some adjustment because the mainstream disciplinary approaches have so far not adequately accounted for their central tenets regarding the productive codetermination and tension between opposite territorialisation forces for homogenisation and differentiation, coding and decoding, and equality and inequality. A better understanding of the capacity of such production is important to refine the conceptual tools used to interpret the fundamental challenges to urban society, environment and culture posed by increasing frequency and intensity of disruptive phenomena at all territorial scales.

Three key notions have informed the radical discourse on deterritorialisation articulating individuations that emphasise the ambivalent power of disruptions generated within established systems. These notions are the Lefebvrian *spatial production*, centred on the interplay of *abstractive* (alienating) and *differential* (emancipatory) forces of social spatial production, the Deleuze-Guattarian *deterritorialising assemblage*, illuminating machinic processes of *overcoding* or *liberatory decoding* of stabilised regimes, and the Rancièrian *distribution of the sensible*, predicated on politics of *disagreement* on authoritarian partitions of resources. Accordingly, my reading is centred on reconstructing the tension of three corresponding processes: the dominative abstractive spatialisation opposing

DOI: 10.4324/9781003196365-6

appropriative differential counterspatialisation (Lefebvre 1991, 2003, 2004); the stiffening, homogenising and halting concatenations that counter creative, diversifying and mobilising territorial destratifications (Deleuze 1992, 1994; Deleuze and Guattari 1983, 1987); and the ordering policed consensus that ruptures political dissensus for social change (Rancière 1999, 2010, 2011).

To address the shortcomings generated by the inadequate reception and mobilisation of these ideas in both *nihilist* and *reformist* camps (as described in the *coda* below), I take into consideration the growing interest in the two-fold endeavour initiated in field geography two decades ago around these lines. Firstly, I continue the process of reconciliation, started by Andy Merrifield (1993), tackling the way in which the Lefebvrian ontology of (social) space subverts the discourse of territory as a Cartesian determination. I focus on the privilege that Lefebvre gave to 'the way in which experience is lived and acted out in place, and how this relates to, and is embedded in, political and economic practices that are operative over broader spatial scales' (517). These are primarily basic social embedded experiences, which include 'banal (an occupation, a piece of work), subtle (meditation, contemplation), spontaneous (a child's game, or even one for adults) or sophisticated' (Lefebvre 2004: 76) instances, that trigger civic and political forces for 'utopian alternatives' of reappropriations and oppose the alienating spatial and temporal abstraction (Lefebvre 1991: 349, 416). Secondly, I develop the critical poststructuralist approach to urbanism, initiated by McFarlane (2011), of revising *assemblage thinking*. This aims to reverse what limits rather than deepens our capacities to thoroughly mobilise the radically liberating prefigurative force of deterritorialisation (Nail 2017) that Deleuze and Guattari indicated as the motor of *series of unclasping* that enables positive and consistent *lines of creation* and *becoming* of open, differential and desiring social bodies (Deleuze and Guattari, 1987: 165, 510).

On this basis, and before discussing the imposing agency of mediatisation and financialisation on contemporary practices of territorialisation in urban space, I provide a definition of territoriality and its constitutive process of creative disruption. Territoriality is a disposition of integrated yet often mutable and mobile concrete, relational and agential components that are engaged in multiple forms. The concrete elements are a variable set of tangible, intangible and hybrid items; the relational networks are connecting systems, patterns and ties subject to continuous actualisations and adaptations; and the activating agents are doctrines, programmes, plans and narratives constantly verified, revised and reformed. The engagements occur through various forms of dynamic individuation, appropriation and association that integrate the actual with the virtual, the Euclidean with the topological, and the synchronous with the multichronic. Such engagement is led by various arrangements of opposing forces either of domination or enfranchisement. The former forces are led by actants[1] aiming to expand their systems through enclosures and engraftments that

1 The term *actant* is a key notion in Actor-Network Theory that indicates both human and non-human actors. As clarified by Bruno Latour (1996), it emphasises

deterritorialise and reterritorialise external domains implanting their own patterns characterised by hierarchical relations of antagonism both internal and external. The latter forces intervene by *commoning* [2] through the establishment forms of *resonant* [3] collaboration and coproduction among actants aiming to reappropriate their own space by affirming the deterritorialisation with open spheres of *agonistic pluralism* where equality is a function of exchange, often conflictual, between the irreducible diversity of the actants (Mouffe 1999).

The multiplicity and variability of these *assembling by dissembling* processes (hereafter, bracketed 'de' or 'dis' indicates this oxymoron) confer the deterritorialised milieus a dynamic status. The destabilisation of the milieus opens them to a continuous becoming with opposite parties of control and liberation in both resistance and transformation camps. The relative stabilising capacity of the former in reaffirming their positions over the latter in constituting them anew, is in their effectivity to set up and implement institutional, strategic/tactical and cultural hegemonic projects to either reterritorialise or affirm deterritorialisation. Yet, both the milieus and the new (de)structurally associated systems are often internally inconsistent as they are constituted by subassemblages with equal semistable territoriality, as exemplarily demonstrated by the case of the contested public space territorialities of Berkeley's People's Park (Mitchell 2017).

Concerning public space, consistent with the Deleuze-Guattarian (1987) *assemblage theory* and its interpretation by Thomas Nail (2017) on the bifurcating production of the deterritorialising concatenations, I maintain that the effects of positive or negative disruptions (hereafter, *affirmative deterritorialisation* and *overcoding reterritorialisation*, respectively, with reference to Richard Sennett's, 2018, notions of *open/over-determined city*) depend on the effectiveness of their support to emancipatory and progressive commoning practices of social and everyday life reproduction. The negative effects typically occur when public space is enclosed to further progress projects of domination through financial extraction, control and homogenisation. The positive effects are typically activated when public space is a commons for the affirmation of equality in *pluralistic counterhegemonic* forms (De Angelis 2012, 2017; Laclau and Mouffe 1985).

the indifference in conferring the primary role to human competence in any network, as anything can be granted to be the source of an action.

2 Extending it beyond the human domain, I adopt Peter Linebaugh's (2008) definition of the commons as harmonious social relations of citizens, equally producers and consumers, that 'vests all property in the community and organises labour for the common benefit of all.' (6)

3 *Resonance* here refers to the definition given by Hartmut Rosa (2018: 58) as a relation based on 'intrinsic connection or correspondence' and 'mutual reaction in the sense of a genuine response,' yet it is extended to nonhuman actors and, more importantly, intended as manifesting its fundamental experiential 'self-efficacy' in spatialised political dimensions.

As discussed in detail in the following two sections, while new forms of stabilisation, normalisation and overcoding formalise the power and capacity of these hegemonic formations, novel creative commoning processes reassemble the counterhegemonic forces of the marginalised, disconnected and delegitimised. On the one hand, overcoding hypostatises the fear of chaos that these very rules generate to institute 'illusions of democracy' (Rancière 1999: 77, 90, 123) that infer the meaning of equality from the very rules that establish its imposed order. Metastability is equated to instability and forcibly suppressed to enable *overcoding reterritorialisations*. On the other hand, embracing chaos facilitates the unmasking of the underlying power motives that negate equality and enables making disagreement an empowering force of *affirmative deterritorialisation*.

Machinic domination through overcoding reterritorialisation

Metastability is not just limited to territoriality, rather it is an effect of the acceleration megatrend that speeds up transformation in all sectors of the contemporary domains of social (Rosa 2013) and spatial (Virilio 1997) spheres. Crucial to this acceleration is the institution of an unprecedented condition of *dynamic stabilisation* that enables the maintenance of the consolidated social and productive structures while fostering disruptive progressive growth and innovation. Dominant economic formations and regimes perpetuate their hegemony by coupling the transformative speeding up of their mode of production dictated by the imperative of exponential expansion with corresponding swift changes in their apparatuses of control. Spatially, such an unprecedented condition of *dynamic (de)stabilisation* was described by Harvey (2001) as the production of provisionally stabilised territorial configurations that reflect the

> *central contradictions of capital: that it has to build a fixed space (or landscape) necessary for its own functioning at a certain point in its history only to have to destroy that space (and devalue much of the capital invested therein) at a later point in order to make way for a new spatial fix (openings for fresh accumulation in new spaces and territories) at a later point in its history.* (25)

Regarding urban space, studies on conception, practices and actions of the spatialisation forms of this alienating metastability have provided extensive descriptions of their links to the escalatory (fixed) fluidity of the territoriality of contemporary urban restructuring and rescaling mediated by globalising capitalism (Harvey 2014; Rosa 2013). Macrodata on urbanisation's global trends, though imprecise and perplexing (Brenner 2019), suggest the strong correlation between territorial metastability and inequality. Macrogeographical areas of high and medium-income countries with higher economic, urban and interurban transformations (IOM – GMDAC 2018; UNDESA 2019) have the highest growth of spatial inequality (UNDESA 2020b). Granular analyses of these transformations indicate how the interconnections between semiemplaced 'broader configurations of capitalist uneven spatial development and geopolitical power' (Brenner and Schmid 2015: 161) generate forms of exploitation, dispossession and socioenvironmental destruction (Brenner 2013, 2019; Moore 2015; Peck 2016, 2017a, 2017b). These studies provide abundant evidence of the effects of escalating uneven spatial distribution of availability, access and decoding of resources for social production and reproduction on spatial justice and urban commoning.

Translocalisation machines and metastability of places

The territorial metastability moderates an irregular expansion of settlement boundaries creating a spatial continuum on multiple scales that progressively materialises what Lefebvre defined as 'planetary urbanisation' (Brenner 2013; Lefebvre 2003). A hybrid urbanity, where the urban unfolds into the rural and vice versa, creates an unprecedented globally interconnected 'differential urbanisation' with configurations unevenly concentrated, integrated and coproduced (Brenner 2019; Grange and Gunder 2018: 389). Cities' spatial properties, elements and parameters are continually redefined. 'Territorial continuity is not necessarily spatial continuity' (Brighenti 2014: 20), as distance has become more a function of the relational strength than a measure of Euclidean proximity. The reduction of spatial barriers was defined by Harvey (1989) as 'annihilation of space through time' and associated with the imperative compound rate of growth that sustains capital accumulation. This entails a mechanism of despatialisation supported by digital technology that enables the development of a global *space of flow* (Castells 2010): a *translocalisation machine* that produces *metastable places* with accelerated production, exchange and consumption.

Such a machine progressively inscribes in space the dynamic stability and unevenness of its socioeconomic forces. Irregular patterns of urbanisation express the contradictions and crises of the dynamic mode of production. Accelerating respatialisation processes led by the *creative destructive* forces of such a mode conjuncturally subvert given spatial orders to improve extractive capacities, often with the complicity of equally mutant and crisis-prone neoliberal regimes (Peck and Theodore 2019). The resulting urbanity is a messy layering of transforming fields with nearly ubiquitous *scale bendings* and *mismatches*, such as central urban areas of many major global cities in which segregative planned communities for expatriate elites juxtaposed to 'degenerated' residential clusters of domestic migrants (Soja 2009). *Translocalisation machines* introduce radical spatial remapping of deep-rooted socioeconomic polarisation, such as centre–periphery and urban–rural, that permanently disconnect and reconnect places, individual, routes and histories.

In a critical articulation of such exacerbated and mobilised fragmentation of the traditional spatial order, Harvey (2018) elaborated on how it is driven by a destructive force that radically restructures both production and consumption practices, disempowering antidominant forces. The translocalisation machines offer opportunities of rapid displacement, relocation and outsourcing of activities, maintaining seamless operations not only to increase direct profit of the dominant actors and corporations, but also to dissolve the conditions (critical mass, continuing relations and consistent frameworks) for the constitution of structured counterforces. This spatial metastabilisation makes the individual life of the disenfranchised extremely precarious as it engenders a condition that combines the illusion of freedom from the attachment to particular systems considered exploitative, and the frustration of increasing dependence on the very same systems that make free, the only available production and consumption options.

Such (in)dependence shreds the whole social fabric and social cohesion of emplaced communities and includes unavoidable debt traps that further increase both the systems' extractive capacity and the individual's subjugation. It undermines the development of the relational subjectivities, discourses, practices, and institutions through which the emancipatory alliances, meanings and political imaginaries are elaborated. The crisis of both political subject and public sphere leads to a condition of *objective alienation* (Harvey 2018: 424) where the internal contradictions of the alienating systems cease to manifest and defy collective opposition. Reflecting on Jameson's (1991) tenet that, in the contemporary world, the concept of alienation is no longer appropriate as 'the alienation of the subject is displaced by fragmentation of the subject' (63), Harvey (1989) submitted that such a loss could be fatal (54) and affect all planetary urbanites, the formal and the newly naturalised.

Transduction machines and mediatised time–space

Unrelenting mediatisation has been a central force of the processes of reterritorialisation in the expansion and integration of all the scales up to the planetary. It has established systems of relations that have progressively expanded the territorial metastability by augmenting the capacity not only to operate translocally, but also to instantly delocalise non-material components of space. The instrumental rationality of information technologies and artificial intelligence has helped hegemonic actors to cope with the dynamic multiplicity and operationalise their expansive domination plans. Yet, it has instituted a *time and space compression* (Harvey 2018: 20) with a multi-dimensional, partial and uneven space–time (May and Thrift 2001) that detaches *reality* from the place where it appears and poses a major threat to situated relationality and its inscription in space[4] (Virilio 1997: 135). The dislocation of reality and its induced multiplication significantly exceed the relational limits that enable us to relate and integrate them due to the desynchronised time structures of their accustomed sets of associations in different social

4 An example of the space–time crisis is the inefficacy of state politics in moderating the growing multidimensional divide in digital capacity in a market driven by global information technology companies that is a crucial emerging factor of social exclusion (Fenton 2016: 350–351; Sloane 2020; UNDESA 2020a).

areas (Rosa 2013, 2018). A novel condition of *constant present* is determined by the temporality of network-time and effaces all spheres of the non-mediated human experience (Hassan 2020: 173; Virilio 1997: 135). For Hassan (2009), the *constant present* introduces spatially emplaced forms of polychronic domination that enable hegemonic powers to exploit the 'seductive lightness' of the digital virtualisation[5] to convert the desire of *participatory ubiquity* into a force of voluntary alienating disparate fragmentation (Hassan 2009, 2018). Such deployment is interpreted by Hassan with a dialectic of technological-temporal change that identifies the institution of a socially dissociating and de-individuating *hegemonic timescape* [6] as a central force of the neoliberal societal revolution (Hassan 2012, 2018). Though today Virilio's catastrophic *post-reality* scenario seems less plausible, the general distancing introduced by the *relational technologies* of the mediatised *society of control* has nonetheless *short-circuited* the socially appropriated circuits of transindividuation (Stiegler 2009: 39) in which both experiences and significations are continuously reproduced in metastable, multiple, diffusive, superposed and multiscalar realities that conjuncturally inscribe translocally embedded practices.

An important contribution to the understanding of the reach of the social dissociation of such a dominative adoption of the new media technologies is given by Brighenti (2010), who unravelled their biopolitical extensions. With the establishment of 'regimes of networked visibility,' he submitted, the control of the new media has made extremely thin 'the distinction between empowerment and vulnerability, between recognition and control,' creating participatory disciplinary systems within mechanisms of exploitation and domination that, as understood by Foucault, transform 'the [collective] subject into *the principle of its own subjection*' (93).

The affordances progressively granted by mediatisation to the established dominative regimes of concentrated power over media have highlighted the role of systems of modulation and variance in resynchronising complacent members and desynchronising threatening agents (Fuchs 2014, 2016). These systems develop on par with the progressive rapidity of shifts in 'tolerance' that traditionally defined compatible social statuses, such as employed/unemployed, host/migrant, capitalist/proletarian and 'organization man'/'flexible woman' (Castells 2005: 9). This includes commanding the whole mediatised integration of private life and public life – i.e., the blurred boundaries that have characterised the modern dualism of production/social reproduction in practices such as play/labour, leisure time/work time and consumption/production. This

5 Restating the critique by Manfredo Tafuri on contemporary 'avant-garde' art, such lightness can be read as the illusion that such ultra-presence 'contains an unexplored richness, unlimited utilizable possibilities, and qualities of the *game* now made into new fetishes for society,' while is in fact just the 'explosion of the irremediable dissonances that escape the plan of advanced capital' (Tafuri 1976: 137, 139).

6 It is worth noting the similarity of Hassan's elaboration to Lefebvre's *rhythmanalytical* description of the supreme abstractive force of *arrhythmic dressage* (Lefebvre 2004: 38–45),

concerns sociality (cognition, communication, cooperation), social roles (e.g., citizens, consumers, workers) and, consequently, the liberal freedoms of speech, opinion, expression, association and assembly (Fuchs 2014: 77, 96). To be effective, such systems of modulation and variance perpetually increase in the precision of case and time-specific systems of individuation. They make the subject into an algorithmically 'resolved identity' (Brusseau 2020) where control is focused on profit and drives granular analysis to identify profiles and predict opportunities. Profiles are no longer describing individual types but dissected transindividual subprofiles integrally embedded into continuous networks. As Deleuze (1992) postulated, we 'no longer find ourselves dealing with the mass/individual pair. Individuals have become *dividuals*' (5).

The restraining effects of mediatisation, Rancière (2010) further emphasised, are due to the superior ability of overpowering parties in assembling multimodal (dis)'information machines' (110) that safeguard their interests by inhibiting actual political action.[7] These parties use such machines to mediate the global networks of computerised intelligence for further intertwining production, exchange and consumption on the global scale, support their appropriations and alliances, and make them their best refuge, the place where they self-legitimise their reality (Rancière 2010: 78–79).

Such capacities, which are activated by transmutative processes that combine heterogeneous and distributed forces with diffusing exogenous activities, reconfigure metastable domains into provisional unities or conditions, making them depoliticising *machines of transduction* (Simondon 2020). Paired with those of translocalisation, these machines guarantee the functionality of the space of flow, becoming the key engine of the current political and economic environments based on the neoliberal faith in self-regulating systems progressively steered by transnational capital (Peck and Phillips 2020). Their coupling is engaged in the inversion of public–private relations at the foundation of the *res publica* and in the subordination of principles of social justice to economic transaction practices, to sustain the concentration of power and market monopoly (Supiot 2013). Their force is demonstrated by the enormous success of platform capitalism (Peck and Phillips 2020; Srnicek 2017) and best exemplifies the contemporary 'cognitive' (Negri 2003: 64) 'informational and computational' (Stiegler 2019) capitalist turn: the formation of a system 'working from that *restricted layer* that Braudel called the antimarket [*a murky but dominating layer located above the competition*], newly constituted as a placeless place in the clouds with its very own breed of great predators' (Peck and Phillips 2020: 93).

Research in the area of social media studies has unveiled and documented, with solid empirical evidence, the primary role gained by these machines in our daily experiences. The contribution of digital technology industries to the

7 Rancière exemplified this with the pioneering Italian 'democratic' conflation of economic and political powers in the hand of the prime media tycoon who was granted the top political executive power.

expansion of inequality has been deemed an inevitable consequence of the irreconcilable democracy/free-market opposition (Caplan and Boyd 2016; Fuchs 2014; Sunstein 2017). The move of these industries 'from competitive to oligopolistic to monopolistic at breakneck speeds' (McChesney 2013: 130) has progressively enabled the affirmation of the *cultural hegemony* of whoever controls them, facilitating the imposition of particular values and norms by transforming them in common sense.

Natalie Fenton (2016) explained the mechanism by which the construction of such a pseudo-public sphere has disempowered the individual, impinging on the constitution of counterhegemonic formations at the basic social level that would develop into civic and eventually political movements. Fenton's description unveils how this disempowerment has been produced by the combined development of technology and capitalism with an 'ever-increasing entanglement of media and communications corporations with politicians and [S]tate agencies' that has increasingly constrained 'the opportunities and possibilities for being political through limiting public knowledge and policing dissent whether covertly or not' (354).

Urban restructuring and expulsion

In the expanded planetary urban space mediated by the machines of transduction and translocalisation the citizenship rights of both assimilated and mobilised urbanites are at high risk. On the one hand, the inurbated-by-extension (who inhabit areas with rural status) are threatened with expulsion by the very same rule presiding over their integration. Their inurbation occurs through an annihilation of space by time that involves displacement from cities of some of their formerly lowest subordinate constituents. This modern form of dioecism of the *space of flow* assimilates ruralists into marginalised urbanite communities. Instances representing this case are found in mega-urban regions, such as McGee's Desakotas, or in emerging distributed networks, such as the Chinese Taobao towns and villages system. The latter is linked to an apparatus co-driven by a governmental economic development programme and an extractive platform capitalist marketplace that restructures rural China by subjecting local communities to an extremely precarious sociospatial relationality and potential economic debasement.

On the other hand, intraurban restructuring is a known cause of mobilising gentrification. Its increasing occurrence expands the number of those who are left behind, displaced and marginalised. Saskia Sassen (2014) widely discussed the condition of the 'radically expelled,' cast out from what had been their lives. She unveiled how these are prevented from appearing and making manifest their disagreement due to the overpowering distance, material and relational, introduced with their eviction from their networks. Yet, these material expulsions through urban restructuring are just the most brutal cases of a much wider dismissal of those who, in various ways, challenge or obstruct the abstractive processes. The dismissed are the nonassimilated, strangers and resistants, such as the poor, the economic migrants and the anti-authoritarian activists. Pseudo-democratic systems target them to eradicate any space of *dissensus* (Rancière 2010: 71) and eliminate, little by little, any emerging 'parasitical entities of political subjectification' (124).

The transduction and translocalisation machines' contribution to the expulsion capacity of the antidissent apparatuses is exponentially growing with the combined application of artificial intelligence and monitoring devices. Prominent examples of State machines of this sort are those using biometric information and facial recognition technologies developed to identify and punish protesting occupants of public space. Foremost cases of the normativity of the disagreement management following the governance transfer of the public–private inversion include the paradoxical contradiction of a recent prominent suspensive order of the prevailing suite of social media platforms. This suspension, which was inflicted on the former president of the United States to, allegedly, end the platform's 'inequal' policy of non-interference with political speech, supremely ratifies the postulated self-legitimating management of disagreement that structurally transforms the public sphere.

Negation of the centre

Among the multiple forms of alienation caused by urban restructuring, the negation of the centre is the reterritorialisation that has most attracted my research. My studies have focused on main centres of multinodal cities which were dislocated, their lived, perceived and conceived dimensions reformulated, and their physical, social and symbolic elements decoded and overcoded. These dislocations mainly result from urban redevelopment plans that deploy sets of policies, measures and programmes to found the new centralities in antagonism with the existing ones. Comprehensive commercial heterotopias have radically 'redistributed the sensible' with compensatory and illusory enclosures of total commodification of daily practices. By establishing semi-fictional conditions they have embodied realities 'supposed to lift us out of the mire of our everyday lives and [move us] into the sacred spaces of ritualized pleasures' (Zukin 1995: 1). Endowed with enhanced control-by-spectacle apparatuses that triangulate actual and digital policing, these heterotopias can be characterised as advanced Baudrillardian *simulacra* where 'everything [belonging to the centre] is already dead and resurrected in advance' (Baudrillard 1994: 6). These simulacra exert their *precession* of the civic through a dynamic stabilisation of their spatialities that deploys powerful (dis)information and translocalisation machines to desynchronise the competing local centralities. Their compensatory–illusory civicness (re)produces 'civic realities' that negate their own illusory nature through their very institutive negation of reality. Yet, their (re)production generates dynamic stabilised copies without actual reference and stages *mise-en-scènes* of fascinating fetishes of relationality, which provide abundant materials for territorial associations and stabilisation of the emerging (pseudo)communities of prosumers.[8]

8 Prosumption is a form of participatory consumption defined by George Ritzer as a condition in which the production and consumption are intimately combined,

Their concrete elements typically include *civic squares, shopping arcades* and *children's playgrounds*, 'creatively' instantiated with Lefebvrian 'induced diversity,' that represent idealised places without originals (Manfredini 2017: 114–115). Their relational apparatuses, constituted with recurring events that typically regarding fashion, lifestyle or entertainment, are based on activities of experiential prosumption and gamification bestowed with powerful, yet discrete, policing systems that minimise even the potential of play to set us free (Han 2017: 52; Manfredini 2019a: 190–191). Their agents, such as elements of behavioural normativity and desire, morph into *spectacularisable* equality and difference the homogenised (Manfredini 2021b: 3). Essential to guarantee their precession is the global overpowering illusive nature of their constructed 'reality,' which affirms their order by ruthlessly decrying the supressing nature of the superstructures of the actual interiors in which 'human life is enclosed and partitioned' (Foucault 2008: 21).

I have examined the territorial capacity of various types of the domination machines that operate dynamically stabilised simulacra of central urban space. By analysing the progressive evolution of their reterritorialisation paradigms, I have identified a novel embodiment of the phenomenon of *creative destruction*. I have described this phenomenon as the transition between the *modern* and *ultra-modern supersessions of the centre* that has occurred with the shift from the consumerist-transactional *inverted city* model of the *modern shopping and entertainment magic spectacle* (Dovey 1999: 123–138) to the postconsumerist-pseudo-participatory *diverted city* paradigm of the virtualising, multiscalar and hypermediated relational *ultra-modern totalising superlative and simulated civicness* (Manfredini 2020).[9] I have highlighted the key role in this transition of three integrated and digitally augmented deterritorialisation processes: transduction, translocalisation and transculturalism (Manfredini 2021a: 4–5). These are processes that disrupt and reconstitute territories by respectively a) associating translocalised concrete elements of the city by relocalising them to constitute rich territorial unities of experiential civicness under simulated or illusory determinations; b) establishing multiassociative transductive relations between scattered spatialities to actualise and give privileged access to the constant present under policed conditions; c) orchestrating transculturalised hegemonic agents to enable the active participatory coformulation of normative elements under disagreement-free pluralistic communities.

My main Aotearoa/New Zealand case study of this superseding centrality is Auckland's Sylvia Park, a shopping mall owned by a single corporation, yet formally designated as top-level metropolitan centre. The compensatory function

discernible for analytical purposes only, and welded in an instrumental fashion that, particularly in the digital age, allows corporations to increase value extraction from participatory activities (Ritzer and Jurgenson 2010).

9 A quintessential example of the ultra-modern paradigm is Westfield's *hyperconnected microcity*, which was presented with the *Destination 2028* vision as a pragmatic heterotopia where consumers are *community-builders* and *hero-hunters* supported by service-synergists that facilitate their total identification with the brand.

of this centre without periphery is to respond to the gross lack of civicness of the extended carpet of distributed domesticity of the city in which it is semi-randomly engrafted. Its illusionary capacity flexes a *creative milieu* with instagrammably styled pedestrian squares and lanes *artistically* counterpointed *à la* Camillo Sitte, segmented sets of transindividually subprofiled active lifestyle precincts *eventfully* curated *à la* Greg Richards and Robert Palmer, mediatised *pacificatory cappuccino made-places à la* Fred Kent, and various multiplatform and cross-identification cultural installations celebrating Richard Florida's 3Ts (talent, technology and tolerance), which also include *reembedding* inscriptions of the local devastated Māori cultural landscape.

Abundant evidence of the metastable associations that produce the negational commodified 'civic' apparatuses shows that the ultra-modern machines of domination have radically deterritorialised and reterritorialised the way users 'live, work and play.' The technological advances that have made it possible to create apparatuses of controlled resonance for self-resolving identities have also allowed the systemic abstraction to implement a new spatial equation. 'Reproducibility, molarity, bounding, rigidness, discreteness and continuous induced mutation … are dissimulated … as [reconfigurations of] their *differential* opposites: individuation, molecularity, openness, suppleness, and continuous produced mutation' (Manfredini 2019a: 190).

The latest and highly revealing manifestation of the axiomatic normativity of the reterritorialisation found in Auckland's Sylvia Park, occurred at the onset of the urban crisis of the COVID-19 pandemic (Manfredini 2020, 2021a). During the first lockdown in March–May 2020, the semipublic space of the centre was promptly fenced off and heavily policed without concertation by the mall management. The outright negation of the centre, which was followed by micromanaged disciplinary measures during the gradual reopening phases, proactively responded to the State *protection-by-restriction* narrative of 'elimination' (of the virus) and 'social distancing,'[10] to which the Aotearoa/New Zealand public overwhelmingly consented. To shed light on the effects of such a radically orthodox spatial embodiment of the negational State paradigm perception, I investigated its collective perception by conducting an analysis on locally crowdsourced data from its main Instagram points of interest (POI, discussed in the following section). Through a triangulation of network and content analyses, findings demonstrated the general acceptance of such negative dynamic (de)stabilisation, confirming the precession capacity of the marketised civicness model. This confirms that, while such a segment of society 'has sacrificed freedom to so-called *reasons of security* and has therefore condemned itself to live in a perennial state of fear and insecurity' (Agamben 2020), the role of the capital in urban governance has become supplementary (Aalbers 2018) in structurally progressing the unevenly formulated and adopted unequal developmental paradigms.

10 The global adoption of the expression 'social distancing' to indicate 'spatial distancing,' was swiftly pointed out by Rosa (Latour and Rosa 2021) as a symptom of the spiralling unchallenged deprivation of social relations.

Machinic emancipation through affirmative deterritorialisation

Assemblages of affirmative deterritorialisation in urban space are characterised by commoning and are centred in institutions that affirm equality and integral sustainability. Commons are complex self-governing concatenations of pooled common resources, activating sets of commoners (De Angelis 2017) and counterhegemonic discursive operations acting against enclosing (Laclau and Mouffe 1985). As these resources, actors and agents are mobilised with universal aims, they involve a large mix of public and private instrumentalities that makes them intrinsically contradictory and permanently necessitating conflictual engagement.

The contradictions constantly bind commons' actors, the *multitude* (Hardt and Negri 2017), to a constant *reconfigurative othering* (Rancière 2010) through a process of *desubjectification* that involves desire as a fundamental force of associative production: a *desiring (dis)articulation* (Deleuze and Guattari 1987) for universal good that assembles, through creative transformative conflicts, othered individual and common interests. A progressive heterogenisation manifests the amplitude, efficacy and agency of the affirmative deterritorialisation against recoding processes of dispossession. As a function of the transformational complexity of their bodies, tasks and programmes, heterogeneity fosters enfranchising processes of becoming that operate concurrently across the three assemblage sets. Concrete counterelements emerge through the (de)identification and (re)association of their overcoded parts and favour the recreative affirmation of their singular corporality and capacity.[11] Relational antisystems come about by (de)networking and (dis)connecting the relations established by policed simulacra and liberating the symbolic from the constraints of its alienating formations, fostering open and emancipated creative association. Insurgent discourses evolve from (de)coding and (re)coding of narratives instituted through simulation and, liberating authenticity from the illusion of authenticity, establish conditions of pluralistic agonism where multiple counternarratives can confront and compete freely.

Positioning affirmative deterritorialisation in urban studies

Core to my recent research aimed to identify the affordances of affirmative deterritorialisation emerging from the digitally augmented translocalisation and transduction machines has been the validation of the affirmative interpretation of alienation as a contradictory condition with intrinsic progressive emancipatory forces (De Angelis 2012, 2017; Hardt and Negri 2017; Harvey 2018). The

11 Deleuze and Guattari (1987) explained such elemental deterritorialisation with the example of the orchid's capacity to attract the wasp for pollination by capturing its code and forming an image that traces it: 'an increase in valence … a becoming-wasp of the orchid and a becoming-orchid of the wasp … operating immediately in the heterogeneous and jumping from one already differentiated line to another' (10).

multiple metastable realities that the *constant present* opens to the possibility to redistribute partitions of the civic along spatial and temporal axes, extraordinarily expands access, collaboration and transindividuation reverting the abstraction and expulsion of desynchronised dividual actants, the biopolitics of controlled networks and the precession of simulacra. Such realities would enable the subversion of the simulated civicness into experimental utopian projects and their expansion into the extended urbanisation towards an effective universality that institutes a *multiscalar planetary relationality of commoning*. The innovations of the very same institutive frameworks that produce the novel compensatory–illusory simulative centres would expand the capacity of commoners to emancipate their daily practice of prosumption and intersectionally formulate scenarios for alternative social processes and, as Don Mitchell (2014) observed for the Occupy Wall Street movement, create a collective 'space for a new kind of world' (239).

My attention to how such realities foster the emerging counterforces of appropriation in the central urban places aims to face with *sober senses* such *melting into air* of the Reality. My stance is equally distant from that of Robert McChesney's (2013: 5–8) 'celebrants' and McKenzie Wark's (2019) 'special idiots.' The former referred to those who adhere to the proclamation that the internet 'would inaugurate a new era of cultural democracy in which the sovereign users—later dubbed prosumers—would call the shots' (McChesney 2013: 5). The latter referred to those who interpret Harvey's objective alienation in the late digital age as a totalising self-administered psychopolitical steering that degrades individuals into *genital organs of capital* 'positivized into things, which can be quantified, measured and steered' (Han 2017: 32).

My approach to the affirmative deterritorialisation adopts the Foucauldian tactic of taking 'the forms of resistance against different forms of power as a starting point' (Foucault 1982: 780). It sheds light on the emerging forms of resistance that subvert 'the locking together of power relations with *relations of strategy* [emphasis added] and the results proceeding from their interaction' (795). Focusing on decoding practices of affirmative deterritorialisation, it emphasises those expressed away from the systems of control of the centres and constitutive of the perceived and lived spatial centralities. These are residual practices (Lefebvre 2016: 16) which are not superfluous or purposeless, rather *irreducible* as they spring from fundamental things like desire, poietic capacity and singularity. Such residues include 'all activity that becomes autonomized [and] tends to constitute itself into a system, a *world*' (211): as clarified by Merrifield (2015), they consist of what is expelled by totalising systems, the 'stuff left over after all the sums have been done, after everything has seemingly been accounted for; le reste after la somme … [the] affirmation of remainders, of marginal dregs, of the power of the ragged and irreducible' (9).

In my recent studies, such residues of public space and urban commons were conjuncturally comparatively analysed as assemblages of constitutive processes of dissenting and (dis)associating that emerge in imposing negative deterritorialisation, such as collectively appropriated debris between commercial enclosures, *malled* urban centres and enclavic cities of spectacle. The focus on translocal and transduced nonconforming, often latent, constellations of actants showed how they manage 'to live with contradictions, to resist contradictions, to innovate and blast through contradictions, to blast through social confinement, through confining totalising contexts and structures' (Merrifield 2015: 10). The conjunctural method enabled engagement with individuation, unveiling *resonant* relationalities and acts of commoning in urban public spaces of transgressive *dividual prosumers translocally* operating in selected instances of major urban centralities of Aotearoa/New Zealand, China, Indonesia and Vietnam.

Communities that speak in Aotearoa/New Zealand

Among my studies on affirmative deterritorialisation, the ones on Auckland and Wellington in Aotearoa/New Zealand are the most articulated explorations of the conditions of the highest algorithmically resolved prosumers that inhabit simulated urban centres (Manfredini, Reeves and Kiddle 2019). These studies enabled us to open a perspective on the (un)mediated granular effects of daily digital practices of encroachments on such overcoded territories in foremost market-driven regimes. We engaged with the pioneering appropriative actions at the basic social level sprouting in the domination gaps opened by the contradictions and conflicts internal to the systems of *financialisation-by-simulation*. Non-harmonised frameworks extended from commerce (e.g., online/offline retail) to governance (e.g., national/international law) and emplacement mode (e.g., space of places/space of flows).

Searching for emerging (dis)alienated progressive emancipatory forces, these studies ventured within a highly mediatised version of what Bruno Latour (2012) defined as multiple, indistinct and mobile *urban plasma*: the inexhaustible source of real-time and real-space instances of materialities, practices and acts of territorialisation of the places we inhabit and the commons we share. Extensive crowdsourced social media datasets from the most popular visual-based, locative social media, Instagram, in the period 2017–19 in these centres were collected and analysed. Integrated methods of network and content analyses of actual and digital spaces, which operationalise the Lefebvrian triplectics of represented, perceived and representational spaces (Manfredini, Tian and Jenner 2017), were developed to compare the modern and the ultra-modern paradigm. Findings revealed a massively outperforming growth in ultra-modern centres of relational counterhegemonic forces that elude the control apparatuses of these civic simulacra by instituting plural, dynamic, cohesive, low-hierarchical, multilineal, open and interconnected emplaced associations (Manfredini 2019b: 407–410).

Longitudinal studies not only provided evidence of the resilience of the associations emplaced in the ultra-modern centres, but also documented the increase of their assertive redistribution of the abstracted commoning spatialities. Findings of both network and content analysis showed a continuous increase of *deviant* relational engagement for the construction and reassembling of discourses, narratives and practices of such disenfranchised commoners. Key results regarding the formation of social networks in the main POIs of the main ultra-modern case study, Sylvia Park, Auckland, showed a constant growth in number and size of independent communities, which involved a large number of individuals (100,000+) and had mostly large clusters (more than 2/3, i.e., 100+, with 500+ members), high dynamism, low centrality and high cross-community interaction (Bueno, Chalermtip and Manfredini 2019).

Topical findings also resulted from the analysis of the digital data of the early phase of the COVID-19 pandemic (Manfredini 2020). During the lockdown, the contradictions intrinsic to the deterritorialisation of these centres exacerbated their manifestation. A greatly amplified difference between the relational behaviour of communities in the two centre types, which as stated above confirmed the normativity excess of the ultra-modern model, concurrently unveiled that the emplaced networks of that centre reacted to the negation of their public space with vigorous and sustained practices of reappropriation. The content of their interaction showed that such reaction to the radical augmentation of the negative reterritorialisation strengthened their countering abstract machines of transduced and translocalised commoning for the coproduction of diversity, partnership and "enjoyment" (Lefebvre 2014). The intensity of animated intersectional ludic practices (e.g., cross–cultural children's play), cultural–identity affirmations (e.g., performative events of ethnic minorities) and poietic action (e.g., creative photographic spatial reinvention) was much higher than in any previous period. Diverted prosumers subverted their scripted actions. Relational networks affirmed the centralities of their centres (via digital POIs) countering their outright negation. Autonomous discourses and imaginaries collectively cocreated in these centres were reaffirmed and further articulated.

These appropriative *lines of flight* found at the core of the preceding simulacra of civicness indicate the strong resilience of social reproduction of subversive prosumer networks that use digital space to redistribute such dominated spheres of the sensible. This confirms Rancière's (2013) understanding of new media as systems that redistribute capacities and support 'new forms of expertise that can be appropriated by anybody in order to help constitute a people of the anonymous, a people of indeterminate individuals at odds with the people governed by the dominant system' (7). More importantly, the strong hike in empowerment of the antisystem forces of affirmative deterritorialisation found in the ultra-modern centre showed that the contradictions intrinsic to radical reterritorialisations that foster the growth of the dominant machines for the creation of consensus and axiomatic normativity, also strengthen the desiring machines for the affirmation of disagreement of digitally empowered communities.

Political movements of affirmation

The disruptive power of forces that subvert the desynchronising apparatuses with affirmative deterritorialisation practices engages in processes of (dis)assembling that

Deleuze and Guattari (1987: 269) defined as contagion-proliferation and creative involution to counter the abstractive, taming and consenting machines that leave society 'short of democracy [and] short of politics' (Rancière 2010: 121). Mobilised by translocally transduced haecceities, technology becomes a powerful instrument of relational capacity building for the production of *differential spaces*. By 'restor[ing] unity to what abstract space breaks up – to the functions, elements and moments of social practice' (Lefebvre 1991: 52), it fosters moments of productive conflict between the discontinuous and oppositional statuses of the modern dividuals. Rancière (2013) described these instances of interruption as the weaving together of intervals of subjectivisation in *heterochronic heterotopies* that 'disrupt the dominant—consensual—combination' to generate 'moments when one of the social machines that structure the time of domination break[s] down and stop[s]' (7–8).

In such a process of *deterritorialisation-by-disagreement* digitally augmented counterhegemonic assemblages are key to the empowerment of disjoined, displaced and alienated *dividuals* (Tufekci 2017). 'Fast resistance transfer' (Purcell 2008: 153) builds dissenting formations' translocal, transformative, transconnective and transcoding capacity, enabling the catalysis and (de)structuration of bottom-up movements claiming the *Right to the conjunctural City* as right to the radical (anti)political against the political abstraction of space. Such an empowering role of digital technology is demonstrated by its agency in major uprisings such as the Occupy, Gezi Park and Black Lives Matter protests, or the recent resistant upheavals in Colombia, Greece or Brazil (Crimethinc 2021).

An exemplary case, the 2013 Gezi Park Movement activated a widespread citizens' resistance to a major government-led abstractive privatisation plan for a foremost urban common, the first public park of modern Turkey. The park became a world of *produced difference* where large scale assemblies established a concrete space of democratic agonistic pluralism (Farro and Demirhisar 2014; Hardt and Negri 2017: 275, 293; Manfredini and Gharaghooshi 2016; Manfredini, Gharaghooshi and Leardini 2017). As counterspace of resistance, it successfully countered the *induced difference* [12] (Manfredini 2021b) of a commercial and cultural 'restorative' project that cunningly conflated consumeristic economic development, pseudo-cultural reidentification and spectacular beautification agendas. Its main actor was the *shadow citizenry* of metropolitan Istanbul – particularly those who Merrifield (2014) defined as 'the disenfranchised constituency haunting the global banlieue… where social exclusion meets spatial marginality' (18). State actions, such as the militarised park clearance aiming to 'give back the park to its users' or the muting of the

12 As defined by Lefebvre (1991), produced difference is a *productive* 'shattering of a system' that 'emerges from the chasm opened up when a closed universe ruptures' when 'a given set gives rise, beyond its own boundaries, to another, completely different set.' By contrast, induced difference is an *unproductive* iteration that 'remains within a set or system generated according to a particular law' (372).

movement by deactivating the key digital messaging application, boosted a *scale jumping* that triggered extended international rhizome-like ramifications. Heterogeneity unfolded, activists coalesced across the spectrum from liberalism to anti-authoritarianism against the homogenisation. Concrete elements included a myriad of actants for subsistence, defence, dialogue and recreation that built and supported the activation of the protest encampment to assert the primacy of such prime public space of social practice and representation. Relational systems comprehended the emplaced, antagonist and grassroot networks instituted on an encrypted social media platform that circumvented the regime's control with glocal tactics that included ingenious practices, such as the ultra-local manually sharing leaflets in the camp indicating steadily changing passwords. Agents collaboratively created in steadily morphing strategies and action plans of resistance were framed by the articulation of a discourse asserting the Right to Difference and Self-Governance. The affirmation of the equality by differentiation was patent in the emplaced assemblage of the encampment, where various allied, yet distinct, groups created semi-autonomous subencampments, such as those of environmentalists and civil right coalitions, and, within them, sub-subencampments of subgroups, such as those of feminist and LGBT activists.

The Gezi Park Protest is an eminent case of the contribution of digitally augmented spatialities to the affirmative deterritorialisation (Tufekci 2017). Progressively diversifying, morphing and embodying *absent presences*, digitalisation made its assemblages ultra-relational *mutable (im)mobiles*, adapting the Latourian description of systems subject to seemingly incompatible systemic interferences that are displaced through transformations but without deformation (Latour 2005: 223). More precisely, these (dis)assemblages embodied *augmented territorial framings with topologies of fire* with conditions of advanced differential individuation in (dis)continuous becoming (Kärrholm 2012: 48–65; Law and Mol 2001: 615–620). Digitally augmented recreative decoding challenged the traditional mechanisms of control of the transformative and innovative emancipatory processes of exchange and acculturation. Global Gezi *constant presents* reduced the differences in local relative power and reordered agency and capacity of the opposite camps, fostering affirmative deterritorialisation dynamics with mechanisms of (de)association and productive relationality. *Insurgent desiring* new worlds of commoning guaranteed the continuous becoming that encumbered the dominant local actors to develop subassemblages of control and rehomogenisation, stabilise identification, normalise connection systems and impose their values as common sense.

By taking a space, making 'it anew as a *public* space' and, by this, redefining 'the meaning of *public*' (245), a multitude of disruptive resistants transformed an instance of *annihilation of space by law* into a springboard for the constitution of a large global counterhegemonic affirmation of what Lefebvre defined as the Right to the Centre. Such affirmation concerns the access and coproduction of the places of converging multiplicities of things and activities, where the different appear, meet, acknowledge and compete with the other (Manfredini,

Gharaghooshi and Leardini 2017: 284ff). In Rancièrian terms, these digitally networked spaces are radically reconfigurative domains in which the egalitarian logic emerges from 'interruptions, fractures, irregular and local' (Rancière 1999: 137), and presents a 'political being-together' that upends dominant orders where the exercise of power is negated to the excluded (Rancière 2010: 69).

Coda: planning and urban design theory between nihilism and reterritorialisation

The theoretical entanglements between coding, decoding and overcoding, which I have articulated in my studies as opposition between dynamics of negative (redeterritorialisation) and affirmative deterritorialisations, have been substantively elaborated in the wider academic discourse on urbanism. However, as stated in the introduction, this has been mostly confined to an expanded area of critical theory that has overlooked the crucial power of certain radical critique – here addressed as that of Lefebvre, Deleuze and Guattari, and Rancière – in affirming the central creative role of disruptive negation and disagreement. Mainstream theoretical elaborations tend to address the crisis of democratic projects, hijacked by the endless variants of neoliberalist embodiments (Peck 2017a, 2017b), either through nihilistic critical narratives *à la* Baudrillard that see the progressive fragmenting homogenisation as *fetishism of cohesiveness* (Lefebvre 1991: 411), or through the articulation of pathways of reform by resistance and empowerment, which see the *shadow citizenry*, along the line of McChesney's *celebrants*, progressively reorient the system's capacity to regulate the convergence and divergence over space and time (Rancière 2013: 5).

Yet, on the one hand, the *nihilists* have raised multiple claims of the failure of contemporary urbanism and exemplarily coalesced in condemning a key discipline for the production of the urban space. Urban design has been identified by eminent scholars (Cuthbert 2007; Sorkin 2009) as incapacitated or incapable (Soja 2009; Vergara Perucich 2019) of responding effectively to the urban problems of our times. They have characterised it as a symptomatic superstructure that expresses the basic negation of inequality structural to the (dynamic) stabilisation of the neoliberal regime. Its manifestations, deemed as ranging through the entire spectrum from ultra-reactionism to (retro-)vanguardism (Sorkin 2009), have been accused of contributing to the completion and dissimulation of extractive processes in urban space by quintessentially representing the amalgamation of governing bodies, industry and academia with the reigning market-driven hegemonic culture. On the other hand, the *reformists*, who have shown a near-heroic attempt to normalise the radical critique in progressive and emancipatory discourses on policies of differential urbanisation, have thereby effaced the power of disagreement. For example, Grange and Gunder (2018) in a Rancièrian critique of contemporary planning failed to engage with the radical power of the *(de)politicising* (liberating) force of dissensus that it entails. By asserting that planning 'must operate as part of the policing order,' (401) they turned this force into a *politicisation* (exercise of power) agent. Instead of using it to introduce elements of contestation, they advocate for a spatial planning practice that allows the play of generic disruptive politics and acknowledges the particularity of place to end exclusionary policing orders. Instead, for Rancière (2010), politics is inherently entangled with policing and its equalitarian agency requires its permanent reassertion. Due to such contradiction, (de)politicisation cannot promote inclusion and reject exclusion, rather it should operate in their interval, as it is a 'supplement to every collective body: that is, the totality of the uncounted, which does not mean the *excluded* but simply anybody at all' (79).

Positive deterritorialisation through non exclusionary planning or otherwise must start from *affirming equality* (not from *ending inequality*) and acknowledging its contradiction as informing non reconciliable social conflicts. Decoupling politics and policing, as such a planning may entail, means achieving *relative deterritorialisation* while negating *absolute deterritorialisation*, that is, not (de)politicising actions of commoning, but rather favouring both their decoding and negative overcoding. Yet, positive deterritorialisation through place-based policies or otherwise must also start from *haecceity* (not from *placeness*), as the *dividual prosumer* of the mediatised age can only reappropriate both the fixed means of production and consumption (e.g., collective intellect's produced algorithms) in *fugitive instances* emerging from the contradiction of the *algorithmically resolved, translocalised and transduced constant present.* The steady affirmation of equality in the haecceity expresses the capability of *total alienation* (as described by Harvey [2018] on Marx's original formulation in the *Grundrisse*) to increment concurrently with reconstructive and recreative revolutionary counterforces. Our study of the reterritorialisation of an ultimate alienating space, the ultra-modern mall of *precessing civicness*, confirmed this positive correlation, providing evidence of the *voice of subversive prosumer communities*: the *production of desire without reference to any exterior agency*.

Acknowledgements

This work was developed as part of the projects *Give Us Space*, funded by the New Zealand Ministry of Business, Innovation & Employment, and *Analysing the Role of Urban Forms in Making Sustainable, Healthy Cities*, funded by the Worldwide University Network. It was supported by the Digital Research Hub and by the Future Cities Research Hub of the University of Auckland.

References

Aalbers, M. B. (2018) 'Introduction to the Forum: From third to fifth-wave gentrification,' *Tijdschrift voor Economische en Sociale Geografie*, 110 (1), pp. 1–11.

Agamben, G. (2020) *Clarifications, An und für sich*. Available at: https://itself.blog/2020/03/17/giorgio-agamben-clarifications/?fbclid=IwAR3y8hIOkUIFgxfITZ4qVxNmhLyHfa2y7QE2rm7dJOLNPpWVNkEjrfFiMr4.

Baudrillard, J. (1994) *Simulacra and Simulation*. Ann Arbor: University of Michigan Press.
Brenner, N. (ed.) (2013) *Implosions/Explosions: Towards a Study of Planetary Urbanization*. Berlin: Jovis Verlag.
Brenner, N. (2019) *New Urban Spaces: Urban Theory and the Scale Question*. New York: Oxford University Press.
Brenner, N. and Schmid, C. (2015) 'Towards a new epistemology of the urban?' *City*, 19 (2–3), pp. 151–182.
Brighenti, A. M. (2010) *Visibility in Social Theory and Social Research*. London: Palgrave Macmillan.
Brighenti, A. M. (2014) 'Mobilizing territories, territorializing mobilities,' *Sociologica*, (1), pp. 1–25.
Brighenti, A. M. and Kärrholm, M. (2020) *Animated Lands: Studies in Territoriology*. Lincoln: University of Nebraska Press.
Brusseau, J. (2020) 'Deleuze's postscript on the societies of control: Updated for big data and predictive analytics,' *Theoria*, 67 (3), pp. 1–25.
Bueno, A., Chalermtip, T. and Manfredini, M. (2019) 'Digital space analysis.' https://cpb-apse2. wpmucdn.com/blogs.auckland.ac.nz/dist/b/596/files/2019/08/1.3.1-Digital-Space-Analysis-Sylvia-Park-Instagram-SMALL-IMGs.pdf.
Caplan, R. and Boyd, D. (2016) 'Who controls the public sphere in an era of algorithms,' *Mediation, Automation, Power*, pp. 1–19. Available at: https://datasociety.net/pubs/ap/MediationAutomationPower_2016.pdf.
Castells, M. (2005) 'The network society: From knowledge to policy,' in Castells, M. and Cardoso, G. (eds) *The Network Society: From Knowledge to Policy*. Washington, DC: Center for Transatlantic Relations, pp. 3–21.
Castells, M. (2010) *The Rise of the Network Society*. Chichester, West Sussex; Malden, MA: Wiley-Blackwell.
Crimethinc (2021) *Crimethinc: Archives 2021*. Available at: https://crimethinc.com/2021.
Cuthbert, A. R. (2007) 'Urban design: requiem for an era – review and critique of the last 50 years,' *Urban Design International*, (12), pp. 177–223.
De Angelis, M. (2012) 'Crises, capital and co-optation: Does capital need a commons fix?' in Bollier, D. and Helfrich, S. (eds) *The Wealth of the Commons: A World Beyond Market and State*. Amherst MA: Levellers Press, pp. 184–191.
De Angelis, M. (2017) *Omnia Sunt Communia: Principles for the Transition to Postcapitalism*. London: Zed Books.
Deleuze, G. (1992) 'Postscript on the societies of control,' *October*, 59, pp. 3–7.
Deleuze, G. (1994) *Difference and Repetition*. New York: Columbia University Press.
Deleuze, G. and Guattari, F. (1983) *Anti-Oedipus: Capitalism and Schizophrenia*. Minneapolis: University of Minnesota Press.
Deleuze, G. and Guattari, F. (1987) *A Thousand Plateaus: Capitalism and Schizophrenia*. Minneapolis: University of Minnesota Press.
Dovey, K. (1999) *Framing Places: Mediating Power in Built Form*. London: Routledge.
Farro, A.L. and Demirhisar, D.G. (2014) 'The Gezi Park movement: A Turkish experience of the twenty-first-century collective movements,' *International Review of Sociology*, 24 (1), pp. 176–189.
Fenton, N. (2016) 'Left out? Digital media, radical politics and social change,' *Information, Communication & Society*, 19 (3), pp. 346–361.
Foucault, M. (1982) 'The subject and power,' *Critical Inquiry*, 8 (4), pp. 777–795.

Foucault, M. (2008) 'Of other spaces,' in Dehaene, M. and De Cauter, L. (eds) *Heterotopia and the city: Public space in a postcivil society*. Abingdon, Oxon: Routledge, pp. 13–30.
Fuchs, C. (2014) 'Social media and the public sphere,' *TripleC*, 12, pp. 57–101.
Fuchs, C. (2016) *Critical Theory of Communication: New Readings of Lukács, Adorno, Marcuse, Honneth and Habermas in the Age of the Internet*. London: University of Westminster Press.
Grange, K. and Gunder, M. (2018) 'The urban domination of the planet: A Rancièrian critique,' *Urban Planning*, 18 (4), pp. 389–409.
Han, B.-C. (2017) *Psychopolitics: Neoliberalism and the New Technologies of Power*. Brooklyn: Verso.
Harvey, D. (1989) *The Condition of Postmodernity: An Enquiry into the Origins of Cultural Change*. Cambridge, MA: Blackwell Publishers.
Harvey, D. (2001) 'Globalization and the *spatial fix*,' *Geographische Revue*, 2, pp. 23–30.
Harvey D. (2014) *Seventeen Contradictions and the End of Capitalism*. London: Profile Books.
Harvey, D. (2018) 'Universal alienation,' *Journal for Cultural Research*, 22 (2), pp. 137–150. doi:10.1080/14797585.2018.1461350.
Hassan, R. (2009) *Empires of Speed: Time and the Acceleration of Politics and Society*. Leiden: Brill.
Hassan, R. (2012) 'Time, neoliberal power, and the advent of Marx's "common ruin" thesis,' *Alternatives: Global, Local, Political*, 37 (4).
Hassan, R. (2018) 'There isn't an app for that: Analogue and digital politics in the age of platform capitalism,' *Media Theory*, 2 (2), pp. 1–28.
Hassan, R. (2020) *The Condition of Digitality: A Post-modern Marxism for the Practice of Digital Life*. London: University of Westminster Press.
Hardt, M. and Negri, A. (2017) *Assembly*. New York: Oxford University Press.
IOM – GMDAC (2018) *Global Migration Indicators*. Berlin. Available at: https://publications.iom.int/system/files/pdf/global_migration_indicators_2018.pdf.
Jameson, F. (1991) *Postmodernism, or, the Cultural Logic of Late Capitalism*. Durham: Duke University Press.
Kärrholm, M. (2012) *Retailising Space: Architecture, Retail and the Territorialisation of Public Space*. Farnham: Ashgate.
Laclau, E. and Mouffe, C. (1985) *Hegemony and Socialist Strategy: Towards a Radical Democratic Politics*. London: Verso.
Latour, B. (1996) 'On actor-network theory: A few clarifications plus more than a few complications,' *Soziale Welt*, 47, pp. 369–381.
Latour, B. (2005) *Reassembling the Social: An Introduction to Actor-Network Theory*. Oxford: Oxford University Press.
Latour, B. (2012) 'Introduction: Paris, invisible city: The plasma,' *City, Culture and Society*, 3 (2), pp. 91–93.
Latour, B. and Rosa, H. (2021) *The world after: Bruno Latour and Hartmut Rosa on the consequences of the coronavirus crisis at the (Frankfurter Buchmesse)*. Available at: https://" t: https://www.buchmesse.de/en/timetable/session/world-after-bruno-latour-and-hartmut-rosa-consequences-coronavirus-crisis.
Law, J. and Mol, A. (2001) 'Situating technoscience: An inquiry into spatialities,' *Environment and Planning D: Society and Space*, 19, pp. 609–621.
Lefebvre, H. (1991) *The Production of Space*. Maiden, MA: Blackwell Publishing.
Lefebvre, H. (2003) *The Urban Revolution*. Minneapolis: University of Minnesota Press.

Lefebvre, H. (2004) *Rhythmanalysis: Space, Time and Everyday Life*. New York: Continuum.

Lefebvre, H. (2014) *Toward an Architecture of Enjoyment*. Minneapolis: University of Minnesota Press.

Lefebvre, H. (2016) *Metaphilosophy*. London: Verso.

Linebaugh, P. (2008) *The Magna Carta Manifesto: Liberties and Commons for All*. Berkeley and Los Angeles: University of California Press.

Manfredini, M. (2017) 'The augmented meta-public space: Interpreting emerging transductive territories in enhanced centres of consumption,' *The Journal of Public Space*, 2 (3), pp. 111–128.

Manfredini, M. (2019a) 'Mobility, translocalisation and transduction,' in Marata, A. (ed.) *Diverse City*. Rome: CNAPPC, pp. 1–10.

Manfredini, M. (2019b) 'Simulation, control and desire,' *The Journal of Public Space*, 4 (2), pp. 179–198.

Manfredini, M. (2020) 'Affirmatively reading post-consumerism,' *The Journal of Public Space*, 5 (3), pp. 207–226.

Manfredini, M. (2021a) 'Envisioning urban commons as civic assemblages in the digitally augmented city,' in Taufen, A. and Yang, Y. (eds) *Sustainable Cities and Landscapes: US Pacific Northwest in Pacific Rim Perspective*. London: Routledge. Manuscript accepted for publication.

Manfredini, M. (2021b) 'The Gezi Park Protest space and the novel urban commons,' in Bravo, L. (ed.) *Resilient Communities, Catalogue of the Italian Pavilion at the* [1]*7th Biennale di Architettura Venezia*. Manuscript accepted for publication.

Manfredini, M. and Gharaghooshi, F. Z. (2016) *Radical Inequalities in and by a Radical Istanbul*, 3rd Istanbul Design Biennial. Available at: http://arewehuman.iksv.org/open-call/.

Manfredini, M., Gharaghooshi, F. Z. and Leardini, P. (2017) 'Instances of emerging agonistic spatialities in the contemporary city,' *Asian Journal of Humanities and Social Studies*, 5 (5), pp. 281–291.

Manfredini, M. and Jenner, R. (2015) 'The virtual public thing,' *Interstices: Journal of Architecture and Related Arts*, 16, 70–82. doi:10.24135/ijara.v0i0.493.

Manfredini, M., Reeves, D. and Kiddle, R. (2019) *Give Us Space: Improving Community Well-being by Enhancing Performance and Communication of semi-public Space in the Evolving Public Realm*. Available at: https://" t: https://www.drh.nz/labs/urban-relational-informatics/.

Manfredini, M., Tian, X. and Jenner, R. (2017) '"Transductive urbanism": A method for the analysis of the relational infrastructure of malled metropolitan centres in Auckland, New Zealand,' *Athens Journal of Architecture*, 3 (4), pp. 411–440.

May, J. and Thrift, N. (2001) 'Introduction,' in *Timespace: Geographies of Temporality*. New York: Routledge, pp. 1–46.

McChesney, R. W. (2013) *Digital Disconnect: How Capitalism is Turning the Internet against democracy*. New York: The New Press.

McFarlane, C. (2011) 'Assemblage and critical urban praxis: Part one,' *City*, 15 (2), pp. 204–224.

Merrifield, A. (1993) 'Place and space: A Lefebvrian reconciliation,' *Transactions of the Institute of British Geographers*, 18 (4), pp. 516–531.

Merrifield, A. (2014) 'The shadow citizenry', *Open Democracy*. Available at: https://www.opendemocracy.net/en/opensecurity/shadow-citizenry/.

Merrifield, A. (2015) 'Towards a metaphilosophy of the urban,' *Antipode Online*. Available at: https://antipodeonline.org/2015/12/04/towards-a-metaphilosophy-of-the-urban/.
Mitchell, D. (2014) 'Postscript (2014): Now what has changed?' in *The Right to the City: Social Justice and the Right for Public Space*. New York: The Guilford Press, pp. 238–246.
Mitchell, D. (2017) 'People's Park again: on the end and ends of public space,' *Environment and Planning A: Economy and Space*, 49 (3), pp. 503–518.
Moore, J. W. (2015) *Capitalism in the Web of Life*. London: Verso.
Mouffe, C. (1999) 'Deliberative democracy or agonistic pluralism?' *Social Research*, 6 (3), pp. 745–758.
Nail, T. (2017) 'What is an assemblage?' *SubStance*, 1 (142), pp. 21–37.
Negri, A. (2003) *Reflections on Empire*. Malden, MA: Polity Press.
Peck, J. (2016) 'Macroeconomic geographies,' *Area Development and Policy*, 1 (3), pp. 305–322.
Peck, J. (2017a) 'Transatlantic city, part 1: Conjunctural urbanism,' *Urban Studies*, 54 (1), pp. 4–30.
Peck, J. (2017b) 'Transatlantic city, part 2: Late entrepreneurialism,' *Urban Studies*, 54 (2), pp. 327–363.
Peck, J. and Phillips, R. (2020) 'The platform conjuncture,' *Sociologica*, 14 (3), pp. 73–99.
Peck, J. and Theodore, N. (2019) 'Still neoliberalism?,' *The South Atlantic Quarterly*, 118 (2), pp. 245–265.
Purcell, M. (2008) *Recapturing Democracy: Neoliberalization and the Struggle for Alternative Urban Futures*. New York: Routledge.
Rancière, J. (1999) *Disagreement*. Minneapolis, MN: University of Minnesota Press.
Rancière, J. (2010) *Dissensus: On politics and aesthetics*. London and New York: Continuum.
Rancière, J. (2011) 'The thinking of Dissensus: On politics and aesthetics', in Bowman, P. and Stamp, R. (eds) *Reading Rancière*. London and New York: Continuum, pp. 1–17.
Rancière, J. (2013) 'In what time do we live?' *European Graduate School*, 4, pp. 1–9. Available at: https://quod.lib.umich.edu/p/pc/12322227.0004.001?view=text;rgn=main.
Ritzer, G., and Jurgenson, N. (2010) 'Production, consumption, prosumption: The nature of capitalism in the age of the digital prosumer,' *Journal of Consumer Culture*, 10 (1), pp. 13–36.
Rosa, H. (2013) *Social Acceleration: A New Theory of Modernity*. New York: Columbia University Press.
Rosa, H. (2018) *Resonance: A Sociology of Our Relationship to the World*. Cambridge, UK: Polity Press.
Sassen, S. (2014) *Expulsions: Brutality and Complexity in the Global Economy*. Cambridge, MA: Harvard University Press.
Sennett, R. (2018) *Building and Dwelling: Ethics for the City*. London: Penguin Books.
Simondon, G. (2020) *Individuation in Light of Notions of Form and Information*. Minneapolis: University of Minnesota Press.
Sloane, M. (2020) 'Inequality in the digital pandemic,' Items: Social Science Research Council, Insights from the Social Sciences. Available at: https://items.ssrc.org/covid-19-and-the-social-sciences/society-after-pandemic/inequality-in-the-digital-pandemic/ (Accessed: 8 March 2021).
Soja, E. (2009) 'Designing the postmetropolis,' in Krieger, A. and Saunders, W. S. (eds) *Urban Design*. Minneapolis, MN: University of Minnesota Press, pp. 255–269.

Sorkin, M. (2009) 'The end(s) of urban design,' in Krieger, A. and Saunders, W. S. (eds) *Urban Design*. Minneapolis, MN: University of Minnesota Press, pp. 155–182.

Srnicek, N. (2017) *Platform Capitalism*. Cambridge, UK; Malden, MA: Polity Press.

Stiegler, B. (2009), 'Teleologics of the snail: The errant self wired to a WiMax network,' *Theory, Culture & Society*, 26 (2–3): 33–45.

Stiegler, B. (2019) *The Age of Disruption: Technology and Madness in Computational Capitalism*. London: Polity Press.

Sunstein, C. R. (2017) *#Republic: Divided Democracy in the Age of Social Media*. Princeton: Princeton University Press.

Supiot, A. (2013) 'The public–private relation in the context of today's refeudalization,' *International Journal of Constitutional Law*, 11 (1), pp. 129–145.

Tafuri, M. (1976) *Architecture and Utopia: Design and Capitalist Development*. Cambridge, MA: MIT Press.

Tufekci, Z. (2017) *Twitter and Tear Gas: The Power and Fragility of Networked Protest*. New Heaven: Yale University Press.

UNDESA (2019) *World Urbanization Prospects: The 2018 Revision*. New York. Available at: https://population.un.org/wup/Publications/Files/WUP2018-Report.pdf.

UNDESA (2020a) *World Social Report 2020: Chapter 2, The Technological Revolution: Winners And Losers*. Available at: https://www.un.org/development/desa/dspd/wp-content/uploads/sites/22/2020/02/World-Social-Report-2020-Chapter-2.pdf.

UNDESA (2020b) *World Social Report 2020: Inequality in a Rapidly Changing World*. Available at: https://www.un.org/development/desa/dspd/world-social-report/2020-2.html.

Vergara Perucich, F. (2019) *Urban Design Under Neoliberalism: Theorising from Santiago, Chile*. London, New York: Routledge.

Virilio, P. (1997) *Open Sky*. London and New York: Verso.

Wark, M. (2019) *Byung-Chul Han: Shanzhai theory, Verso Blog*. Available at: https://www.versobooks.com/blogs/4283-byung-chul-han-shanzhai-theory.

Zukin, S. (1995) *The Cultures of Cities*. Oxford: Blackwell.

Chapter 7

Rendering territory (in)visible

Approaching urban struggles through a socio-territorial lens

Anke Schwarz and Monika Streule

Introduction

The grainy picture shows a group of about twenty people – most of them male, some uniformed – standing in front of a colorful mural. Behind their backs, a large portrait of the Mexican revolutionary Emiliano Zapata seems to make direct eye contact with the photographer. However, only one eye is visible. The other is in the process of being covered with white paint by two men standing on ladders and wielding paint rollers on extension poles, who are painting over the entire mural. This photograph of the destruction of the mural 'Alerta mi general Emiliano Zapata en la lucha de Atenco' [Alert my general Emiliano Zapata in the struggle of Atenco] on December 12, 2013, was published the following day on the blog of the *Frente de Pueblos en Defensa de la Tierra* [People's Front in Defense of the Land, or FPDT] (FPDT 2013), a social movement set out to stop the large-scale infrastructure project of a new international airport on land of the municipality of San Salvador Atenco on the eastern outskirts of Mexico City. The image, taken by an unnamed photographer, is illustrative of what we have introduced elsewhere as 'contested urban territories' (Schwarz and Streule 2020). Taking the violent erasure of the mural as a starting point for this chapter, we examine contemporary urban contestations through a socio-territorial lens. Like layers of paint, the transformation of urban territories always leaves traces of former uses and points to the ways in which questions of representation, identity, and group formation as well as economics and ecology are constantly being negotiated over, in and through space. Such contested spatial representations – or, as Andrea Brighenti (2010) puts it, inscriptions in the (publicly) visible – are but one of the myriad ways of how urban territories are appropriated, adapted, and transformed. Whereas the mural of Atenco serves to illustrate one of the many means of how ordinary people produce urban territories on an everyday basis, the erasure of the mural exemplifies a specific take on 'territoriology,' differing significantly from prevailing definitions of the term which we will further develop in this chapter and condense here in two basic points. First, territorial practices are not always directly related to

DOI: 10.4324/9781003196365-7

the nation state or to state actors. Second, territorial practices are not limited to human or animal behavior of a group or individual defending a 'home turf.'

In this chapter, we outline a socio-territorial perspective on the urban that puts non-state actors and everyday practices center stage.[1] Urban territories, as we understand them, emerge from collective imaginaries as well as spatial regulations, both of which materialize in space and are in constant transformation. We therefore conceive of territory as a social process, always in the making. Framing territory as a social process highlights the significance of urban territories as both the site of and what is at stake in contemporary contestations in cities. As urban scholars, our main questions analyzing social struggles in the context of urbanization are: What is contested? Who are the involved actors? What are their claims, what are their strategies? And where are these different actors socially and geographically situated? To tackle these questions, we propose to move beyond statism and its narrower definitions of fixed and bounded territory closely associated with the nation state to open new perspectives on relational territory. This conceptual engagement implies joining in a critical debate about relational power, a central tenet of any socio-territorial approach providing a way to avert the 'territorial trap,' as John Agnew (1994) famously called a problematic reification of territory.

To drive a shift of perspective in the anglophone human geography field – a 'transposition of territory,' as we have called it elsewhere (Schwarz and Streule 2016) – we draw on socio-territorial concepts emerging from Latin American Indigenous, Afrodescendant and feminist social movements and scholarship.[2] Currently, it seems that large-scale natural resource extraction – framed as neoextractivism with dramatic transformation of landscapes, usually accompanied and driven by large-scale infrastructure projects – is the main domain in which activists and scholars fruitfully apply the concept of territory (e.g. Svampa 2015; Bartra 2015; Escobar 2016; Anthias 2018). Neoextractivism also applies to the urban context, as Maristella Svampa and Enrique Viale (2014: 10) show by using this lens to analyze the process that produces exclusive urban territories. Closely related is the work of feminist decolonial scholars linking questions of bodies with territories through collaborative methods of research and reflection (e.g. Ulloa 2016; Colectivo Miradas Críticas del Territorio desde el Feminismo 2017; Zaragocín and Caretta 2020).

These various recent approaches generally build on longstanding debates on a relational approach on territory, particularly put forth by Latin America-based

1 Methodologically, our chapter draws on methods including cartography, document research, interviews and ethnographic insights into the case study of San Salvador Atenco in Mexico City to elaborate on a situated understanding of territorialization as a social process (Streule 2020).

2 This relational concept of territory differs significantly from the common definition in anglophone geography where territory is mainly considered to be a political technology, resulting from social and political strategies to delimit and control space (see Sack 1986; Sassen 2013; Elden 2019).

scholars, in which territory is mainly understood as a spatial social product deeply shaped by unequal power relations (e.g. Becker 1985; Porto-Gonçalves 2001, 2006; Saquet and Sposito 2009; Haesbaert 2013; Santos 2017). An interdisciplinary approach at the intersections between human geography, sociocultural anthropology, architecture, planning and sociology forms the basis for research in this emerging field of inquiry. Explicitly urban perspectives, while still somehow fragmented, are receiving increasing interest in recent debates (see Echeverría and Rincón 2000; Lindón 2019 and other contributions in our 2018 *Geographica Helvetica* special issue: Schwarz and Streule 2020). We thus consider territory an analytical category that is crucial to understand today's urban transformations because it is a particularly helpful focus for inquiring into the social production of urban space and 'the spatial dimension of power relations' (Haesbaert 2011. By grasping the epistemological and empirical complexities of a socio-territorial approach, this contribution aims to put territory to use for the transdisciplinary field of urban studies.

Zapata at Atenco: Defending the commons

In the municipality of San Salvador Atenco at the periphery of Mexico City, plans for a new international airport have been the focal point of resistance by local inhabitants, many of whom work in farming. A quick overview of the recent history of contestations over land in the context of this large-scale infrastructure project will help to gauge the relevance of rendering a mural visible or invisible.

Adorning the walls of the municipal auditorium on the main square of Atenco until its destruction in 2013, the mural by Mexican artist Javier Campos 'Cienfuegos' was originally painted in 2001 (Figure 7.1). It is a telling example of our understanding of territories as being produced precisely in moments of social struggle over the practices, meanings and tenures of urban space.

Prior to the start of construction of the airport on the plains of the former Lake Texcoco – a vast area of state-owned land in the eastern part of Mexico City – the government planned to expropriate land adjacent to the municipality of Atenco as early as 2001. It abandoned the plans in the following years and never carried out this large-scale confiscation in part a result of successful local organizing by the social movement around the People's Front in Defense of the Land. Brutal police repression, including sexualized violence against protesters, followed in 2006 and was condemned internationally (see Giordano 2006).

However, plans for the airport have been relaunched since the state governor responsible for this police operation, Enrique Peña Nieto, became president of Mexico in 2012. The very same land was again earmarked for an upscaled project pushing a massive urban transformation: a private developers' project, the *Ciudad Futura* [Future City], not only intended to build a major international airport hub serving the whole region of the Americas and with a passenger capacity four times bigger than that of the existing airport, but also

Figure 7.1 Original mural 'Alerta mi general Emiliano Zapata en la lucha de Atenco' by J. Campos 'Cienfuegos' before it was erased with white paint (Image: Monika Streule, 2013).

intended to develop large parts of the former lake bed of Texcoco Lake into a business district with condominium towers and other real estate projects.

This is the backdrop upon which to measure the symbolic value of the destruction of the mural, which stands for the collective memory of socio-territorial struggles in Atenco since at least 2001. The mural serves as a highly visible reference to the unfinished project of the Mexican Revolution some eight decades before. The huge portrait of Mexican revolutionary Emiliano Zapata, considered an icon of radical land reform, provides the most direct hint towards the main issue at stake in this whitewashing: communal land used for agriculture according to *ejido* territorial regulation, a form of collective land use established in the 1930s in the aftermath of the Mexican Revolution and modeled upon precolonial agricultural commons.

From a socio-territorial perspective, ejidal land tenure is key to understanding the ongoing conflict in Atenco and other peripheral communities of Mexico City. Its main feature is collective ownership of plots which are cultivated for the individual usufruct of each member of the ejido. Land uses were originally restricted to agricultural purposes, and land could not be legally sold nor urbanized. Even after a reform in 1992 introduced drastic legal changes, the commodification of ejido land still depends on the consent of a majority of the Ejidatarixs, the members of the ejido committee (Varley and Salazar 2021). This unique form of territorial regulation thus represents a major obstacle to urbanization and land use change. At the same time, the ejido as a territory is also stabilized and reproduced through agricultural practices. Tilling the soil means defending the land, as one of the leaders of the People's Front told us during an interview in 2013:

> The land is not for sale. No. Our slogan is: The land is loved and defended … Because we know it, because we grew up there, because this is where we have experienced happiness and also a lot of sadness. We know it and therefore we defend it. How do we defend it? By planting the land, cultivating it.
>
> (Interview with Doña Trinidad Ramírez, Mexico City, November 19, 2013; authors' translation)

This illustrates how making and sustaining territory is an active process: one of active and ongoing production much more than of passive inheritance or autochthonous entitlement. It also shows how territory serves as both a source and an expression of power in several ways, as two following examples will further clarify.

A very different kind of territory is, for instance, sketched in urbanist visions and architects' renderings of the same time. Inspiring or inhibiting certain future actions through territorialization is particularly present in design interventions of urban planners and architects alike. Bearing the programmatic title Ciudad Futura, the airport project displayed glowing landscapes full of greenery and modern buildings. Despite drafting an infrastructural megaproject such as an international airport with several runways and significant environmental impact, it also claimed to promote sustainability. Absent in these computer-generated images and the accompanying texts are current inhabitants and their uses of the land, in particular ejidal agriculture. Through these omissions, architectural discourses mirror the symbolic violence of the destruction of the mural in Atenco. Making territory is, in other words, by no means automatically a counter-hegemonic exercise. On the ground, the lines between acting 'from above' and 'from below' are blurred in multiple ways, complicating attempts to narrate these contestations in binary terms. We will return to this point later. As such, these symbolic strategies resemble each other in striving to render certain territorial practices and land uses invisible in what could be called a strategic appropriation based on de-territorialization. The apparent void which results from rendering pre-existing territorialities invisible may then be filled with a multiplicity of new visions.

Although the mural bearing the memory of Atenco's socio-territorial struggles was effaced with white paint, the vision of ejidal land as commons lives on in other forms. The People's Front blog, reporting about a local festival titled *¡La memoria y la cultura, no se borran con pintura!* [Memory and culture cannot be erased by paint!] held a couple of months later, recalls the mural not only as a victim but as a protagonist and motivation to continue organizing: 'This time we will not have our mural as a witness and, at the same time, a testimony of so much history, for by "erasing" it, it has already turned into another reason to fight' (FPDT 2014, authors' translation). As of early 2021, the municipal auditorium of Atenco continues to bear Zapatas's name, and the mural has been temporarily resurrected, printed on a makeshift plastic tarp. After years of conflict and confrontations, the airport project was partly built but was ultimately stopped by the incoming López Obrador administration in late 2018, with plans to construct a new airport elsewhere. Recent satellite images of the area reveal that little in terms of architectural features of the airport terminals has been realized. However, a widespread network of access roads and highways has been constructed, providing a strong incentive for and acting as a driver of further urbanization of the lacustrine zone. Alternative visions for the region are being put forward through the *#YoPrefieroElLago* campaign, addressing past, present, and future human and non-human inhabitants of the lake bed through a 'letter to the lake' (Hackear el Aeropuerto 2018; see also Rivera 2020). Socio-territorial urban struggles over forests, land, and water are currently reaching well beyond this specific case and include contested urban territories in the wider urban peripheries of Mexico City (Streule 2019; Sawyer et al. 2021).

Urban territories: A socio-territorial approach

Conceptualizations of territory, territoriality, and territorialization are subject to profound, longstanding debates in the field of human geography. A relational understanding of territory – of critical importance for examining urban socio-territorial struggles – is widely debated by francophone geographers in particular (e.g. Gottmann 1973; Raffestin 1980; Moine 2006; Giraut 2013) and increasingly discussed in the field of urban studies (e.g. Schwarz and Streule 2016) and related disciplines such as architecture (e.g. ETH Studio Basel 2016). Others have shed light on the concept's widespread use in fascist ideologies, particularly nativist reifications in National Socialist-slogans such as 'blood and soil' (Barnes and Minca 2012; Minca and Rowan 2016; Michel 2018). Taking a critical stance against essentialist and exclusive understandings of territorialization, current debates in political and social geography also oppose prevailing understandings of territoriality because they too often serve as an aggressive defense of home or place against 'others;' they misleadingly suggest seemingly fixed and clearly defined borders.[3]

3 Such a reified idea of territory is commonly employed in the natural sciences, specifically in animal ecology – though even within this field, definitions of territoriality tend to differ significantly (e.g. Maher and Lott 1995; Bartlett and Light 2017). For example, research along this line observes song birds' use of acoustic markers to outline their territory during breeding time, or herbivorous fish defending 'their'

The socio-territorial approach proposed here contributes to the analysis of urban contestations and radically challenges essentialist and behavioristic approaches to territoriology through (1) understanding urban territory as a relational social product and (2) analyzing territorialization with a focus on power relations. This goes together with the study of different key dimensions of urban territory, namely: (3) materiality and the built environment, (4) urban imaginaries and representations of territory, and (5) lived experiences and everyday practices. In the following, we will briefly outline each of these interrelated aspects.

(1) Urban territory as a relational social product

Research in line with the socio-territorial approach is attentive to the ways in which territories are made and remade in constantly shifting coalitions and situations rather than assuming an intrinsic or innate human territoriality. A socio-territorial perspective is interested in the process of territorialization and its diverse actors. Beyond the scale of the nation state, which is often prioritized in political geography, a socio-territorial approach helps to shift focus towards processes of territorializations related to urban transformations. Here, the oeuvre of Henri Lefebvre (1991) and other debates on relational space (e.g. Massey 1994; Hart 2018) provide a particularly useful backdrop as they propose to conceive urbanization as an ongoing social process:

> Spatial practice regulates life – it does not create it. Space has no power 'in itself,' nor does space as such determine spatial contradictions. These are contradictions of society … that simply emerge in space, at the level of space, and so engender the contradictions of space.
>
> (Lefebvre 1991: 358)

A similar relational approach to urban territories provides a socio-territorial lens that is useful for analyzing ongoing processes of de- and reterritorialization and their inherent questions of power, as the next section will illustrate in more detail. Latin America-based conceptualizations of territory revolving around such questions of relationality are closely linked to an understanding of urban space as socially produced.

(2) Territorialization through power relations

Socio-territorial perspectives revolve around the above outlined understanding of territory as a relational concept and additionally engage with a particular focus on power relations (see e.g. Raffestin 1980). Such a notion of territory seeks to lift the veil on 'the spatial dimension of power relations' (Haesbaert 2011: 281). Being able to exert influence upon processes of territorialization is

algae against competing corals. Applications of this approach to humans and human territorial behavior have also been made, particularly in the field of anthropology.

crucial for gaining and increasing social visibility and recognition (Zibechi 2008; 2012). We can observe a diverse set of social subjects with individual and collective memories, interests, capitals and powers, who express and practice their territoriality from a broad set of different social positions (Echeverría and Rincón 2000: 12). In this context, it is pertinent to link a subject's spatial practices and knowledge production back to their social position, and consequently, questions of power (e.g. Best 2014; Schwarz 2017). These subjects are always situated in contexts which both circumscribe and affect them. Social inequalities organized along categories such as gender, race, and class are reproduced or contested by every subject through their everyday practice. The meaning of such contestations and struggles is, as Fernandes (2009) argues, basic to the territory concept. Territory, understood as a social product, is thus made by these subjects and is at the same time aware of social contradictions:

> Territories do not exist if not for the social relations and power relations that form them and thus, they always affirm the social subjects by whom they are realized. Therefore, rather than idealizing any territoriality, it is necessary to verify the relations which shape them.
>
> (Porto-Gonçalves 2006: 179; authors' translation)

Rather than something arising from a certain geographical location or ecology, territories are contingent and fragile products in constant need of stabilization and renegotiation. Therefore, 'conflicts, powers, subversions and resistances belong to all territorial construction, which means to recognize the constantly fragile quality of territory. Its consistency is permanently imprecise, its coherence is an illusion, a never-ending search' (Echeverría and Rincón 2000: 12; authors' translation). The production of urban territory is the precise instance in which social relations are disputed, stabilized, and mediated. At the same time, it seems prudent to keep things complicated. The task ahead is to carefully analyze 'ordinary' socio-territorial urban constellations and negotiations rather than to romanticize them. Just as ordinary lifeworlds, and very much as part of them, heterotopian places, resistances, and alternative worlds are messily interwoven with social contradictions and unequal power relations.[4] Yet there are, as Penelope Anthias (2019: 71) writes with a view to Indigenous lifeworlds affected by extractivism, 'challenges to sustaining a pluriverse on a gas field.' To understand how such exceptional and ordinary urban territories are produced and contested, a socio-territorial approach attends to materiality, meaning, and the everyday as key dimensions of urban territorializations.

4 Along the way, it would appear that such a relational stance also has the potential to respect and include latent territories created by human/non-human interactions and interspecies relations, such as those beautifully traced by Anna Lowenhaupt Tsing (2015) in *The Mushroom at the End of the World*. To live (and die) well together in capitalist ruins may depend on our skills to track down, create, and shape possible future territories (Tsing 2015; Haraway 2016).

(3) Materiality and the built environment

Power relations and social processes of negotiation concerning territorial practices and meanings unfold in the material conditions of urban territories. As it applies a specific focus on the concrete, material conditions of urbanization, a socio-territorial perspective is particularly useful for an urbanist analysis (Schmid 2015: 293). Current debates on the concept of territory in the social sciences are further nourished by interpretations stemming from the field of architecture. The concept of territory has circulated for a while particularly in the field of architectural research and is based strongly on conceptualizations by André Corboz (2001) along with Saverio Muratori (1967) and Alberto Magnaghi (1998). Thus, in this approach of architectural research, territory differs also from the conventional framing as the bounded space of the anglophone tradition. Conversely, it is mainly understood as a concrete, physical reality with its own specific characteristics. In that sense, social processes like urbanization are inscribed into territory and materialize as such in a particular space and time. Corboz, for instance, describes this inscription as follows:

> Most layers are both very thin and filled with lacunae. Above all, we do not just add to these layers, we erase. Some strata have even been deleted on purpose. ... The territory, so heavily charged with traces and with past readings, seems very similar to a palimpsest.
>
> (Corboz 2001: 228; authors' translation)

In this view, urbanization – or more specifically, large-scale urban infrastructures like dams, highways or airports – comes up against concrete conditions: that is, the land with its specific characteristics and social and economic constellations as it is shaped and transformed by processes of urbanization (Schmid 2015: 290). Moreover, power relations are profoundly embedded in territory; they tend to reproduce themselves through materialization and hence intensify hegemonic territorial relations. Thus, processes of territorialization are deeply engraved in the land, materialized in the built environment with its specific features of long duration and sometimes resistant to change, like transport infrastructures, real estate, or landscape engineering. This interpretation resonates productively with the relational conceptualization of territory defined above, upon which we draw in this chapter for the elaboration of a relational socio-territorial approach (see also Schwarz and Streule 2016; Streule 2018).

(4) Urban imaginaries and representations of territory

Despite this material inertia, a conceptualization of territory as socially produced renders urban territory contestable – and it does so via both materiality and meaning:

> In this process of territorialization, space undergoes variations of meaning over time. This can take millenniums, decades, or years, but … it can also happen fast, as in transformations through the abrupt impact of planned or incidental interventions, or due to the emergence of protagonists with a strong ability to control pre-existing logics. Those expressions … constitute a system of codes, which provide it with a particular meaning. In this context, space, while territory, is only as stable or instable as the practices of territoriality it stems from.
>
> (Echeverría and Rincón 2000: 18; authors' translation)

Territorial protagonists, equipped with diverse individual and collective memories and urban imaginaries (Silva 1992), establish relations and negotiate with each other to fix particular meanings of territories. Hence, a socio-territorial perspective on urbanization foregrounds the intentions of social actors and the meanings they assign to territory. Or, as Carlos Walter Porto-Gonçalves writes, 'places do not exist a priori but are constructed in the shifting terrain of social struggles, which are also struggles over the attribution of meaning' (2001: 15). This attribution of meaning is a collective, a social endeavor, and again, it is deeply inscribed with social contradictions and inequalities reflected in multiple concurrent representations of territory.

To name just three of the many sources of such representations of territory in the context of our case study, there are, first, the visual devices of professional planners, cartographers, and engineers – maps, master plans, and architectural renderings. Computer-generated images such as the ones employed by Ciudad Futura described above frequently serve as tools of neoliberal urbanism, representing 'distinctive forms of visualizing and marketing the urban' (Degen et al. 2017: 3). Second, complex sets of spatial regulations and legal frameworks regarding land use and urbanist development plans of all kinds stand for another, closely related path: statist territorial representations (Wilson 2014). Yet urban territories come forth through powerful collective imaginaries which emerge along, beyond, and, at times, in spite of such professional or statist interventions. Third, these representations of territory emerge from an everyday making-sense-of-the-urban guided by urban imaginaries, and take a wide spectrum of shapes. They range in scale and scope from reproducing a dominant status quo to engaging in resistance and radical change (Lindón 2019), as well as from an outward-looking 'global sense of place' (Massey 1994) to an identitarian and exclusionary perspective creating seemingly 'authentic communities' (Ince 2011). Such homogenizing or essentializing visions regarding the shape and character of urban entities – say, 'the banlieue' or 'the European city' – are conjured up (Schwarz 2022). Some of these tropes tend to feed on and contribute to territorial stigmatization (Wacquant et al. 2014) and related struggles for recognition (Sisson 2021). Understanding territorial representations thus as contingent and in constant transformation, a socio-territorial approach focuses on urban imaginaries to highlight various representations of diverse and powerful territorializations. As such, this approach mirrors affects along representations' entire spectrum, from hope to despair.

(5) Lived experiences and everyday practices

Following Milton Santos's call to heed 'banal spaces' (2000), Latin America-based scholars propose to examine the 'territories of the everyday' (Fernandes 2009) to understand the impact of global spatial regulations in the production of specific urban territories.

> Consequently, there is an escalating conflict between local space, a space lived by all neighbours, and global space, inhabited by a rationalizing process and with an ideological content of distant origin. This process and content arrive at each place with objects and rules established to serve them; hence, the interest in reclaiming the notion of banal space, that is, the territory of everyone, which is often contained in the limits of the work of everyone.
>
> (Santos 2017: 29)

It is in the vast terrain of everyday practices that people's territorial practices are most intimately interwoven with the co-production of materiality and meaning. Ordinary urban situations are when and where 'to territorialize is to turn stone, clay, or even dust into a vehicle of transformative power' (Brighenti and Kärrholm 2020: 2).[5]

In contrast to other already fully built up municipalities in the peripheries of Mexico City, many inhabitants of Atenco work cultivating the ejido land. 'These projects, the airport or Ciudad Futura, are not for us,' says Trinidad Ramírez in an interview conducted 19 November 2013. 'We know that urbanization will happen, but we want to control these processes ourselves' (*ibid.*). A specific use value is given to land as it is often the only income source for families and thus the sole inheritance for future generations. Back in November 2013, everything seemed peaceful in Atenco, but Ramírez was expecting the next 'blow of the beast,' as she puts it. 'The government conceals its intentions and keeps sending other people into the village to buy up land' (*ibid.*).

At the same time, there were other struggles over urban territories going on in Atenco: The election for leaders of the ejidal committee was just won over by the members in favor of the airport project in October 2013 – the

5 That resonates strongly with Sylvaine Bulle's (2019: 215) reflection on ordinary discourse in the context of the Zad, a former land occupation against the construction of an airport near Nantes, France, describing the occupation as a set of customary practices, gestures, and even aesthetics that brings people together to evaluate events and to assemble individual stories in a collective narrative with a particular attention to living spaces.

representation of the more than 950 Ejiditarixs, which until then had been made up of people loyal to the People's Front in Defense of the Land. Though the vote was corrupted, offering 2,500 pesos for those who put their cross in the right place, this change in local politics is an example of the different interests and urban imaginaries within the inhabitants themselves. It remains uncertain where the new airport for Mexico City will actually be built. The government is keeping a low profile, considering a compromise in which the landing strips would be laid on the state-owned land of the lake basin before the project was just completely stopped in 2018. Although the territorial conflict over the construction of the new airport seems to be over, the dispute over urban development in the much sought-after territory of the former Texcoco Lake has not yet been decided. In Atenco, urban imaginaries and everyday practices as well as the future of Mexico City are contested; expressed clearly in their opposition to the idea of their land being accessed again, as Ramírez concludes: 'The land is not for sale.'

It is important to note that we separate the socio-territorial approach into five aspects here for narrative clarity; whereas on the ground, the reality is much messier and more entwined. When urban territories are created, all above-mentioned aspects are present at the same time, and only reveal themselves as distinct when analyzed from a specific angle. The urban understood as territory can be analyzed simultaneously in its material dimension, as everyday urban experiences, and as techniques of spatial regulation and representation, each with a focus on unequal power relations (Schwarz and Streule 2020: 13). Moreover, it is key to remember that territorialization, while conducted by individual subjects, is always a collective undertaking.

Conclusions

Prevailing understandings frame territory to be a spatial unit that has a certain extent, is delimited from neighboring territories by borders, and is often characterized by specific forms of governance. Basically, this definition regards territory as a bounded area over which a social or political institution, foremost the nation state, exerts power and control. Although the national state territory has not remained the only scale of analysis, territorial conflicts are generally interpreted as struggles for hegemony and an aggressive defense of one's home or place against 'others.' Instead, this chapter suggests approaching contemporary social struggles in Mexico City through a socio-territorial lens based on an understanding of urban territories as a relational social product, and by analyzing territorialization with a focus on power relations. By looking at materiality, urban imaginaries, and representations, as well as at everyday practices such as the mural at the municipality hall, the professional renderings of real estate development, or the cultivation of the land and defense of the commons by inhabitants, it is possible to delineate different yet deeply interrelated dimensions of urban territories. In understanding the ways and strategies in which the social movement around the People's Front in Defense of the Land resisted the airport project, the focus on processes of urbanization and territorialization proved significant.

The socio-territorial approach offered here has highlighted the destruction of the Atenco mural as an attempt to efface the urban imaginary of inhabitants resisting the airport project and defend instead their vision of urbanity based on collective land tenure in which community members have usufruct rights rather than individual ownership rights to land. A socio-territorial approach can move the discussion of territoriology beyond a focus on borders and boundaries and towards a more relational understanding of space and power. In sharp contrast to essentializing both ideas of territoriality and the territorial nation state, the relational urban territories in question are conceived as contingent, multiple, potentially unbounded, ambiguous, and/or overlapping. Drawing, stabilizing, and defining sharp boundaries is not imperative to a socio-territorial approach. Rogério Haesbaert (2013) has fittingly named this 'multi-territoriality:' It is precisely in these more-than-bounded territories that multiply-scaled processes of urbanization are most approximately reflected.

We have argued that a socio-territorial approach in urban studies allows us to see the possibilities of emphasizing unequal power relations among social subjects involved in the making of urban territories, as they are reflected in contradictions, contingencies, and stakes of urban struggles. This perspective takes us beyond the limitations of a simplified understanding of territorialization either involving actors 'from above' or 'from below' by replacing them with a more careful analysis of unequal power relations and social difference. As the case study of Mexico City has demonstrated, such a territorial complexity does often happen through blurred adversaries between urban social movements and state actors such as functionaries, urbanists, or planners. Yet even where it appears to play out almost horizontally such as between members of the ejidal committee associated to different political parties, such struggles are infused with and informed and formed by unequal positions of power. Tackling the complexity of territorialization is messy but crucial for a situated analysis of socio-territorial relations that render questions of power and difference visible in urban analysis. Approached through a socio-territorial lens, a relational concept of urban territory can make discernible how people struggle for different lifeworlds, meanings, and everyday practices, and how they can find ways to begin to lay the basis for more just urban worlds.

Acknowledgements

The authors are grateful to Doña Trinidad Ramírez for sharing her knowledge, and to the editors for feedback on an earlier version of this text.

Funding

The Heinrich Böll Foundation and the Swiss National Science Foundation provided funding for our research in Mexico in 2013. Research and writing by

Monika Streule leading to this publication has received funding from the European Union's Horizon 2020 research and innovation programme under the Marie Sklodowska-Curie grant agreement No 101024446.

References

Agnew, J. (1994), 'The territorial trap: The geographical assumptions of international relations theory,' *Review of International Political Economy*, 1 (1), 53–80.

Anthias, P. (2018), *Limits to Decolonization: Indigeneity, territory, and hydrocarbon politics in the Bolivian Chaco*. Ithaca: Cornell University Press.

Anthias, P. (2019), 'Beyond territories of resistance,' *Human Geography*, 12 (3), 66–72.

Barnes, T.J. and Minca, C. (2012), 'Nazi spatial theory: The dark geographies of Carl Schmitt and Walter Christaller,' *Annals of AAG*, 103, 669–687.

Bartlett, T.Q. and Light, L.E.O. (2017), 'Territory,' in Fuentes, A. (ed.), *The International Encyclopedia of Primatology*. Hoboken: Wiley, 1–3.

Bartra, A. (ed) (2015), *Se hace terruño al andar: Las luchas en defensa del territorio*. México: UNAM-X; Itaca.

Becker, B. (1985), 'El uso político del territorio: Consideraciones a partir de una visión del Tercer Mundo,' *Revista Geográfica de América Central*, 2, 13–26.

Best, U. (2014), 'The Debate about Berlin Tempelhof Airport, or, A Lefebvrean Critique of Recent Debates about Affect in Geography,' in Stanek, Ł., Schmid, C. and Moravánszky, Á. (eds), *Urban Revolution Now: Henri Lefebvre in social research and architecture*. Ashgate: Surrey & Burlington.

Brighenti, A.M. (2010), 'At the wall: Graffiti writers, urban territoriality, and the public domain,' *Space and Culture*, 13 (39), 315–332.

Brighenti, A.M. and Kärrholm, M. (2020), *Animated Lands: Studies in territoriology*. Lincoln: University of Nebraska Press.

Bulle, S. (2019), 'A Zone to Defend: The utopian territorial experiment of Notre Dame Des Landes,' in Frère, B. and Jacquemain, M. (eds), *Everyday Resistance: French activism in the 21st century*. Cham: Palgrave Macmillan, 205–227.

Colectivo Miradas Críticas del Territorio desde el Feminismo (2017), *Mapeando el cuerpo-territorio. Guía metodológica para mujeres que defienden sus territorios*. Quito: CLACSO.

Corboz, A. (2001), *Le territoire comme palimpseste et autres essais*. Besançon: Les Editions de l'Imprimeur.

Degen, M., Melhuish, C. and Rose, G. (2017), 'Producing place atmosphere digitally: Architecture, digital visualisations practices and the experience economy,' *Journal of Consumer Culture*, 17 (1): 3–24.

Echeverría, M. and Rincón, A. (2000), *Ciudad de territorialidades, Polémica de Medellín*. Medellín: Centro de Estudios del Hábitat Popular/Universidad Nacional de Colombia.

Elden, S. (2019), 'Territory/Territoriality,' in Orum, A.M. (ed.), *The Wiley Blackwell Encyclopedia of Urban and Regional Studies*. Oxford: Wiley, 2167–2177.

Escobar, A. (2016), 'Thinking-feeling with the earth: Territorial struggles and the ontological dimensions of the epistemologies of the South,' *Revista de Antropología Iberoamericana*, 11 (1): 11–32.

ETH Studio Basel (eds) (2016), *Territory: On the development of landscape and city*. Zurich: Park Books.

Fernandes, B.M. (2009), 'Sobre a tipologia de territórios,' in Saquet, M.A. and Sposito, E.S. (eds) *Territórios e territorialidades. Teorias, processos e conflictos*. São Paulo: Espressão Popular.

FPDT (Frente de Pueblos en Defensa de la Tierra) (2013), *Comunicado del FPDT, 7 Diciembre 2013*. Blog post, December 7, 2013, at https://atencofpdt.blogspot.com/2013/12/comunicado-del-fpdt-7-dic-2013.html, (last access 2 February 2021).

FPDT (2014), *¡La memoria y la cultura, no se borran con pintura!* Blog post, 18 February 2014, at: https://atencofpdt.blogspot.com/2014/02/la-memoria-y-la-cultura-no-se-borran.html (last access 10 February 2021).

Giordano, A. (2006), 'Mexico's presidential swindle,' *New Left Review*, 41, 5–26.

Giraut, F. (2013), 'Territoire multisitué, complexité territoriale et postmodernité territoriale: Des concepts opératoires pour rendre compte de territorialités contemporaines?, *L'Espace Géographique*, 42 (3), 293–305.

Gottmann, J. (1973), *The Significance of Territory*. Charlottesville: University of Virginia Press.

Hackear el Aeropuerto (2018), *Carta del Lago de Texcoco*. http://yoprefieroellago.org/carta/ (last access 14June 2021).

Haesbaert, R. (2011), *El mito de la desterritorialización: Del 'fin de los territorios' a la multiterritorialidad*. México D.F.: Siglo XXI.

Haesbaert, R. (2013), 'A global sense of place and multi-territoriality: Notes for dialogue from a "peripheral" point of view,' in Featherstone, D. and Painter, J. (eds), *Spatial politics. Essays for Doreen Massey*. Malden: Wiley-Blackwell, 146–157.

Haraway, D.J. (2016), *Staying with the Trouble. Making kin in the Chthulucene*. Durham, London: Duke University Press.

Hart, G. (2018), 'Relational comparison revisited: Marxist postcolonial geographies in practice,' *Progress in Human Geography*, 42 (3), 371–394.

Lefebvre, H. (1991), *The Production of Space*. Malden: Blackwell Publishing.

Lindón, A. (2019), 'The lived city: Everyday experiences, urban scenarios, and topological networks,' *Geographica Helvetica*, 74 (1), 31–39.

Maher, C.R. and Lott, D.F. (1995), 'Definitions of territoriality used in the study of variation in vertebrate spacing systems,' *Animal Behaviour*, 49 (6), 1581–1597.

Magnaghi, A. (1998), 'Territorial heritage: A genetic code for sustainable development,' in International Network for Urban Research and Action (ed.), *Possible Urban Worlds*. Basel: Birkhäuser, 114–121.

Massey, D. (1994), *Space, Place and Gender*. Cambridge: Polity Press.

Michel, B. (2018), 'Anti-semitism in early 20th century German geography: From a "spaceless" people to the root of the "ills" of urbanization,' *Political Geography*, 65, 1–7.

Minca, C. and Rowan, R. (2016), *On Schmitt and Space*. London, New York: Routledge.

Moine, A. (2006), 'Le territoire comme un système complexe: Un concept opératoire pour l'aménagement et la géographie,' *L'Espace Géographique*, 35 (2), 115–132.

Muratori, S. (1967), *Civilità e territorio*. Roma: Centro Studi di Storia Urbanistica.

Porto-Gonçalves, C.W. (2001), *Geo-grafías: Movimientos sociales, nuevas territorialidades y sustentabilidad*. México D.F.: Siglo XXI.

Porto-Gonçalves, C.W. (2006), 'A reinvenção dos territórios. A experiencia latino-americana e caribenha,' in Ceceña, A.E. (ed.), *Los desafíos de las emancipaciones en un contexto militarizado*. Buenos Aires: CLACSO.

Raffestin, C. (1980), *Pour une géographie du pouvoir*. Paris: Librairies Techniques.

Rivera, S. (2020), 'Atenco y los imaginarios en resistencia frente al 'areopuerto simbólico,' in Mendoza Álvarez, C.; Rafael de la Cruz, R.; Chima Ortiz, V.M. and Olvera

Castillo, A. (eds), *El corazón de la tierra: Pueblos en resistencia.* Cuaderno Narrativas de Resistencia 2, 16–26.

Sack, R. (1986), *Human Territoriality: Its theory and history.* Cambridge; New York: Cambridge University Press.

Santos, M. (2000), 'El Territorio. Un agregado de espcios banales,' *Boletin de Estudios Geográficos*, 96, 87–96.

Santos, M. (2017), 'The return of the territory,' in Melgaço, L. and Prouse, C. (eds) *Milton Santos: a pioneer in critcal geography from the Global South.* Cham: Springer, 25–31.

Saquet, M.A. and Sposito, E.S. (eds) (2009), *Territórios e territorialidades. Teorias, processos e conflitos: Geografia em movimento.* São Paulo: Editora Expressão Popular.

Sassen, S. (2013), 'When territory deborders territoriality,' *Territory, Politics, Governance*, 1 (1), 21–45.

Sawyer, L., Schmid, C., Streule, M. and Kallenberger, P. (2021), 'Bypass urbanism: Re-ordering center-periphery relations in Kolkata, Lagos and Mexico City,' *Environment and Planning A: Economy and Space*, 53 (4), 675–703.

Schmid, C. (2015), 'Specificity and urbanization. A theoretical outlook,' in Diener, R., Herzog, J., Meili, M.de Meuron, P., Herz, M., Schmid, C., Topalovic, M. (eds), *The Inevitable Specificity of Cities.* Zürich: Lars Müller, 287–307.

Schwarz, A. (2017), *Demanding Water: A sociospatial approach to domestic water use in Mexico City.* Stuttgart: Franz Steiner Verlag.

Schwarz, A. (2022), 'Parochial imaginations: The 'European city' as a territorialised entity,' in Ha, N. K. and Picker, G. (eds), *European cities: Modernity, race and colonialism.* Manchester: Manchester University Press.

Schwarz, A. and Streule, M. (2016), 'A transposition of territory: Decolonized perspectives in current urban research,' *International Journal of Urban and Regional Research*, 40 (5), 1000–1016.

Schwarz, A. and Streule, M. (2020), 'Introduction to the special issue "Contested urban territories: Decolonized perspectives,"' *Geographica Helvetica*, 75 (1), 11–18.

Silva, A. (1992), *Imaginarios Urbanos.* Bogotá: Tercer Mundo Editores.

Sisson, A. (2021), 'Territory and territorial stigmatisation: On the production, consequences and contestation of spatial disrepute,' *Progress in Human Geography* 45(4), 659–681.

Streule, M. (2018), *Ethnografie urbaner Territorien: Metropolitane Urbanisierungsprozesse von Mexiko-Stadt.* Münster: Westfälisches Dampfboot.

Streule, M. (2019), *El bosque de vuelta: Indigenous socio-territorial movements claiming the right to urban territory.* Working Paper. Zurich: ETH Zürich Department of Architecture.

Streule, M. (2020), 'Doing mobile ethnography: Grounded, situated, and comparative,' *Urban Studies*, 57 (2), 421–438.

Svampa, M. (2015), 'Commodities consensus. Neoextractivism and enclosure of the commons in Latin America', *The South Atlantic Quarterly*, 114 (1), 65–82.

Svampa, M. and Viale, E. (2014), *Maldesarrollo: La Argentina del extractivismo y del despojo.* Buenos Aires: Editorial Katz.

Tsing, A.L. (2015), *The Mushroom at the End of the World: On the possibility of life in capitalist ruins.* Princeton: Princeton University Press.

Ulloa, A. (2016), 'Feminismos territoriales en América Latina: Defensas de la vida frente a los extractivismos,' *Nómadas*, 45, 123–139.

Varley, A. and Salazar, C. (2021), 'The impact of Mexico's land reform on periurban housing production: Neoliberal or neocorporatist?' *International Journal of Urban and Regional Research*, online first.

Wacquant, L., Slater, T. and Pereira V.B. (2014), 'Territorial stigmatization in action,' *Environment and Planning A*, 46 (6), 1270–1280.
Wilson, J. (2014), 'The violence of abstract space: Contested regional developments in southern Mexico,' *International Journal of Urban and Regional Research*, 38 (2), 516–538.
Zaragocín, S. and Caretta, M.A. (2020), 'Cuerpo-Territorio: A Decolonial Feminist Geographical Method for the Study of Embodiment,' *Annals of the American Association of Geographers*, 1–16.
Zibechi, R. (2008), 'Espacio, territorios y regiones: La creatividad social de los nuevos movimientos sociales en América Latina,' *Revista Chuchará' y paso atrá'*, 18, 95–119.
Zibechi, R. (2012), *Territories in Resistance: A cartography of Latin American social movements*. Oakland: AK Press.

Chapter 8

The Territorialisation of the Grocery Shopper

Eco-ethical asceticism and environmental nostalgia

Mattias Kärrholm and Anna Petersson

Introduction

Establishing oneself in a new neighbourhood takes time. It involves getting to know one's way around and finding daily routines, as well as starting to recognise some people in the area, and over time perhaps getting to know some of them. A routine that often establishes itself after a short time is that of going to the store for groceries. Sometimes this might involve choosing the shortest way to the nearest store, but in general it grows more complex. Even if picking the shortest route might be a first starting point (but it often is not), there are many reasons why we might not keep to this decision. Bad weather, the need for a specific item, the need to run other errands, etc., are examples of reasons for a temporary change of plans. Nevertheless, we tend to establish certain shopping practices over time and thus territorialise our role as grocery shoppers (on the notion of territorial roles, see Brighenti and Kärrholm 2018; Brighenti and Kärrholm 2020:182 f.). But how and why do we establish our routines around grocery shopping?

In this chapter, we are interested in how the role of the grocery shopper and the territory of grocery shopping are established and stabilised. How is the association between the shopper and the spatio-temporal peculiarities of her environment territorialised? Based on the findings, we then look at ethical and aesthetical concerns in this process, and more specifically how people struggle to take on the role of the 'eco-ethical grocery shopper.' Eco-ethical shopping seems to be a very specific type of shopping, involving a specific kind of attention, information, selectivity and 'energy investment' on the part of the shopper, all of which can be translated into territorial factors that go into the specific formation of this role. In the article we thus discuss how eco-ethical practices are developed in relation to the environment, as well as how feelings and uses related to environmental nostalgia are part of stabilising the specific territorial role of the grocery shopper in general and the eco-ethical shopper in particular.

The chapter starts with a short introduction to the theoretical perspective followed by an introduction to the case of our study – a relatively new urban district in Malmö, Sweden, called the Western Harbour – as well as an account

DOI: 10.4324/9781003196365-8

of the methods in the study. After a discussion of the different concerns and struggles related to grocery shopping, we discuss the formation of the grocery shopper as related to ethical aspirations and refinements, as well as to aesthetic concerns and decisions related to nostalgia. In the concluding discussion, we argue that moving between different urban areas could be seen as a kind of (minor) life phase shift that sets off new processes of individuation (Simondon 2017; 2020). Here, we also argue that the territorialisation of the grocery shopper involves at least a double process, where the stabilisation of a territorial appropriation is informed by different kinds of associations to situations of shopping beyond the formation of the territory at hand. This chapter thus seeks to add to territoriological research by expanding on the notion of the territorial role, as well as showing how territorialisation often is a complex process involving several interrelated forms of territorial production.

Territorialised mobilities

In the last few decades, we have seen an increasing amount of research into the mundane mobilities of the consumer (Brembeck et al. 2015; Hagberg and Normark 2015; Calvignac and Cochoy 2016), a field sometimes called consumer logistics (Granzin and Bahn 1989). In market and consumption studies, this could be described as a move from what has been called framing practices, like retail marketing, organisation and design, to the agency of the consumer, as well as a move from a focus on the consumer in the shop or at home, to the consumer on the move. The rise of consumer logistics as a field of study is related to the increasing number of objects that we carry around (Cochoy, Hagberg and Canu 2015; Cochoy et al. 2019), and to how pedestrian mobility patterns have changed in the wake of self-service retailing and new technologies, such as the shopping cart (Cochoy 2009) and the shopping bag (Hagberg and Normark 2015). Consumer logistics also includes the study of how the shopper as an assemblage changes during different phases of a shopping trip (Brembeck, Cochoy and Moisander 2015), as well as in different phases of life (Brembeck et al. 2015). The theoretical perspective is here one of 'vehicular agency' where the assemblages, rather than people or things that make up these assemblages, set the course of action (Calvignac and Cochoy 2016; cf. Goffman 1972: 7 on 'vehicular units').

So far, many of the studies in consumer logistics have been based on observation studies, sometimes quantitative studies, sometimes walk-alongs, focusing on what can perhaps be called spatial practices (Lefebvre 1991) and in-the-moment concerns (Pink 2012). In this article, we want to add a territorial perspective to this promising research on consumer logistics, investigating the moving consumer as an expressive actor of aspirations, associations, and longings over time. We also see this actor as firmly related to a certain environment that is formed through the very activity of everyday shopping. That is, the shopper is not only an autonomous – albeit heterogeneous and ever-transforming – assemblage; the shopper is also rooted in a certain environment and affected by atmospheres, designs, paving, smells, emotions, memories, etc. Where we shop depends not only on how our retail is framed by marketing, or by how we as shoppers are able (or not) to form assemblages on our way to the store, but also on how we territorialise and produce ourselves as grocery shoppers in a specific environment, and how we make sense of this in the context of our everyday life.

A relational territorial perspective (Brighenti 2010; 2014; Brighenti and Kärrholm 2020; Kärrholm 2017) allows us to follow territorialisation processes as well as territories on the move. Territories can be associated to a specific space, object, cognitive domain, etc., but also to mobile entities such as the emerging and recurrent pattern of a moving actor, a certain duration (e.g., lunch hour, or the journey home from work) or a specific role. In the case of the grocery shopper, routines and meanings related to grocery shopping become connected to a certain way of conduct and its associated spatio-temporal formations and trajectories. The grocery shopper is a well-known figure in everyday life, and it is also a specific kind of territorialised and embodied role that we form over time through our interactions with the lived environment. The territorialisation of grocery shopping is related to many things: practical things in the moment, but also longer processes of territorial appropriation and association, whereby grocery shopping (or certain aspects of it) becomes associated to certain places, sentiments, values, etc. This territorial association might, for example, be responding in part to specific retail strategies and designs, expressed in a phrase such as 'this is my kind of shopping place,' or developed as part of an ongoing territorial appropriation – such as 'this is my shopping place' (Kärrholm 2012).

Investigating a new city district

The study focuses on everyday decisions and practices regarding grocery shopping in the relatively new city district Western Harbour in Malmö (see Figure 8.1). The Western Harbour is a former industrial area in Malmö that was the location for a housing exhibition 'Bo01' in 2001 and subsequently developed to an urban district with predominantly housing and offices (about 9 500 inhabitants and 16 000 workplaces in 2018). The area has been under construction for twenty years, and for a long time, the zone between the district and the rest of the city has acted as a barrier of sorts, with construction sites, temporary traffic solutions, deserted plots, etc.

From early on, the Western Harbour was launched as a district that combined contemporary architecture with ecological sustainability, and it has played an important part in the branding of Malmö as a green and sustainable city (Kärrholm 2011; Anderberg and Clark 2012; Holgersen and Malm 2015). The area has several flagship projects, the most famous of which is Turning Torso – a residential skyscraper designed by Santiago Calatrava and inaugurated in 2005.

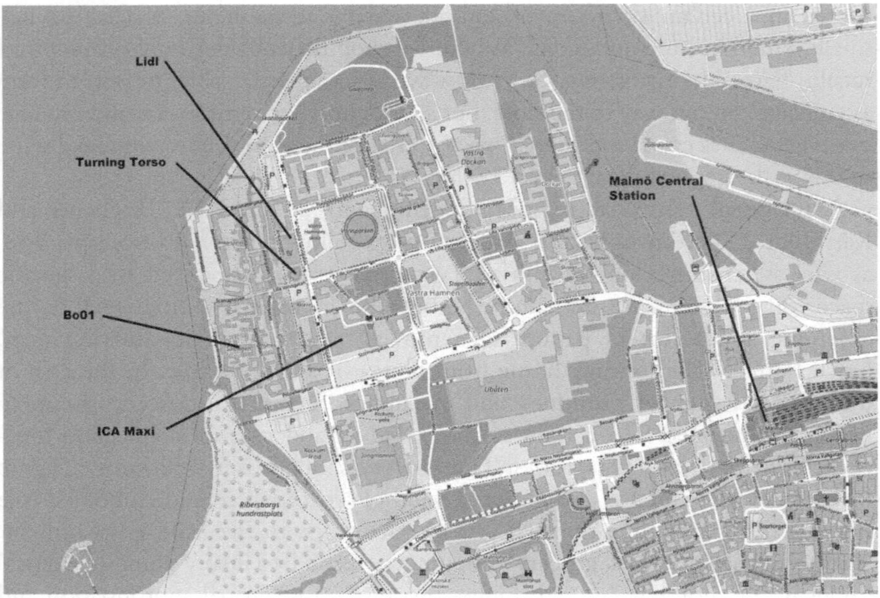

Figure 8.1 Map of the Western Harbour, Malmö (map made by authors, based on OpenStreetMap).

In this article, we have investigated six residents' experiences of and thoughts about their shopping routines and routes, using qualitative interviews supported by participant-produced photographs and captions (Rose 2001; Brinkmann 2013). In 2019–2020, contact was established and maintained with the six informants: three males (aged 19, 30 and 78) and three females (aged 46, 48 and 49). We selected the first informants from a convenience sample, and more informants followed in the manner of snowballing (cf. Gerhardsson 2021). The informants in this study are hence not chosen as representatives of a specific group, but rather seen as individual voices of lived experience (Brinkmann 2013). In a first step, the informants were asked to take five photographs (with a mobile phone or digital camera) on their regular shopping trips in the Western Harbour. Only two of the informants followed our instructions, however; the rest chose to take more than five photographs (we received a total of 39 photographs), which could perhaps be seen to reflect the informants' engagement in the task or enthusiasm for photographing in general. The informants were encouraged to both take photographs of things that they appreciate in their shopping environment or on the way to and from the store, and of things that they consider to be obstacles to their shopping routine or on their shopping route. The informants were also instructed to write captions for their images: a few lines per image about what the image shows and why they chose that particular motif.[1]

1 Translation from the original Swedish by the authors.

In a second step, each informant was interviewed for about 40–50 minutes about his or her habits related to the purchase of food and other groceries. The semi-structured interview included open-ended questions about possible transport to and from the store, and questions related to the actual shopping routine and to the environment of the shopping route as such, as well as to grocery shopping at the informant's country home or summer house (if they had one), and to online shopping. We added more questions to the interview template during the interview process, resulting in a kind of iterative interview design that developed as the interviewing progressed (Brinkmann 2013). The informants' photographs and captions were also discussed in the interviews, both in relation to the open-ended questions and by introducing specific situations and settings that would not have been noted or targeted by the interviewer otherwise. The participant-produced photographs and captions prompted the participants to reflect on the topic of the interview in advance (Harper 2002). One informant did not send the photographs before the interview, and when they later arrived, they were captionless. But since the informant had already planned what to photograph, we could still talk about the motifs of the (future) photographs in the interview situation. The photographs and their captions also helped us to better plan for the interview talk (cf. Gerhardsson 2021), and the images and captions were recurringly referred to in the interview and served as a checklist. This further allowed the informants to bring discussion points of their own to the interview situation, which affirmed that their views were important to us and created a collaborative interview milieu (Pain 2012; cf. Rose 2001; Gerhardsson 2021). In our analysis of the collected material, we looked for situations and settings that were both common to, and included qualitative variations between, the different informants' interviews and photographs/captions.

We also searched for conceptual themes that could link these different situations and settings in an overarching way. In this text, we discuss and contextualise some of these themes by connecting them to earlier research.

Going shopping

Moving to a new area that is branded as ecologically sustainable might perhaps suggest an inclination to act or shop in an 'environmentally friendly' way. The ecological identity of the area was not specifically given as a reason for moving there, however. Instead, the proximity to nature and the sea, the relatively car-free urban living environment, and the location itself were mentioned by informants as reasons for moving to the Western Harbour. The high-end architecture was also singled out as a contributing factor for moving there. One informant, who lives in Turning Torso, mentioned that he chose an apartment quite high up in that building because it was newly built, spectacular, and had a good view of the strait Öresund (which forms the border between Sweden and Denmark). He has fond memories of the time spent during his youth in the bar at the top of another building overlooking Öresund and the city of Copenhagen: *Kronprinsen* ('The Crown Prince'), which was the first proper high-rise building in Malmö, built in 1964 (Torisson 2021). Another informant also mentioned the high architectural profile of the new city district as a reason for choosing to live in the Western Harbour.

The diversity of architectural expressions and different designs was very high in the area, especially in the beginning. The shopping facilities, however, were initially quite poor. Some informants also moved to the area before shops and schools were in place and were thus aware that living there would initially require a car, bus, or bike for moving between the home and work/school as well as to grocery stores. This meant that they at first went to their old grocery stores, i.e., where they had shopped before moving to the Western Harbour. As one informant mentioned, it also takes time to change and learn one's way around a new grocery store, and the informant therefore initially went to his old store, where he used to live, although ICA Maxi had already opened in his new neighbourhood. A territorial appropriation such as 'my grocery store' takes time to produce, and as it becomes familiar and incorporated as a terrain on which we depend (Steinbock 1995), it also takes time to undo.

Over time, several grocery stores opened and became established in the area. First came *Handlaren* ('The merchant'), a small on-call shop, and then came the large supermarket ICA Maxi in 2005 with 4500 square meters of sales area (Svantesson 2005). On *Masttorget* ('The mast square') in front of ICA Maxi, there has been a small open-air marketplace hosted by *Cityfrukt* ('City fruit') since 2017, where locally grown vegetables, fruit, berries, herbs, flowers etc., are sold under a tent-like construction. The large food market Green, with fine organic goods, opened in the Turning Torso Gallery in 2007, but closed in 2017, leaving room for Lidl to open a store in the same premises. The low-price grocery shop Netto also moved in, and has recently been acquired by Coop. Informants mention ICA Maxi's size as a probable reason why smaller supermarkets have difficulty establishing themselves in the Western Harbour. Several smaller stores have opened but have had to close again, such as Nesta Gastro delicacies, which closed in 2009, and the kiosk Time, which closed in 2010. Informants also mentioned how difficult it is for businesses to establish themselves in the location behind the Turning Torso, where the food market Green used to be. A wish for a better mix of supermarkets and more local stores was expressed in the interviews, as it would broaden the supply and perhaps the competition would also improve the quality of food, which would be good for the city district as a whole.

Several informants mentioned the good service to which all shops in the Western Harbour contribute, but the choice of where to shop might depend on other things. Some mentioned the price of the goods as what affects their choice of supermarket. For example, informants sometimes choose Lidl over ICA Maxi precisely because it is cheaper, even if the range of goods there is not as broad as at ICA Maxi. At other times informants do the opposite, choosing ICA Maxi because it is well stocked and well organised, even though it is regarded as quite expensive. The ongoing clustering of different services around ICA (like the liquor store *Systembolaget*, a pharmacy, and Instabox) obviously also works in its favour. Additionally, the interviews touch upon the issue of animal companions influencing one's choice of store. Two informants mentioned that since they do not have the time to go to multiple stores, they choose to shop in the store that sells the brand of cat food their cats want. It thus seems as if animal companions and convenience sometimes overrule the preferences of the grocery shopper.

Eco-ethical concerns and asceticism

The eco-ethical turn in shopping is the focus of a number of recent studies (Giesler and Veresiu 2013) that are interested in e.g. why people shop ethically (Schoolman 2019), and under which circumstances people choose to buy organic food (Williams et al. 2010; Hjelmar 2011; Katzeff et al. 2020). In our study, it soon became clear that eco-ethical concerns were high on the agenda of most of the informants, and for one informant this issue also seems to have increased in importance over the years. Replying to the direct question of whether she could describe when she last made an active choice in a shopping situation that was caused by anxiety related to climate change, the informant answered: *I do that almost every day* [...] *Now. But that was not the case just two years ago.* [...] *It's new.* (Woman, 46). In fact, eco-ethical concerns appeared to be an important part of grocery shopping, suggesting that eco-ethical grocery shopping might even be seen as a specific (sub)type. Four different themes or concerns were brought up in the findings that support this claim to some extent.

First of all, the question of what to buy seems to be an important concern. Some informants try to buy eco-friendly groceries and products, but the higher price of organic products is a problem for several of them. If the product is too expensive in relation to the price of the non-organic product, they do not buy the eco-friendly variant, although they would really like to. Cleaning products and detergents were also mentioned as a problem by a couple of informants. Here they might prefer to buy more expensive, environmentally unfriendly variants because they know that these work, and because they do not think that the eco-friendly equivalent has an equally good effect. Another example of failure to make an eco-friendly product choice is when one decides not to buy goods that are transported from far away, but then realises that the grocery store or the online shopping site has neglected to clearly declare the relevant information and one unintentionally does just that, according to two informants. Eco-ethical approaches in everyday life mentioned in the interviews include choosing game meat, having a vegetarian day every week, and growing one's own vegetables in an allotment garden. When we asked the informants about how the area could be improved, this issue was also high on the agenda. Among the ideas were e.g. cultivation beds for growing one's own vegetables. However, one informant does not dare to grow edibles directly in the ground of her garden plot and instead uses high pallet collars; since the Western Harbor is located on backfills outside the old shoreline, she fears the soil might be contaminated.

A second theme in our study was the importance of recycling. Recycling was initially difficult in the Western Harbour, when the nearest recycling station was by the beach in Ribersborg, but a new recycling station was eventually set up in front of ICA Maxi, and people can now synchronise their recycling with their grocery shopping (see Figure 8.2). But even after this, it

Figure 8.2 With recyclables and the shopping trolley (photo and caption by informant, Woman, 46).

was mentioned in the interviews that better recycling opportunities would be good and could encourage people to recycle more. Recycling centres for recycling and sharing things (such as tools, box bikes, outgrown toys and clothes and more) also came up as an idea for improving the area further. By having a place to share things, some people's abundance could benefit people who are less well-off.

A third concern that was raised especially in relation to transport was the outdoor climate. The greatest obstacle to walking appears to be the weather. Particularly in the newer parts of the area, there are long and windy streets, and it is clear to anyone walking there that the question of weather was not prioritised by planners and designers. Doing their work in the comfort of an office, perhaps the planners managed to forget the windy days so typical of this part of Malmö, and Sweden more broadly (Prieto de la Fuente 2020; cf. Remm 2016). In fact, the wind around Turning Torso is at times so strong that the residents are advised not to use the building's main entrance, but to use the garage entrance on the back of the building instead. A small dog was once lifted from the ground by the strong wind when leaving the main entrance and had to be drawn back by its leash (according to the informant living in Turning Torso). The square in front of ICA Maxi was also singled out by the informants as a specifically windy area (see Figure 8.3). One of the informants also joked

Figure 8.3 The outdoor environment of the square in the Western Harbour is dark, empty and windy, especially in the autumn (photo by informant, Man, 30).

about the windy environment in one of his figure captions, justifying his choice of transport with bad weather while also playing with the dual meaning of the word climate: *Despite the proximity to Lidl, I usually go up* [by lift] *to the garage two storeys above Lidl to take the car to ICA MAXI for the purchase of groceries. I do this for a couple of reasons, among other things for 'climate reasons'!* (Man, 73). Windy and bad weather means that informants sometimes make choices in their everyday life that are not so good for the environment. In the quote above, the man writes that he usually takes the car to ICA, even though it is just one block away – when we talked to him however, we discovered that this was not just because of the wind, but also to help him transport the heavy goods.

The first part of the Western Harbour, Bo01, was built to shelter from the wind to some extent, and some informants also mentioned that the green environment with its winding paths inspires walking or cycling and adds a positive aesthetic value and an experience of nature to everyday life that beats the comfort of the car. One informant particularly likes that the greenery is left 'wild' in the older parts of the Western Harbour, as it reminds her of nature: *So there is some wild shrubbery left and… and I like that too. That you let things be like a little* [pause] *like eh… yes, not so planned.* […] *Anyway, but… you get the feeling of like… a little nature.* (Woman, 48). Allowing unkempt greenery in the urban environment could also be seen as playing a part in making Malmö a 'climate-smart' city by increasing biodiversity (cf. Wingren, Alsanius, Karlén and Lidström 2015). Aesthetic attraction can be a valuable tool here for changing the norm of what a proper green space should look like in terms of maintenance and care (Lintott 2006). There can however be a dangerous downside to the wilder and more 'natural' greenery, such as a lack of visibility. Another informant even teaches her kids not to walk on hidden paths behind vegetation that is too high, since there was a sexual assault in the area: *Elephant grass is nice, but it can also be scary.* (Woman, 46). As the Western Harbour expanded, the design strategy was changed to an orthogonal grid with more large-scale buildings and tightly maintained green areas.

The fourth theme that our informants brought up was accessibility. Besides wind and bad weather, the poor functionality of the traffic environment was also consistently mentioned. The area is not very well connected to the rest of the city, and everything is also constantly being rebuilt. There is a feeling of being isolated at the outer limits of the city, and long and empty stretches still form a kind of barrier between the Western Harbour and the rest of Malmö. In addition, the street network seems to be undersized and planned in a modernist fashion with a tree-like structure. There are long queues in the afternoons when all of the commuters who work in office complexes in the Western Harbour are travelling home from work. However, even something that is bad for the environment – such as traffic jams – can lead to everyday choices that are good for the environment. Several informants prefer to walk or bike when shopping for food, leaving the car at home so as not to get stuck in traffic on the way to and from the store: *The walkway home is much nicer and more easily accessible than the car road. A bike or a shopping trolley is the easiest and most relaxed way to go. For me, it has been like 'rather two visits a day* [to the grocery store], *than one big visit by car', just because of this, otherwise I'm lazy.* (Caption by informant, Woman, 46).

Rental e-bikes are also mentioned as an easy and low-cost alternative for avoiding traffic jams while going to and from work and when doing shopping: *It is fantastic. So, we do not have our own bikes, but accounts at 'Malmö by bike'.* [...] *so, my boyfriend uses that, he goes into town and, and works. So, he has such a bike and parks it on* [ICA] *Maxi, goes in and shops.* (Woman, 49).

Twenty years after the city district's inauguration, the Western Harbour is still a large construction site with construction dust blowing around in the streets, especially during the windy winter months. The noise (because of the constant construction in progress) can also be problematic at times, and the bad traffic solution in relation to the unfinished walkways is a twofold problem for the inhabitants. One informant took a picture of a torn-up street, writing in the caption that *This may be a consequence of the construction work that destroys the road and can hinder you from taking the shorter route.* (Man, 19). Another strategy related to accessibility is online shopping. This was used by several informants and for different reasons: convenience (as one's grocery bags are delivered to the front door); ecological sustainability (many households are served with one large van, instead of each household taking its own car); and product choices linked to proximity and personal taste (some products, especially clothing, pharmacy and health products, are not available in the stores in the area).

In sum, we could argue that there seems to be a strong ethical aspect in the formation of grocery shopping as a territorialised role. Peter Sloterdijk has pointed to the way in which modernism also aims at training and forming humanity, producing us as good citizens, and how a certain amount of self-improvement goes into this project (Sloterdijk 2013, cf. Brighenti and Kärrholm 2018). This is not least true for eco-modernism (Hagbert, Wangel and Broms 2020), where we as consumers are constantly encouraged to improve ourselves, for example through design techniques such as nudging (Lehner, Mont and Heiskanen 2016). The trend of so-called ethical consumers, who shop eco-friendly, healthy, local, fair-trade, etc., can also be discussed in terms of an *eco-ethical asceticism* (cf. Brighenti and Kärrholm 2018). Asceticism is an exercise related to abstinence and in this case to the process of taming consumption: it cannot be all joy. This ascetic process, with its rhythms of success and failure, of course also plays a part in how we get territorialised as shoppers. We constantly try (but sometimes fail) to improve ourselves through our grocery shopping, by walking or biking to the store rather than taking the car, in buying healthier or more ecologically friendly food and goods that have not been transported from across the world, or even by growing our own vegetables.

The formation of the grocery shopper is not ours alone, but instead depends on social interaction and 'civilized consumption' (Ranasinghe 2011). This process of imitation (and self-imitation) contributes to the territorialisation and intensification of our role as grocery shoppers, where this also becomes a role that supports other roles in our life. For the connoisseur, the eco-shopper, the vegan, etc., the role of the grocery shopper might even develop to become a role *par excellence* in a mixed gallery of differently formed and utilised self-presentations (Goffman 1959). The grocery shopper might thus become a key role, one on which other roles depend.

Importantly, the development of the role of grocery shopping is integrated into a narrative of everyday life, as a specific kind of ethic and aesthetic story. Everyday consumer choices are placed in a narrative that fits with the respondents' overall idea of what respectable grocery shopping is and should be (cf. Skeggs 1997). Commodities are placed in a social and cultural perspective, where ethical consumer choices could be seen as symbolically good (Appadurai 1986). Walking with a shopping trolley, taking an e-bike, growing one's own vegetables, eating game meat and plant-based food or buying eco-friendly products seem to play an important part in the production of this specific territorialised role, and these choices and material objects also become part of the respectable eco-ethical shopping persona. The different paths towards the role of a 'grocery shopper of the Western Harbour' were also shaped through ongoing negotiation and struggle with different actors, such as prices, quality, animal companions, weather conditions, traffic, paving (or the lack thereof), aesthetic values and experiences of nature. In navigating these different assets and obstacles, we find our way, our allies, and our enemies in the ascetic refinement of our new role.

Environmental nostalgia

The role of providing food has always been important and is directly related to our economy, health, social relations, etc., and in a society with a growing ecological crisis, issues of sustainability obviously come into play as well (see Hall 2011). In fact, an ecological tone had already been set during the building and branding of the area and, as we have seen, this tone has been given a variety of melodies by the different informants. However, the formation of the territorial role also needs to resonate personally, and thus connect back to other times and places that one has experienced previously – in short, it needs to align with a territorial association to a type of grocery shopping that feels right. The strategic planning of the shopping infrastructure might work, and one has perhaps found one's tactics within it as one moves to and through the store (or one's own kitchen garden). One may possibly even carve out a route and a routine that make the specific practice of shopping feel like 'yours and yours alone', i.e., one has appropriated them, and they have become a part of one's life. Yet, if the territorial role one has formed is associated as being e.g. dangerous, boring, unhealthy, or not ethical enough, one might not associate it with a good or proper routine. It is a routine that needs to change. As we saw above, we can change it through further training and drilling, but the energy might also need to be imported from other times and places.

Besides the aspects mentioned above, there are also actors that bring one outside a situation and connect to other spaces (like different production sites around the globe) and other times; the latter of these seem to be of particular interest to our informants. If possible, shopping routes and routines are chosen so that they add aesthetic value to the respondents' everyday life, for instance experiences of nature and beauty (cf. Kaplan and Kaplan 1989). Whilst the aesthetics and form of the environment were important for many different reasons (walkability, comfort, etc.), there were also clear signs of what we will call *environmental nostalgia.* The term nostalgia is often used to encompass a search for home, identity, authenticity and reimagination (cf. Niemeyer 2016; Chrostowska 2010). Nostalgia appears to be a universal feeling (Bonnett 2016): a bittersweet longing for home and past times, as is reflected in the composition of the Greek *nostos* (homecoming) and *algos* (pain or ache). Its historical roots emanate from Homer's *Odyssey*, where the Greek king Odysseus longs for his homeland and his loved ones and eventually pursues his goal to return; it has been considered a medical or neurological disease confined to the Swiss; a mental disorder; a psychiatric or psychosomatic disorder; and finally, a psychological resource that motivates a person to pursue certain goals (Boym 2001; Chrostowska 2010; Sedikides et al. 2015; Niemeyer 2016). From a philosophical viewpoint, nostalgia could be seen to mix memory with the desire to find a way 'home,' where home stands for an absolute truth about the world and ourselves (Chrostowska 2010; Sedikides et al. 2015). It is a creative force that can be used to cope with painful memories, a difficult present, and an uncertain future (Sedikides et al. 2015; Niemeyer 2016). Nostalgia, like daydreaming, 'is rebellion against the modern idea of time' (Boym 2001: xv).

In our investigation, several informants pointed to nostalgic sentiments that called forth a time and a place from the past, including the ideas and values that accompany these sentiments. The informants' nostalgic emotions were evoked by both built and nature environments, and they were as much a longing for an idealised past as a creative force giving the present a meaning and stimulating actions for an improved future.

One example here is the idea of the marketplace. In the interviews, *Cityfrukt*'s tent-like outdoor market with locally grown fruits and greens on the square in front of ICA Maxi is mentioned as a good addition to the grocery stores in the Western Harbour, although a couple of informants stated that it is hard to discern where the market goods really originate from. The small market on *Masttorget* is thus valued, although the square itself is almost unusable due to the cold weather and strong winds throughout most of the year. It is also mentioned as a place with the potential to be developed further in the future, especially as it could both support climate-smart shopping and be an attractive venue: *It would have been quite nice to have an eh… a good, high quality market as well. A real market* [where] *you could buy food from small… ehm… where people come* […] *with organically* [and] *locally grown* [food] *and such.* (Man, 19). Another informant even offered suggestions for the conceptual format and design of the future market, giving the example of a farmer's market consisting of fixed wooden huts on the square in the Western Harbour.

The environmental nostalgia for the marketplace relies on both first-hand and second-hand memory (Chrostowska 2010). Although most of the informants might not have experienced a time when the open-air markets of the past were an important part of food shopping – let alone the only option available – they can still have a conception of what a marketplace could be, how it should look, and what it stands for in the form of authenticity and honesty. The association to bygone spatial types might actually be a strength here, since it tends to make the type more fluid. As Chrostowska has suggested, this also plays into the hands of the commercial agents as a capitalised and commodified nostalgia: The more distant a past, the better it can serve as a playground for the commercially bound imagination.' (Chrostowska 2010: 54). This longing for the authentic open-air market, where goods are sold in wooden huts placed at the centre of a square, is also something that for example ICA Maxi has tapped into with its indoor vegetable 'market,' where fruit and vegetables are sold under a sign that reads *Torget* ('The market square') placed on top of a wooden construction (see Figure 8.4). Here, ICA Maxi has

Figure 8.4 *Torget* ('The market square') with fruit and vegetables at ICA Maxi. It smells good, and it is colourful, nice, and open. It puts you in a good mood and makes you hungry, said one informant (photo by the informant, Man, 30).

attempted to create a marketplace atmosphere, using a kind of open-market design, even transgressing the idea of the traditional Swedish market by using a scent-machine that spreads the scents of exotic fruits such as apricot and mango in the fruit section.

Another strong object of environmental nostalgia that we found in the interviews was the dream of countryside living. Several informants mentioned that the Western Harbour is somewhere in between city life and countryside; this is something that they both appreciate and see as a problem. On the plus side, the city district is close to nature (by the open sea) and at the same time it is close to the pulse of the city. As the district grows and new high-rise buildings are added, further strengthening the urban image, one can perhaps imagine that the dream of the countryside might grow even stronger. However, there appears to be some disparity between the dream of the countryside and the reality of the countryside, i.e., between the ideal way to provide food in the countryside and the actual reality of shopping for groceries and food items in the countryside. Several informants said that they would like to shop more locally and perhaps even grow their own food if they could dream freely, and that dream also includes an existence far away from city life. For some, this dream also includes a critique of the current way of living: *Because I think that this* [pause] *we forget, traditions and all that humans could do themselves, before.* [...] *And we have lost... in that everything has become incredibly... yes, commercial and... and mass-produced.* (Woman, 49). But those who talked about their everyday lives in their actual country houses recalled how they must drive even longer stretches by car to get groceries in the countryside than at home in the city, where everything is close by. Even if a selection of locally-produced food is available near the country house, binge-shopping by car in the nearest town with a large enough grocery store seems to be a necessity, *especially* in the countryside. Grocery shopping at the country home is often preceded by more careful planning however, precisely because one cannot go shopping anywhere and at any time. This in turn prevents the purchase of unnecessary things, something that can ultimately be good for the environment since it reduces consumption, suggested an informant.

The third and final object of environmental nostalgia concerns the Western Harbour district itself, or rather the older Bo01 part. Several of the informants mentioned that the old part of the Western Harbour is completely different from the newer part being built right now. The old part is perceived as more organic, more natural and more human in scale, and more carefully planned and built than the newer part. The new part, on the other hand, is seen as more commercial and mass produced, which does not go well with the mediated eco-ethical and aesthetic architectural values of the original neighbourhood. *It does not feel like these new buildings, I do not think... that it is someone actually... a skilled architect who designed them, I feel. It's more that they want to make money out of these buildings.* (Man, 19). Here, the informant's feelings of loss for their neighbourhood borders on 'Solastalgia' (e.g. Albrecht et al. 2007), which refers to feelings of pain and distress caused by negative environmental changes to the home environment that affect one's 'sense of place' (cf. Tuan 1974), such as for example large-scale extractions of natural resources, or natural catastrophes related to climate change (Arnason and Hafsteinsson 2020).

The branding of the residential area as architecturally innovative and ecologically sustainable seems to be of importance to the informants. However, this association is an ongoing and changing process of 'resemiotization' (cf. Remm 2016; Hiller and Goodbrand 2016), where a difference between the old and new Western Harbour has already emerged. This affects the residents' experiences of their neighbourhood, causing them to reposition themselves within the changing context. It also affects their visions for the future, expressed by one informant as a desire for a direct application of this study: [...] *my biggest wish for this study is that one continues to build eh... or do everything one started with Bo01.* (Woman, 48).

The image of the old Western Harbour may however not be more than just an image created to 'resemiotize' the area from an industrial land to an eco-friendly neighbourhood with high quality architecture (cf. Remm 2016) – the original housing in the area has proven to be quite poorly built, for example – but this image has nevertheless affected the identity of the area, as well as its residents. The informants' environmental nostalgia for the old Western Harbour hence resides somewhere between individual and collective memory, and between personal and branded ideals (Boym 2001; Remm 2016). This nostalgia can also be related to a fear of change in the neighbourhood (Miller et al. 1998: 109), and it is interesting that nostalgia of this kind seems to be thriving even in a newly built area such as the Western Harbour, which is no more than 20 years old. The critique of malls and hypermarkets often takes the form of nostalgia for 'local corner store shopping' (Miller et al. 1998: 88), or for the old neighbourhood and its characteristics. This has already emerged in the Western Harbour: both by looking back in admiration at its older parts, and by looking forward and wishing for a farmers' market as well as more carefully planned additions to the built environment of the new Western Harbour.

The territorialisation of grocery shopping

Our main question in this article was about the formation of grocery shopping as a territorial role, and we set our investigation to study this through the moment and context of a double formation: the formation of a new urban district and the formation of the inhabitants moving there and settling down. The territorialisation of a role such as the grocery shopper depends on many things. In the above, we have highlighted aspects relating to wind, urban morphology, dreams (e.g. of the countryside), animal companionship, eco-friendly ambitions, traffic, recycling, paving, etc. But how do these aspects play into the process of territorialisation?

In their book *Life Phases, Mobility and Consumption, An Ethnography of Shopping Routes,* Brembeck et al. (2015) talk about life phases as a way of acknowledging the non-linearity of aging (2015: 11 f.). Ageing is neither a straightforward trajectory nor a strictly individual experience, but also a social and a cultural one. A new phase of life can, for example, start when one retires from work or when one becomes single after a long relationship. Life phases can, however, also take on shorter durations and other temporal scales than those related to the traditional and often longer life phases of childhood, parenthood, etc. For example, one could say that moving from one part of a town to another triggers a dephasing of a certain pattern and sets a new individuation process in motion (Simondon 2017; 2020). This seems to be connected to the territorialisation of new roles. In our case, we can say that an individual harbours a collection of different territorial roles. We are, as Simondon suggests, more-than-one (see also Combes 2013: 3). The passage from one (micro) life phase to another is thus not necessarily catastrophic, since the being as a unity of more-than-one can exist across different individuation processes and through their diverse phases.

The individuation process, i.e., both the process of dephasing and rephasing, is stabilised through the environment. Since the individuation process is always co-produced with its environment, we cannot have one without the other, and even a prosaic change of milieu, such as that of a move to the Western Harbour, can and will result in a new individuation process. It is this process, the reformation of a territorialised role, that we have begun to trace above.

The ascetic process can be seen as a contributing part to the process of individuation in our case – the production of a specific territorial role among others, the dephasing of old habits and the production of new ones. These new practices were related to an eco-ethical imperative and formed through the environment in which they take place. This role-taking could also be described as a process of territorial appropriation, the exhausting (yet unplannable) ways in which the shaping and refinement of certain practices and environments becomes personal: *my way (both in terms of conduct and place) of shopping*.

Environmental nostalgia might be a person's way of reckoning with a new environment, but it also allows this new individuation process (me, the grocery shopper) to connect to one's inner environment of different roles and territorialisations (as well as to other occasions and places), allowing an individual to be both more-than-one and a unity of sorts. The notion of environmental nostalgia is a process oriented both backwards and forwards. For example, countryside-living might be a resource that gives meaning to life and makes the nostalgic strive for a better future (cf. Sedikides et al. 2015); it thus helps us to reproduce territorial associations while also reforming them, even if ever so slightly. As Boym (2001: xvi) notes: 'consideration of the future makes us take responsibility for our nostalgic tales.' A modern nostalgic can be homesick and sick of home at the same time, using critical thinking and judgement in 'reflective nostalgia' (Boym 2001: 49–55). In short, nostalgia may be related to both self-examination and self-improvement.

In summary, we could thus say that the production of a territorial role in our case is a double one – although we of course realise that more than two nuances could be added to this – and that these two processes are deeply interrelated. We have a territorial association to grocery shopping where the notion of what it is and can be is set in relation to former experiences, ideas, and dreams – this process is slow and can resonate back to collective memories formed even before we were born, but it can also inform and be used to develop our idea about what grocery shopping should be. Furthermore, there is the territorial appropriation formed (among other things) by a constant process of self-improvement, self-imitations and rhythmic returns. In short, the transformation and re-formation of a territorialised role, such as that of grocery shopping, must be seen as an interrelated process where territorial associations and appropriations – and their ongoing interactions with both the environment at hand and each other – work together. Both aesthetic experiences (former and present) and our more practical interrelations with the immediate environment seem to play an important part in our struggles to maintain a sustainable urban lifestyle.

Acknowledgement

The research of this study was supported by the Swedish research agency Formas, through the project 'Urban design and everyday life choices,' 2017–01943.

References

Albrecht, G. Sartore, G.-M., Connor, L., Higginbotham, N., Freeman, S., Kelly, B., Stain, H., Tonna, A. and Pollard, G. (2007), 'Solastalgia: the distress caused by environmental change.' *Australasian Psychiatry*, 15, 95–98.

Anderberg, S. and Clark, E. (2012), 'Green sustainable Øresund region – eco-branding Copenhagen and Malmö,' in Vojnich, I. (ed.), *Urban Sustainability: A Global Urban Context*. East Lansing, MI: Michigan State University Press, pp. 591–610.

Appadurai, A. (ed.) (1986), *The Social Life of Things: Commodities in cultural perspective*. Cambridge: Cambridge University Press.

Arnason, A. and Hafsteinsson, S. B. (2020), 'A funeral for a glacier: Mourning the more-than-human on the edges of modernity.' *Thanatos*, 9(2), 46–71.

Bonnett, A. (2016), *The Geography of Nostalgia: Global and Local Perspectives on Modernity and Loss*. London: Routledge.

Boym, S. (2001), *The Future of Nostalgia*. New York: Basic Books.

Brembeck, H., Cochoy, F. and Moisander, J. (2015), 'Moving consumption.' *Consumption markets & culture*, 8(1), pp. 1–9.

Brembeck, H., Hansson, N., Lalanne, M. and Vayre, J. S. (2015), *Life Phases, Mobility and Consumption: An ethnography of shopping routes*. Farnham: Ashgate.

Brighenti, A. M. (2010), 'On territorology: Towards a general science of territory.' *Theory, culture & society*, 27(1), 52–72.

Brighenti, A. M. (2014). 'Mobilizing territories, territorializing mobilities.' *Sociologica*, 8(1), 1–25.

Brighenti, A. M. and Kärrholm, M. (2018), 'Atmospheres of retail and the asceticism of civilized consumption.' *Geographica Helvetica*, 73(3), 203–213.

Brighenti, A. M. and Kärrholm, M. (2020), *Animated Lands: Studies in Territoriology*. Lincoln: University of Nebraska Press.

Brinkmann, S. (2013). *Qualitative Interviewing*. Oxford: Oxford University Press.

Calvignac, C. and Cochoy, F. (2016), 'From "market agencements" to "vehicular agencies": Insights from the quantitative observation of consumer logistics.' *Consumption Markets & Culture*, 19(1), 133–147.

Chrostowska, S. D. (2010), 'Consumed by nostalgia?' *Substance #122*, 39(2), 52–70.

Cochoy, F. (2009), 'Driving a shopping cart from STS to business, and the other way round: On the introduction of shopping carts in American grocery stores (1936–1959).' *Organization*, 16(1), 31–55.

Cochoy, F., Hagberg, J. and Canu, R. (2015), 'The forgotten role of pedestrian transportation in urban life: Insights from a visual comparative archaeology (Gothenburg and Toulouse, 1875–2011).' *Urban Studies*, 52(12), 2267–2286.

Cochoy, F., Hagberg, J., Normark, D., Ducourant, H., Holmberg, U. and Calvignac, C. (2019), 'Bicycles, cyclists and loads: a comparative analysis of cycling practices in Gothenburg and Toulouse'. *Applied Mobilities*, *4*(1), 1–25.

Combes, M. (2013), *Gilbert Simondon and the Philosophy of the Transindividual*. Cambridge MA: MIT Press.

Gerhardsson, K. M. (2021), 'Benefits and challenges of adding participant photography to qualitative residential research.' *NAAR Proceedings Series*, (1), 45–76. Giesler, M. and Veresiu, E. (2014), 'Creating the responsible consumer: moralistic governance regimes and consumer subjectivity..' *Journal of Consumer Research*, 41(3), 840–857.

Goffman, E. (1959), *The Presentation of Self in Everyday Life*. New York: Doubleday.

Goffman, E. (1972). *Relations in Public: Micro Studies of the Public Order*. New York: Harper & Row.

Hagberg, J. and Normark, D. (2015), 'From basket to shopping bag: Retailers' role in the transformation of consumer mobility in Sweden, 1941–1970.' *Journal of Historical Research in Marketing*, 7(4) 452–475.

Hagbert, P., Wangel, J. and Broms, L. (2020), 'Exploring the potential for just urban transformations in light of eco-modernist imaginaries of sustainability.' *Urban Planning*, 5(4), 204–216.

Hall, S. M. (2011), 'Exploring the "ethical everyday": An ethnography of the ethics of family consumption.' *Geoforum*, *42*(6), 627–637.

Harper, D. (2002), 'Talking about pictures: a case for photo elicitation.' *Visual Studies*, 17 (1), 13–26.

Hiller, H. H. and Goodbrand, P. T. (2016), 'From slum to village: A semiotic analysis in reimaging urban space.' *Canadian Journal of Urban Research*, 25(2), 48–61.

Hjelmar, U. (2011), 'Consumers' purchase of organic food products: A matter of convenience and reflexive practices.' *Appetite*, 56(2), 336–344.

Holgersen, S. and Malm, A. (2015). '"Green fix" as crisis management. or, in which world is Malmö the world's greenest city?' *Geografiska Annaler: Series B, Human Geography*, 97(4), 275–290.

Kaplan, R. and Kaplan, S. (1989), *The Experience of Nature, A Psychological Perspective*. Cambridge: Cambridge University Press.

Kärrholm, M. (2011), 'The scaling of sustainable urban form: A case of scale-related issues and sustainable planning in Malmö, Sweden.' *European Planning Studies*, 19(1), 97–112.

Kärrholm, M. (2012), *Retailising Space: Architecture, Retail and the Territorialisation of Public Space*. Farnham: Ashgate.

Kärrholm, M. (2017), 'The temporality of territorial production – the case of Stortorget, Malmö.' *Social & Cultural Geography*, 18(5), 683–705.

Katzeff, C., Milestad, R., Zapico, J. L. and Bohné, U. (2020), 'Encouraging organic food consumption through visualization of personal shopping data.' *Sustainability*, 12 (9), 3599.

Lefebvre, H. (1991), *The Production of Space*. Oxford: Blackwell.

Lehner, M., Mont, O. and Heiskanen, E. (2016), 'Nudging: A promising tool for sustainable consumption behaviour?' *Journal of Cleaner Production*, 134, 166–177.

Lintott, S. (2006), 'Toward Eco-Friendly Aesthetics.' *Environmental Ethics*, 28(1), 56–76.

Miller, D., Jackson, P., Rowlands, M., Thrift, N. and Holbrook, B. (1998), *Shopping, Place, and Identity*. London: Routledge.

Niemeyer, K. (2016), 'Digital nostalgia.' *Media Development*, 4, 27–30.

Pain, H. (2012), 'A literature review to evaluate the choice and use of visual methods.' *International Journal of Qualitative Methods*, 11(4), 303–319.

Pink, S. (2012) *Situating Everyday Life*. London: Sage.

Prieto de la Fuente, P. (2020), 'Guilt-tripping: On the relation between ethical decisions, climate change and the built environment.' *Urban Planning*, 5(4), 193–203.

Ranasinghe, P. (2011), 'Public disorder and its relation to the community–civility–consumption triad: a case study on the uses and users of contemporary urban public space.' *Urban Studies*, 48(9), 1925–1943.

Remm, T. (2016), 'Textualities of the city – from the legibility of urban space towards social and natural others in planning.' *Sign Systems Studies*, 44(1/2), 34–52.

Rose, G. D. (2001), *Visual Methodologies: An Introduction to the Interpretation of Visual Materials*. London; Thousand Oaks, California: Sage.

Schoolman, E. D. (2019), 'Doing right and feeling good: Ethical food and the shopping experience.' *Sociological Perspectives*, 62(5), 668–690.

Sedikides, C., Wildschut, T., Routledge, C., Jamie, A., Hepper, E. G. and Zhou, X. (2015), 'To nostalgize: Mixing memory with affect and desire.' *Advances in Experimental Social Psychology*, 51, 189–273.

Simondon, G. (2017), *On the Mode of Existence of Technical Objects*. Minneapolis: Univocal Publishing.

Simondon, G. (2020), *Individuation in Light of Notions of Form and Information*, Volume 1, Minneapolis: University of Minnesota Press.

Skeggs, B. (1997), *Formations of Class and Gender: Becoming Respectable*. Thousand Oaks, CA: Sage.

Sloterdijk, P. (2013) *You Must Change Your Life*. Polity Press: Cambridge.

Steinbock, A. J. (1995), *Home and beyond: Generative phenomenology after Husserl*. Evanston, IL: Northwestern University Press.

Svantesson, E. (2005), 'Stormarknad öppnar i Västra hamnen.' *Sydsvenska dagbladet*, 15 November 2005. (https://www.sydsvenskan.se/2005-11-15/stormarknad-oppnar-i-vastra-hamnen, accessed 3 November 2021)

Torisson, Fredrik (2021), *Malmhattanism: Skyskrapan i Malmös utveckling*. Lund: Nordic Academic Press.

Tuan, Y.-F. (1974), 'Space and place: Humanistic perspective.' *Progress in Geography: International Reviews of Current Research*, 6, 211–252.

Williams, J., Memery, J., Megicks, P. and Morrison, M. (2010), 'Ethics and social responsibility in Australian grocery shopping.' *International Journal of Retail & Distribution Management*, 38(4), 297–316.

Wingren, C., Alsanius, B., Karlén, H. and Lidström, V. (2015), *Urbana nyanser av grönt – om grönskans roll i en klimatsmart stad*. Stad & Land, 187. Alnarp: Movium.

Chapter 9

The territories of music in public space

Scenes from Warsaw and Lisbon

Cláudia Casquilho, Pedro Gonçalves, Caio Mourão, Paula Nunes and Daniel Paiva[1]

Introduction

Music has been understood by urban authorities as a strategic asset to market cities as lively, dynamic and refreshing in order to promote tourism, leisure, consumption, and real estate investment (Krims 2007). While some cities attempt to promote themselves as 'music cities' through the development of the music industry (Watson 2008), others have defined themselves as 'festival cities' or 'party towns' where one can find bustling musical events and nightlife districts (Van Aalst and van Melik 2012; Hollands, Berthet, Nada, and Bjertnes 2017). These strategies of urban marketing aim to cultivate and commercialize hip and fun atmospheres that cater to the youthful desires to experience life at its fullest while at the same time incorporating aspects of local culture and identity, be it traditional or multicultural identities (Wynn 2015). Perhaps paradoxically, while the use of music as a strategy for urban development is on the rise, the development of musical districts has also been associated with a decrease in the quality of life due to the increase of noise generated by the loud volume of music and the bustle of crowded spaces, which can lead to negative effects on physical and psychological health, including sleep disturbances, increased stress, and cardiovascular problems (Nofre, Giordano, Eldridge, Martins and Sequera 2018; Paiva and Sánchez 2021).

In this context, a number of conflicts between music promoters and residents have emerged in several cities in the world (Hae 2011). In the public debate, such conflicts have often been framed solely through the lens of the dichotomy between noise and silence, in which musical practices are conceived as noisy, and silence is valued as the resource that residents claim (Wissmann 2014). This framing has often reduced the matter to a quantitative question revolving around the number of decibels that musical practices are permitted to make, which neglects the complex social, cultural, economic, historic, and urbanistic entanglements of these conflicts (Thibaud and Amphoux 2013; Amphoux 2017). It is our contention that addressing the territorial dimension of these

1 List of authors is alphabetical. All authors contributed equally for this work.

DOI: 10.4324/9781003196365-9

matters can underpin a more nuanced approach to these issues. With this in mind, this chapter sets out to explore the territories that music makes in urban space and the ways in which these territories overlap. To do so, we draw on recent territoriological work that has unveiled the performative and dynamic ways in which territories are assembled and disassembled (Brighenti 2010; Kärrholm 2017; Brighenti and Kärrholm 2020). This work has paved the way to a better understanding of how sound participates in the making of territories, a novel topic which has received some attention of late (LaBelle 2010; Bertoni 2019; Paiva and Cachinho 2018). In this chapter, we draw on two non-fictional vignettes of musical practices in everyday urban space to demonstrate how music produces territories and how they overlap. The first vignette focuses on the musical installation of Chopin's works in public benches in the streets of Warsaw, Poland. In contrast, the second vignette describes a sonic conflict in which a local resident used loud music playing in sound columns to expel street musicians from a public square in Lisbon, Portugal. While the first vignette demonstrates that music can produce territories by diluting existing sonic and bodily boundaries and connecting individuals, the second vignette shows the potential of music to territorialize spaces by establishing sonic boundaries and disconnecting individuals. With this in mind, we reflect on the differentiated impacts that music has in the making and unmaking of urban territories, and its social, cultural, and political entanglements, and we conclude the paper by arguing that the way forward is to recognize the right to acoustics as an element of the right to the city.

From performative territories toward sonic territoriology

The recent emergence of a research agenda on territoriology has paved the way for a better understanding of how sound makes, unmakes, and remakes territories. A territory can be defined in simplistic terms as a bounded segment of space which is claimed, appropriated, and owned by an individual, a group, or an institution. While the concept of territory has traditionally been understood in formal juridical terms, often as the spatial underpinning of the nation state, research has expanded the concept beyond this context. By doing so, the performativity and inherent instability of territories has also been unveiled. Territory is no longer understood as a stable, perennial entity. Rather, it is understood as a dynamic spatio-temporal assemblage of elements that carve out spaces of appropriation and property.

Such understanding of territory as dynamic has emerged from two research strands. First, anthropological, geographic, psychological, and sociological research on territoriality has demonstrated that the making of territories is not exclusive to formal political entities (Dyson-Hudson and Smith 1978; Edney 1974; Lyman and Scott 1967; Paasi 1998; Sack 1983, 1986). Instead, research on territoriality has shown that the making of territories is a spatial strategy used to claim space for certain practices and define boundaries between bodies that can be found in the behaviour of both humans and animals, individually or collectively. Territoriality is thus understood as a vital strategy shared by all living bodies that affords opportunities for social exchanges within its boundaries and the construction and expression of personal and collective identities.

On the other hand, recent territoriological research has noted that such territorial production is not the consequence of the action of humans alone, but rather of the ecological relation between bodies, objects, and space (Brighenti and Kärrholm 2018a). This leads our attention toward how bodies appropriate spaces by using them and what kind of objects and technologies are employed in these practices (Kärrholm 2007; Prieto de la Fuente 2015; Bertoni 2018). Likewise, it guides our attention to how the morphology of space itself is adapted by these practices in a way that reinforces those uses. In this sense, territorial production is something that requires time, it is achieved through repetition (Kärrholm 2017). In practice, there are no perennial territories, but cycles of territorialization that encompass two movements: reterritorializations in which a territory emerges from the territorial actions of an ensemble of agents, and deterritorializations in which those agents disperse and form new connections to make new territories (Brighenti and Kärrholm 2019). This temporal understanding of territories situates territorial production in everyday life, rather than the writings of legislation or the discourses of those in power (Brighenti and Kärrholm 2018b). However, it does not present a horizontal or a-political conception of territory in which any body has the same power to claim, appropriate, or own space (Warnaby 2018). Indeed, the uneven distribution of the power to territorialize is best captured when the material and spatial resources needed to produce territories are taken into account (Smith and Hall 2018). On the other hand, looking at the assemblages that constitute territorial production is also helpful for addressing the power dynamics within a certain territorialization. In other words, it allows us not only to understand who and what is part of a territory and who and what is excluded from it, but also to clarify who imposes practices within that territory and on whom those practices are imposed (Brighenti and Kärrholm 2020). For Brighenti (2010), this implies attuning to both the expressive and the functional components of territories. That is, it implies understanding the expressive communicative features within territories which may encompass speech, writing, or symbols, and the way in which space becomes organized to allow certain functions and deter others. Such expressive and functional components enforce territories by imprinting specific rhythms and effects that promote certain practices (Brighenti and Kärrholm 2018c). The literature has described several cases of such territorialized practices, for instance, in music halls (Cascudo 2018; Bertoni 2019), public space (Johansson, Sternudd, and Kärrholm 2016; Paiva and Cachinho 2019a), or shopping districts (Kärrholm 2008; 2009).

This performative understanding of territory allows us to consider the role that sound might play in territorial production, which is something that strict juridical conceptions of territory cannot conceive. While sound is a fundamental aspect for human existence as a crucial medium for both communication and environmental perception, it is also a highly ephemeral phenomenon (Voegelin 2015). Sound can be defined as the perception of vibrations in mediums such as the air or water by the human ear, and in this sense the constant production of such vibrations is required for the continuity of sound. On the other hand, soundmaking is present in all kinds of human activities, even when a certain activity is not intended to generate sounds (Paiva and Cachinho 2019b). Thus, sound is a highly volatile field which is nevertheless deeply entangled in everyday practices. As such, it is also deeply affective in many ways. The different perceived qualities of sound – including volume, pitch, timbre, rhythm, and meaning – not only provide environmental and trans-personal information, but also affect the mood and emotions of the individual (Eidsheim2015). This affectivity of sound is largely unescapable. As sound theorists often note, we cannot turn the ear away or shut the ear like we can do with our eyes (Chion 2016). Sound encapsulates the human body, and it becomes permeable to its effects.

In this sense, sound can be a crucial medium for the expressive components of territories. LaBelle (2010) focuses on how sound forms territories by connecting individuals in shared spaces. He argues that sound 'opens up a field of interaction, to become a channel, [...] to ultimately carve out a micro-geography of the moment, while always already disappearing, as a distributive and sensitive propagation' (LaBelle 2010, p. xvii). In this micro-geography of the moment, he argues, sound as a field of interaction is also a medium for participation that inevitably leads to the formation of communities of listeners and soundmakers. On the other hand, sound can be an instrumental tool in the practices of space-claiming and boundary-making that make up territorial production. This is evident in Goodman's (2010) work, which has explored the ways in which sound has been used as an instrument of violence for the purpose of making war or torturing individuals. While the cases Goodman outlines are extreme forms of claiming or maintaining territory through the use of sound, his work shows that sound is a powerful affective medium to establish boundaries. Thus, sound plays a dual role in the making of territories. On one hand, it connects bodies within territories by imprinting new rhythms onto space and allowing communication. On the other hand, it disconnects bodies by communicating and enforcing spatial borders. That notwithstanding, the sonic environment is a lively arena in which several agencies of bodies and other materialities compete with each other to perform social practices (Paiva, Cachinho, Barata-Salgueiro, and Amílcar 2017). For this reason, sound also contains a potential for conflict as it produces multiple territories that often overlap and collide. As noted in the introduction, music has been a particularly important source of such conflicts in many cities across the world. In the next sections, we will present two vignettes to address the potential of music to make and unmake multiple territories in urban space.

Warsaw's Royal Route: territories

I, Daniel, am sitting on a bench under the shadow of a tree at the ks. Jana Twardowskiego Square near Krakowskie Przedmieście street in Warsaw. It is late morning, almost noon, and so far the day has been sunny. The square is silent, and the very soft buzz of the street behind me seems very far away. I am in the company of a few crows that tip toe around me and, on the other benches, there is a woman reading and an older man resting with his cane beside him. Suddenly, piano notes. They sound very faint at first, but quickly the air is filled by a prodigious piece. I look behind me, but I cannot see where the sound comes from. The man and the woman must be accustomed to hearing music playing in this square because they do not seem surprised in any way. Later that afternoon, I am strolling along the Krakowskie Przedmieście street and again, out of the blue, a piano piece resounds. I look into the other side of the street, where the sound is coming from, and I see a woman with two children on a bench slightly darker than the others. She is sitting down with one child reading something in the bench, while the other child jumps around. There are a few people on the other benches looking at them, amused by this endearing moment. Krakowskie Przedmieście is a busy street in the city centre of Warsaw where throughout the day workers and tourists walk up and down the street. It is not usual to see people stopping and spending time on this street, aside from the occasional group of visitors on a guided tour. It is, using the words of Amin (2012), a land of strangers. However, the introduction of a musical piece in this urban passage seems to have temporarily created a space of connections.

Getting closer to one of these dark benches, I discover what they are. On the occasion of the 200th anniversary of Chopin's birth in 2010, the city transformed a significant part of the touristic Royal Route into a tribute to the composer. This historical route guides visitors along the path that the kings took when they left their winter residences to transfer to their summer palaces. The route starts at Zamkowy Square and ends in Wilanów Palace, connecting some of the most representative monuments of the city. Along this route, fifteen black granite benches were installed in front of monuments and historic buildings associated with important times in Chopin's life. Each bench contains a map of its location on the street, information about the monument, and a small button that can be pressed to reproduce thirty-second-long excerpts of Chopin's compositions.

The introduction of music augments the historical experience of the Royal Route. The combination of the visual content of the Royal Route, which consists of historical monuments, museums, churches, squares, and sculptures that were built prior to the twentieth century, and the musical experience of Chopin's work, allows people to be transported to another time with an idealized imaginary of peace: the heyday of Poland in the nineteenth century, before the devastation of the Second World War. This way, Chopin's work becomes a soundscape for Warsaw's Royal Route. While the soundscape is most often used to refer to the ensemble of sounds one can hear at a specific location, it can also refer to a sonic environment associated with a certain time (Hill 2015). However, knowing and experiencing the sonic environments of the past is a particularly treacherous task, due to the lack of recordings and the reliability of the documentation (Bijsterveld 2013). In this case, Chopin's music emerges as an alternative window to the sonic past, providing perceptual coherence in the experience of an historical city.

However, the benches not only add a sonic element to the landscape for aesthetic pleasure; they also generate musical territories. As sounds are produced and propagate, they encapsulate all those within its reach. In this sense, the music of the benches forms spatio-temporal communities of listeners who share the experience of the same acoustic events (LaBelle 2010). However, the field of interaction of the Chopin bench is not a mere flow between a sound source and a listener. Music allows multiple connections between listeners and soundmakers, and anyone can switch between these two roles. People listen to the bench's music, but also comment, ask questions, move around, or dance. Indeed, it has been argued that music in public space facilitates connections between individuals (Doughty and Lagerqvist 2016). For Doughty (2019), musical interventions in public spaces are moments of affective connections between time and space that promote feelings of belonging and interconnectedness with the world and can foster greater public engagement. Chopin's benches are meant to generate this sort of engagement in situations such as the one we describe in Krakowskie Przedmieście.

The territories generated by music foster specific types of public engagement which are politically structured. As Ouzounian (2013) argues, when soundmaking practices relate to space as socially and politically constituted, they emerge not only as aesthetics and poetry, but also as an ethical and political act. In the case of Warsaw, the production of musical territories by Chopin's benches plays a significant role in the construction of the city's sense of place and identity, which in turn is central for the marketing of Warsaw as a touristic city. A city's sense of place largely stems from the use of symbols capable of creating a common identification, and public memory is a crucial aspect in this process. For Brandellero and Pfeffer (2015), place is an active element in the formation and negotiation of identity, as well as the context in which certain practices are reproduced and sustained. Place is not just 'spatial aggregation,' but also 'a stock of knowledge, traditions, memories, and images that reinforce your identity' (Scott 2010, p. 123). The association of Chopin's music with the city of Warsaw contributes to the identity processes of the city by territorializing an historical reference in urban space through its insertion in the city centre's soundscape. Simultaneously, the benches of Chopin can be understood as a way of suggesting certain practices that generate value for the city, namely tourism. In this sense, the soundscape is inextricable from the commercial and economic intentions of the conscious effort made by local authorities to use Chopin's music to legitimize and promote local marketing and the tourism industry.

Nevertheless, this process also contains its silences: for instance, the materialization of Chopin's life on Warsaw's Royal Route omits the wider mobility of the musician. Chopin migrated to Paris and was influenced by the conventions of French music, and so his music is not only related to Polish musical identity, although he was certainly influenced by Polonaise music. Brandellero and Pfeffer (2015) note that the significance of place for music is generally based on the assumption that there is a connection between a real place and the characteristics of the sound produced in that place. However, the relationship between music and place often entails co-production, in which music 'reflects but also produces a place' (Cohen 1995, p. 444). In this regard, Chopin's benches are also a matter for the production of narratives as a way of uniting people and reinforcing a national identity, rather than promoting musical cosmopolitanism by putting diverse spaces and musical traditions in contact with each other.

While musical territories can link bodies within territories to promote affective connections, public engagement, sense of place and identity, they can also disrupt urban relations. In the next section, we turn to Lisbon to explore the disconnecting potential of music in urban space.

Lisbon's city centre: multiterritorialities

On October 24, 2019, the Portuguese newspaper *Público* reported a peculiar situation taking place in Carmo Square, Lisbon: a local resident was fighting street musicians with a loudspeaker playing Salsa music. Carmo Square is a bustling place in the Chiado area, which is well-known as a shopping and touristic zone in the city centre of Lisbon. As a place with a number of touristic attractions, including two museums, an historic public fountain, and several restaurants, Carmo Square is quite attractive for street musicians seeking a stage where donations can be easily collected. This is a relatively new phenomenon, undoubtedly related to the surge of tourism in the city. Indeed, street performances have become common in several locations of the city centre of Lisbon, and there have been several complaints about the excessive noise they produce (Silva and Paiva 2021).

In Carmo Square, one of the residents grew annoyed by the sound of musicians using sound amplifiers day and night. He argued that raising his two seven-year-old children had become an impossible task, as they could not do their everyday homework. Frustrated with the ineffectiveness of the police to put an end to this situation after filing several complaints, he decided to take matters into his own hands. His solution was to place a loudspeaker on his window and play a 2018 Salsa music mix whenever street musicians were playing loudly in the square. The purpose was to force musicians to leave by making the square's ambiance inadequate for their performances, but sometimes this led to extended conflicts between the resident and the performers in which they would battle to see who could endure the loud noise the longest. Eventually, the local restaurants also started asking musicians to leave because the noise of the acoustic battle was such that they were unable to talk to their clients.

The music battle between the Carmo resident and the street musicians was a clear disputing of musical territory in which both parties were trespassing the sonic boundaries of the other, while at the same time imposing their musical identities on the wider community. The Carmo resident felt threatened and annoyed by the constant music – which he considered to be noise – near his residence, and tried to win back his territory by imposing his music on the community and the musicians who were playing at the square. This imposition is not only a matter of volume. It can also be understood as an imposition of identity, since the Carmo resident was a former Portuguese ambassador in Cuba, and choose to use Cuban music to territorialize the square. This action can be described as a form of acoustic violence, a term put forth by Miyara (1999) to describe how sound comes to threaten bodies by imposing an abusive volume onto the everyday. As he states,

> [a]coustic violence is just violence exercised by means of sound. Often, such sound will be loud noise, but it might also be the neighbor's music going through the party wall or the constant hum of a busy city late in the night while one is trying to sleep.
>
> (Miyara 1999, p. 18)

Acoustic violence in this case also entails sonic coercion, that is, the use of loud music to torture individuals with the purpose of inducing certain behaviours or choices (Goodman 2010, p. 20). While acoustic violence and sonic coercion have been described mostly in extreme terms, namely as weapons of war, they are also a significant part of everyday life (Paiva and Cachinho 2019a).

Indeed, sonic conflicts such as this one are now common in several busy squares not only in Lisbon but also across Europe. It has been noted that these sonic conflicts are entangled in wider urban territorial struggles. More precisely, Kusiak (2014) notes that class lines largely define those who have a voice regarding crucial issues, such as what is music and what is noise, and what kind of spaces are appropriate for music or for noise. On the contrary, marginal groups are stripped away from their rights to make sounds in certain spaces. But this also means that the changes that take place in the acoustic ecology of the city are entangled with the social changes in the city itself, such as processes of gentrification or touristification.

The political and economic entanglements of acoustic disputes in the city often reduce the multiplicity of musical and acoustic practices to a dichotomy between noise and silence. In turn, the management of territorial conflicts related to music and sound is often guided by the pursuit of silence. The way to find a balance in complex societies and communities, with different musical and acoustic identities and preferences, has often led to a policy of silence, in the sense of enabling the emergence of a personal space of musical experience without challenging the territorial space of each other. This is however not without its critics. For instance, Labelle argues that

> [s]ilence, in acting as a social ordering principle through which domestic life finds balance, comes to perform a homogenizing effect. Functioning as

> an imagined base for harmonious living, a quieter environment necessarily reshapes the possibilities for social interaction, characterizing 'the other' as a noise always already breaking commonality. In this way, silence is a slippery ideal as it gathers within the imagination a set of seemingly positive values that when overlaid onto social behavior and community lends to understandings of place and placement a contentious intolerance.
>
> (2010, p. 55)

Indeed, ongoing events present scenarios that are more complex than the noise–silence dichotomy. The Carmo vignette illustrates this complexity. It is not a mere dispute between one resident and street musicians, but a larger field of play that encompasses the territorialities of the multiple people who use the square. This includes not only the several tourists who visit the square individually or in guided tours to get to know the museums, but also the restaurant owners who attempt to provide tranquil premium ambiances for their clients. As an urban square in the city centre, the square is likewise traversed by workers of the local shops throughout the day. In this sense, the Carmo vignette leads us to think about the multiterritoriality of music. Haesbaert (2004, 2007) presents the concept of multiterritoriality as an alternative to the use of the term deterritorialization to describe the proliferation of mobile practices such as migration or tourism which, for some authors such as Augé (1992), detach the individual from the significance of place. Haesbaert, following the perspectives of authors such as Massey (2005) and Cresswell (2006), argues that rather than detach individuals from place, increasing mobility generates multiple belongings and the proliferation of territorial identities and belongings. Similarly, Brighenti and Kärrholm (2020) argue for a pluralistic understanding of territories as overlapping, rather than mutually exclusive, belongings. These multiple belongings operate in different spatial and temporal scales. In this regard, we can think about multiple spatial scales in Carmo square: the city centre, the square, the restaurant terrace, the apartment, the window, the room, etc. We can likewise consider different temporal scales: the resident who lives there, the street musician who plays for an hour, or the tourists who visit the city during a weekend. On the other hand, as multiterritoriality implies the overlapping of different territories at the same time-spaces, it also potentiates a series of personal and collective conflicts. Following Haesbaert and Mondardo (2010), we can think about the conflicts in Carmo Square as transterritorial, in the sense that they emerge within the transient experience of multiple territories. That is, they emerge from the spatio-temporal movements of the territories of tourists and street musicians, and their touching points with the territories of the square's residents. However, unlike the case of Chopin's benches in Warsaw's Royal Route, music in Carmo Square highlights these touching points, fostering disconnection between different urban territories. Such disconnections should however not be understood as negative or sterile outcomes. We must take into account that disconnections might foster other connections or different ways of thinking about space (Massey 2005). We can allude, for instance, to Kopljar's (2016) experiments in urban design in which she used sound installations to unsettle the expectations of urban planners regarding specific sites as a way to generate new views and approaches.

Conclusion

Thinking about musical practices in urban public life from a territoriological perspective not only unveils the differentiated impact that music can have in the making and unmaking of urban territories, but also the profound social, cultural, and political entanglements of this territorial production. The Warsaw and Lisbon cases demonstrate that music can make territories by being either a force of connection that pulls individuals into a common territory, or a force of disconnection that pushes individuals away from an exclusive territory. Both processes have their underlying political and cultural entanglements. While the Warsaw case demonstrates how musical territories can serve to materialize and perform a specific historical, cultural, and political narrative, the Lisbon case unveils the complex interactions of musical territories with the social and economic disputes of the city. In this sense, music in urban space becomes political not because its aesthetic content contains a political message, but because – as a sonic practice – music participates in the politicized making of urban territories. This leads us to think about music as a practice of social or everyday acoustics, which is defined by LaBelle (2021) as the everyday practice of ordering or arranging space through the modulation of sound. In this sense, acoustics is not something exclusive to professionals or experts, but a performative care for soundmaking and how it allows acoustic communities to emerge. Understanding acoustics as an everyday social practice is key to think how acoustic justice can be thought beyond the noise–silence dichotomy. For LaBelle (2021), acoustic justice involves a work of reorientation, from normative top-down understandings of what can be heard toward a practice of enabling more voices, desires, and other practices to be heard.

With this in mind, we argue that one way to achieve acoustic justice is to recognize the right to acoustics as an element of the right to the city. Stemming from Lefebvre's (1972 [1968]) proposal for a more just access to city life, the right to the city has been defined not only as a right to access the amenities of cities, but also as a right to participate in the processes of urban change (Harvey 2003; Marcuse 2009; Brenner et al. 2012). Recently, it has been acknowledged that the right to the city must be extended to less obvious urban activities, such as data processing (Shaw and Graham 2017), walking (Middleton 2018), or branding (Masuda and Bookman 2018). Duff (2017) has pointed out that the right to city has an affective dimension, which is linked to how the right to the city is expressed through the performative relation of the human body with urban materiality, but this affective dimension must be expanded. More precisely, the practices of acoustic production and experience must be understood as a crucial aspect of urban everyday life that must be justly distributed. The acknowledgement of the territoriality of sound practices must be expanded into an acknowledgement of personal and collective rights to acoustic production and experience, taking into account that the multiterritoriality of sound means that soundmaking always possesses a potential for conflict.

Acknowledgements

This work has been supported by the Fundação para a Ciência e a Tecnologia (FCT) through grants no. CEECIND/03528/2018, no. UIDP/00295/2020, no. UIDB/00295/2020, and no. LA/P/0092/2020.

References

Amin, A. (2012). *Land of Strangers*. London: Polity.

Amphoux, P. (2017). Nuisances sonores: réflexion critique et principes opérationnels. *Revue de la BNF*, 2(55), 88–101.

Augé, M. (1992). *Non-Lieux: introduction à une anthropologie de la surmodernité*. Paris: Editions du Seuil.

Bertoni, F. (2018). Segretamente pubblici: il parkour e lo spazio pubblico come soglia. *Rivista Geografica Italiana*, 125(2), 175–188.

Bertoni, F. (2019). Resounding heterotopias: breakdance, caporales and the re-appropriation of the city. In *Sounding the World: More-than-representational Accounts of Sound and Music*, edited by Karolina Doughty, Michelle Duffy, and Theresa Harada. London: Edward Elgar, pp. 52–62.

Bijsterveld, K. (2013). *Soundscapes of the Urban Past: Staged Sound as Mediated Cultural Heritage*. Bielefeld: transcript Vertag.

Brandellero, K. and Pfeffer, K. (2015). Making a scene: exploring the dimensions of place through Dutch popular music 1960–2010. *Environment and Planning A*, 47, 1574–1591.

Brenner, N., Marcuse, P., and Mayer, M. (2012). *Cities for People, Not for Profit. Critical urban theory and the right to the city*. London: Routledge.

Brighenti, A. M. (2010). On territorology: towards a general science of territory. *Theory, Culture and Society*, 27(1), 52–72.

Brighenti, A. M. and Kärrholm, M. (2018a). Morphogenesis and animistic moments: on social formation and territorial production. *Social Science Information*, 57(2), 249–272.

Brighenti, A. M. and Kärrholm, M. (2018b). Domestic territories and the little humans: understanding the animation of domesticity. *Space and Culture*, 21(4), 395–407.

Brighenti, A. and Kärrholm, M. (2018c). Beyond rhythmanalysis: towards a territoriology of rhythms and melodies in everyday spatial activities. *City, Territory and Architecture*, 5(4). doi:10.1186/s40410-018-0080-x

Brighenti, A. M. and Kärrholm, M. (2019). Three presents: on the multi-temporality of territorial production and the gift from John Soane. *Time & Society*, 28(1), 375–398.

Brighenti, A. and Kärrholm, M. (2020). *Animated Lands: Studies in Territoriology*. Lincoln: University of Nebraska Press.

Cascudo, T. (2018). Territory is the key. A look at the birth of 'national music' in Spain (1799–1803). In *Confronting the National in the Musical Past*, edited by Elaine Kelly, Markus Mantere, and Derek Scott. Oxon: Routledge, pp. 196–207.

Chion, M. (2016). *Sound: An Acoulogical Treatise*. Durham: Duke University Press.

Cohen, S. (1995). Sounding out the city: music and the sensuous production of place. *Transactions of the Institute of British Geographers*, 20(4), 434–446.

Cresswell, T. (2006). *On the Move: Mobility in the Modern Western World*. London: Routledge.

Dyson-Hudson, R. and Smith, E. (1978). Human territoriality: an ecological reassessment. *American Anthropologist*, 80(1), 21–41.

Doughty, K. (2019). Rethinking musical cosmopolitanism as a visceral politics of sound. In *Sounding Places: More-than-representational Geographies of Sound and Music*, edited by K. Doughty, M. Duffy, and T. Harada. Cheltenham: Edward Elgar, pp. 189–201.

Doughty, K. and Lagerqvist, M. (2016). The ethical potential of sound in public space: migrant pan flute music and its potential to create moments of conviviality in a 'failed' public square. *Emotion, Space and Society*, 20, 58–67.

Duff, C. (2017). The affective right to the city. *Transactions of the Institute of British Geographers*, 42, 516–529.

Edney, J. J. (1974). Human territoriality. *Psychological Bulletin*, 81(12), 959–975.

Eidsheim N. (2015). *Sensing Sound: Singing and Listening as Vibrational Practice*. Durham: Duke University Press.

Goodman, S. (2010). *Sonic Warfare: Sound, Affect, and the Ecology of Fear*. Cambridge: MIT Press.

Hae, L. (2011). Dilemmas of the nightlife fix: post-industrialisation and the gentrification of nightlife in New York City. *Urban Studies*, 48(16), 3449–3465.

Haesbaert, R. (2004). *O Mito Da Desterritorialização. Do Fim dos Territórios à Multi-territorialidade*. Rio de Janeiro: Bertrand.

Haesbaert, R. (2007). Território e multiterritorialidade: um debate. *GEOgraphia*, 9(17), 19–46.

Haesbaert, R. and Mondardo, M. (2010). Transterritorialidade e antropofagia: territorialidades de trânsito numa perspectiva brasileiro-latino-americana. *GEOgraphia*, 12 (24), 19–50.

Harvey, D. (2003). The right to the city. *International Journal of Urban and Regional Research*, 27, 939–941.

Hill, L. (2015). More-than-representational geographies of the past and the affectivity of sound: revisiting the Lynmouth flood event of 1952. *Social & Cultural Geography*, 16 (7), 821–843.

Hollands, R., Berthet, M.-A., Nada, E., and Bjertnes, V. (2017). Urban cultural movements and the night: struggling for the 'right to the creative (party) city in Geneva. In *The SAGE Handbook of New Urban Studies*, edited by John Hannigan and Greg Richards. London: Sage, 295–310.

Johansson, M., Sternudd, C., &and Kärrholm, M. (2016). Perceived urban design qualities and affective experiences of walking. *Journal of Urban Design*, 21(2), 256–275.

Kärrholm, M. (2007). The materiality of territorial production: a conceptual discussion of territoriality, materiality, and the everyday life of public space. *Space and Culture*, 10 (4), 437–453.

Kärrholm, M. (2008). The territorialisation of a pedestrian precinct in Malmö: materialities in the commercialisation of public space. *Urban Studies*, 45(9), 1902–1924.

Kärrholm, M. (2009). To the rhythm of shopping: on synchronisation in urban landscapes of consumption. *Social and Cultural Geography*, 10(4), 421–440.

Kärrholm, M. (2017). The temporality of territorial production: the case of Stortorget, Malmö. *Social and Cultural Geography*, 18(5), 683–705.

Kopljar, S. (2016). *How to Think about a Place not yet: Studies of Affordance and Site-based Methods for the Exploration of Design Professionals' Expectations in Urban development processes*. Lund: Lund University, Faculty of Engineering.

Krims, A. (2007). *Music and Urban Geography*. Oxon: Routledge.

Kusiak, J. (2014). Acoustic gentrification: the silence of Warsaw's sonic warfare. In *The Acoustic City*, edited by M. Gandy and B. J. Nilsen. Berlin: JOVIS, pp. 206–211.

LaBelle, B. (2010). *Acoustic Territories: Sound Culture and Everyday Life*. London: Bloomsbury.

LaBelle, B. (2021). *Acoustic Justice: Listening, Performativity, and the Work of Reorientation*. London: Bloomsbury.

Lefebvre, H. (1972). *Le Droit à la ville suivi de espace et politique*. Paris: Anthropos. (Originally published in 1968.)

Lyman, S. and Scott, M. (1967). Territoriality: a neglected sociological dimension. *Social Problems*, 15(2), 236–249.

Marcuse, P. (2009). From critical urban theory to the right to the city. *City*, 13 (2–3), 185–197.

Massey, D. (2005). *For Space*. London: Sage.

Masuda, J. R. and Bookman, S. (2018). Neighbourhood branding and the right to the city. *Progress in Human Geography*, 42(2), 165–182.

Middleton, J. (2018). The socialities of everyday urban walking and the 'right to the city.' *Urban Studies*, 55(2), 296–315.

Miyara, F. (1999). Acoustic violence: a new name for an old social pain. *Hearing Rehabiliation Quarterly*, 24(1), 18–21.

Nofre, J., Giordano, E., Eldridge, A., Martins, J., and Sequera, J. (2018). Tourism, nightlife and planning: challenges and opportunities for community liveability in La Barceloneta. *Tourism Geographies*, 20(3), 377–396.

Ouzounian, G. (2013). Sound installation art: from spatial poetics to politics, aesthetics to ethics. In *Music, Sound and Space: Transformations of Public and Private Experience*, edited by G. Born. Cambridge: Cambridge University Press, pp. 73–89.

Paasi, A. (1998). Boundaries as social processes: territoriality in the world of flows. *Geopolitics*, 3(1), 69–88.

Paiva, D. and Cachinho, H. (2018). Artistic practices and the redistribution of the sensible in Largo do Chiado: attention, corporeal isles, visceral politics. *Tijdschrift voor Economische en Sociale Geografie*, 109(5), 597–612.

Paiva, D. and Cachinho, H. (2019a). Soundmaking and the making of worlds and territories: a case of street football games in Quinta da Piedade. *Social & Cultural Geography*. doi:10.1080/14649365.2019.1704046.

Paiva, D. and Cachinho, H. (2019b). The sounds we make: environmental feedback and the entanglements of sonic presence. In *Sounding the World: More-than-representational accounts of Sound and Music*, edited by Karolina Doughty, Michelle Duffy, and Theresa Harada. London: Edward Elgar, pp. 109–126.

Paiva, D., Cachinho, H., Barata-Salgueiro, T., and Amílcar, A. (2017). A criação de geoetnografias como metodologia para o estudo dos ritmos urbanos: uma aplicação no Chiado, Lisboa. *Scripta Nova. Revista Electrónica de Geografía y Ciencias Sociales*, 21. http://revistes.ub.edu/index.php/ScriptaNova/article/view/19342/21750.

Paiva, D. and Sánchez, I. (2021). The territoriality of atmosphere: rethinking affective urbanism through the collateral atmospheres of Lisbon's tourism. *Transactions of the Institute of British Geographers*, 46(2), 392–405. doi:10.1111/tran.12425.

Prieto de la Fuente, P. (2015). Discrete architectures: rhythms of public eating in Värnhemstorget in Malmö. In *Urban Squares: Spatio-temporal Studies of Design and Everyday Life in the Öresund Region*, edited by Mattias Kärrholm. Lund: Nordic Academic Press, pp. 57–86.

Sack, R. (1983). Human territoriality: a theory. *Annals of the Association of American Geographers*, 73(1), 55–74.

Sack, R. (1986). *Human Territoriality: Its Theory and History*. Cambridge: Cambridge University Press.

Scott A. J. (2010). Cultural economy and the creative field of the city. *Geografiska Annaler: Series B, Human Geography*, 92(2), 115–130.

Shaw, J. and Graham, M. (2017). An informational right to the city? Code, Content, control, and the urbanization of information. *Antipode*, 49, 907–927.

Silva, A. and Paiva, D. (2021). A economia urbana e os artistas de rua: performance, mobilidades e conflitos em um espaço público turistificado. *Geotextos*, 17(1), 129–149.

Smith, R.J. and Hall, T. (2018). Everyday territories: homelessness, outreach work and city space. *The British Journal of Sociology*, 69, 372–390.

Thibaud, J.-P. and Amphoux, P. (2013). Silencing the city? *SoundEffects. An Interdisciplinary Journal of Sound and Sound Experience*, 3(3), 62–70.

Van Aalst, I. and van Melik, R. (2012). City festivals and urban development: does place matter? *European Urban and Regional Studies*, 19(2), 195–206.

Voegelin, S. (2015). *Sonic Possible Worlds: Hearing the Continuum of Sound*. London: Bloomsbury.

Warnaby, G. (2018). Taking a territoriological perspective on place branding? *Cities*, 80, 64–66.

Watson, A. (2008). Global music city: knowledge and geographical proximity in London's recorded music industry. *Area*, 40, 12–23.

Wissmann, T. (2014). *Geographies of Urban Sound*. London: Ashgate.

Wynn, J. (2015). *Music/City: American Festivals and Placemaking in Austin, Nashville, and Newport*. Chicago: University of Chicago Press.

Chapter 10

Passage Territories

Reconstructing the Domestic Spatiality of an Indonesian Urban Kampung

Kristanti Dewi Paramita

Rethinking domestic territoriality in urban kampungs

This chapter aims to redefine the understanding and formation process of domestic territory in the context of urban *kampungs*. *Kampung* is a term for a densely populated neighbourhood in Indonesia, largely occupied by a low to middle class community (Kusno 2015). In the urban context of Indonesian cities, kampungs are often home to particular ethnic groups or people of a particular religious affiliations (Martinez and Masron 2020), or instead based on the dominant occupation or reliance on a particular production system (e.g agriculture or fishing) (Martinez and Masron 2020, Putri 2019). Some kampungs have existed for a long time as a particular cultural heritage (Yuliastuti and Sukmawati 2020, Simone and Rao 2012), but the literature has mainly defined the kampung as a temporary settlement that emerges on informally obtained land (Martinez and Masron 2020, Kusno 2015).

Discussions of informal settlements tend to frame their territoriality in terms of power and control (Roy 2011), and this includes urban kampungs (Dovey, Cook, and Achmadi 2019, Kusno 2020). The kampung can be defined based on Chatterjee's (2006) discussion of a political society, where its territory emerges through persistent claims to habitation and livelihood. Similarly, Kusno (2020) has highlighted that a kampung is organised from the outside by the government, since it is the latter that provides access to some state-run programs and infrastructures. However, the set-up of household livelihood and access to wider infrastructural systems are also organised from the inside by local communities (Kusno 2020, Yatmo and Atmodiwirjo 2013, Putri and Moulaert 2017). Kampungs are often at risk of eviction. In Jakarta, the capital of Indonesia, kampungs located in central locations are often displaced to give way to new estate and infrastructure developments (Putri 2019). Some kampungs have been displaced for sanitary reasons: these settlements have limited access to waste infrastructure, and are routinely stigmatised in public discourse as threats to public health (Putri 2019, Tilley, Elias, and Rethel 2019). In short, kampungs recurrently originate territorial conflicts and are often depicted as riotous, since local communities enter into conflict with the government over claims to

DOI: 10.4324/9781003196365-10

ownership of the settlement. In most occasions, evictions and displacements are not the final word, as the same kampung gets repeatedly re-occupied (Widyaningsih and Van den Broeck 2021).

This chapter explores the creation of domestic territoriality in an urban kampung. Inherently, the kampung transforms the mainstream meaning of domesticity: here, a domestic territory becomes a product of interacting forces in the neighbourhood and the city. In this vein, Kusno (2020) discusses how some dwellings in urban kampungs are converted into rental spaces and food stalls to support the labour needs from the surrounding city establishments, e.g workers of offices and malls. Despite that, discussions of domesticity in urban kampungs tend to focus on localised, bounded spatial appropriations by the dwellers (Ellisa 2016), rarely investigating the larger spatiality of interacting social forces. Beyond understanding territory as an act of the controller over the controlled (Sack 1983), multiple organisations give shape to a territory formed by a heterogeneous 'ensemble of subjects and agents who form it' (Brighenti 2010: 68).

The domestic territoriality of kampungs is also powerfully shaped by environmental degradation and the risk of natural disasters, such as flooding (Hawken and Sunindijo 2018, Jones 2017). It is thus important to unpack how the instability of the kampung influences the formation of local domestic territoriality. As an explanatory tool, I adopt in particular the concept of 'passage territories,' a term coined by Richard Sennett (2006). Sennett describes passage territories as territories constructed by movements. A similar emphasis on passages as a framework of territorial discussion is also outlined by Brighenti and Kärrholm (2020), exploring territory as driven by mobility instead of stability. These theories highlight that territory is a process of inhabitation rather than a sheer spatial condition (Paramita and Schneider 2018), a process that deals with 'boundary, limit, inhabitation, transition, and difference' (McCarthy 2005: 120).

This chapter expands on the dynamic relevance of passage territories. The chapter starts by outlining some stories of passage in Kampung Pulo, an urban kampung in Jakarta. It explores the different passage territories that emerge as responses to the instability affecting the kampung. I then discuss how the entanglement between these different forms of passages illuminates the issue of domestic territoriality in interior architecture, neighbourhood, and urban design. The chapter concludes by elaborating on theoretical and practical implications of passage territories for contested urban areas.

Stories of passages in Kampung Pulo

Kampung Pulo is located in Jatinegara, East Jakarta. The overall neighbourhood is situated in 8.5 hectares of pocket-shaped land alongside the Cilliwung river. It hosts nearly 4,000 households and about 10,000 residents (Sumardi 2015, Meilasari-Sugiana, Sari, and Anggraini 2018). The neighbourhood is accessible through five gates situated alongside the Jatinegara Barat road (see Figure 10.1). Opposite to Kampung Pulo is Jatinegara Market, a large traditional market in the city. Some Kampung Pulo dwellers work in the market as store employees, street vendors, parking attendants and cleaners, while a large majority rely on small-scale, home-based businesses: selling cooked food, snacks and beverages, raw ingredients (vegetables, meat, and poultry) as well as a variety of products for households (from soap to tools) (see Figure 10.2).

Kampung Pulo has faced both environmental and political challenges. The kampung developed at various altitudes and some parts of the neighbourhood are lower than street and river levels. In the rainy season the kampung is subjected to floods that last for up to three weeks (Kompas 2014). According to the altimetry, while some houses in the neighbourhood are completely submerged, others may remain dry. Such environmental vulnerabilities are also worsened by inadequate sanitation and sewerage (UN Habitat 2003). This environmental issue has become the cause of political debate. In 2015–2016, the kampung was forcibly evicted by the regional government, displacing over around 1,000 households and a about third of its inhabitants (The Jakarta Post 2016). These households were evicted to give way for the river regeneration project that took place in the city, which aimed to widen the river by 15 m and create a hardened embankment (The Jakarta Post 2015). The justification for the forcible eviction was in part built upon the claim that the residents pollute the river and contribute to the causes of flooding, despite there being little evidence for such claims (Wilson 2015, Vollmer and Grêt-Regamey 2013).

Kampung Pulo suffers from lack of space and infrastructures: the majority of dwellings consist of modest two-story houses with varying floor plan sizes, from as small as 2 x 2.5 m up to 4 x 4.5 m per floor. There are only a few bigger houses, often owned by older dwellers who have resided there for generations. The two-story houses are important as places of temporary escape

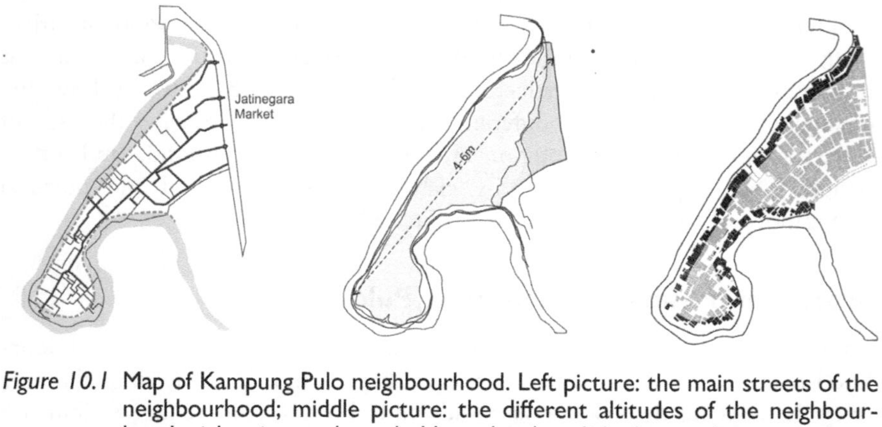

Figure 10.1 Map of Kampung Pulo neighbourhood. Left picture: the main streets of the neighbourhood; middle picture: the different altitudes of the neighbourhood; right picture: households to be demolished according to the river regeneration project (maps by author).

Figure 10.2 A typical two-storey dwelling in the neighbourhood (photograph by author).

from floods. Not all dwellings are equipped with bathrooms and toilets, and many dwellings rely on community toilets built around the riverbanks. This has created difficulties since the river regeneration project started, as the project eliminated community toilets, leading to a sanitary crisis in the neighbourhood (Hamanongan 2015). Along with its environmental and political strife, spatial scarcity and infrastructural crisis compound the basis for the emergence of passage territories. Based on a study of Kampung Pulo neighbourhood[1], four types of passage-territorial patterns can be observed.

1 The study was conducted in 2015–2016 and consisted of interviews and observations towards 41 dwellers of Kampung Pulo. The dwellers that were being

Passages of child-rearing strategies

The first pattern responds to childcare needs, where dwellers utilise multiple dwelling spaces to care for young children. To begin with, domestic territory is a distinct living terrain, which does not exist in isolation but is strengthened by its territorial associations with the homes of neighbours, friends and family (Brighenti 2010). In the existing literature, the role of kinship is mostly studied in the context of collective uses of a particular dwelling space (Yatmo and Atmodiwirjo 2013). Nevertheless, local relations define spaces that can be used by networks of families or neighbours beyond any rigid spatial ownerships (Thrift 2005). Such kinship patterns enable multiple dwellings to collectively take care of young children as a distinct form of domestic territory. The literature on informal urban settlements has also pointed out the ambiguity of the boundary between private and public spaces (Dovey and Polakit 2012).

There are different scenarios for how the child-rearing pattern unfolds. Some dwellers leave their young children with their parents, siblings, or acquaintances for a particular period, before leaving for work, which can be in the morning or the night, and can sometimes even last for whole days, depending on their work. The children will move back to their parents' home after school. Other dwellers may have many children, so they class them by age and assign them to different places. Some of the older children may live permanently with their grandparents or with their aunts and uncles. In this scenario, children do not move back and forth between houses, but some of them may go to their parents' house during the day to help caring for siblings or to do other household chores. Other than these more regular, routine scenarios, there is another more intermittent pattern that does not follow any schedule. For example, one dweller stated that one of her grandchildren, who is a teenager, prefers to move in with her every now and then since her parents are too strict with her. The child may then spend several nights in their grandparents' dwelling before moving back to their parents' place for the rest of the week.

The configuration of passage territories for these needs varies depending on the positions of the existing dwelling spaces and the paths connecting them. Some of these dwellings are close to each other, in the same alley or a few blocks away, and proximity facilitates movements back and forth through the day: this leads to the temporal and dynamic occupation of connecting paths (see Figure 10.3), such as the appropriation of terraces and alleys by children. Paths themselves become living spaces also thanks to objects that are moved in and through them so as to expand the domestic territory (Atmodiwirjo, Yatmo, and Ujung 2015, Deluchi 2018). Some dwellers have even built bridges between the houses' second floors, creating further new connecting paths. Some passage territories that respond to childcare needs may include dwelling

observed live in a variety of altitudes within the neighbourhood, with different occupations and family configurations to ensure a comprehensive reading towards the various domestic lives in Kampung Pulo.

Figure 10.3 Occupation and movement of young children cared for by their extended families across the neighbourhood (photograph by author).

spaces located further away, in different quarters of the settlement, about 200–500m away. Yet, these dwelling spaces are often interwoven with the routes which the dwellers take during the day: usually, they are positioned along the routes to work, shop, or school. In short, dwellers' everyday routes enable the activation of dispersed dwelling spaces, rather than just transits generated by starting and destination points (Hillier 2015).

Passages of economic activity distribution

The second pattern of passage territories emerges as a way of supporting local economic activities. Urban kampungs rely particularly on home-based enterprises (Hawken and Sunindijo 2018). The literature has highlighted that similar business tend to cluster in an area (Newberry 2008), and that dwellers put in place a number of survival strategies in both private and public spaces (Tunas 2008). But it is also important to underline that economic enterprises can occur in dispersed spaces, in response to economic needs and working systems. Some dwellers scatter their dwelling spaces to obtain a more profitable location to sell their products, for example they rent a living space near more crowded areas, while also continuing to live in their other house. Other dwellers use their parents' or adult childrens' houses located in more strategic areas and go back and forth for work.

Besides ensuring more profitable locations, dispersal may be required to get more storage space for their productions, due to the limited stock of spaces in the neighbourhood. Some dwellers prepare and cook in one space and then continue their selling activities in their other dwelling spaces. Such

Figure 10.4 One of the profitable locations for economic activities in the street alongside a mosque in the middle of the neighbourhood (photograph by author).

arrangements often bind extended families who own a family business and actually occupy and live in both dwelling spaces; similarly, close neighbours may also share their business and split the job between them (See Figure 10.4).

The configuration of passage territories for economic activities varies: the most profitable areas in Pulo follow a logic of street-level hierarchy, with spots along the neighbourhood street, where the proximity to junctions, street markets or mosques is especially valued (see Figure 10.4). Dwellers who rent spaces around these areas will occupy the whole dwelling space and use it for business in its entirety; on the other hand, dwellers who use their relatives' dwelling space would usually use only a part of the dwelling for business, such as a small part of the room or the terrace area in front of the dwelling. An example is a dweller who sells *kolak* (a sweet dessert made from banana) in front of her daughter's dwelling, while her own house is located in a narrower alley that faces the river, which is rarely passed by anyone.

Dwellers who spread their economic activities usually occupy dwellings as close as possible to their own, going back and forth between them and thus creating a more compact passage territory. These processes are made of multiple trajectories within and across the connected spaces. For example, a mother and daughter live next to each other, owning and operating a rice stall together. This type of home business requires a lot of cooking of vegetables and meat in large quantities. The mother lives alone, using her house for cleaning and preparing the ingredients, such as washing and cutting vegetables, or arranging spices and blending them. The daughter, who lives next-door, then collects the ingredients and cooks them in her kitchen. When the food is ready, they go and operate the stall located on the daughter's terrace, taking turns to keep the food hot and serve the customers.

Such a spreading and sharing of economic activities enables a convenient allocation of resources across the neighbourhood, valorising both economic investment and family or neighbourly relations. Such a spatial dispersal creates a more open classification of home-based enterprise that is not limited to dwellings, but is based on the dwellers' social position in the neighbourhood.

Passages of infrastructural access

The third pattern evolves from the tactics created by dwellers to access basic domestic services, in particular sanitation and waste disposal. Literature on informal settlements has highlighted how basic infrastructural resources such as water, sanitation, and electricity are often disrupted, failing, or even absent (McFarlane 2010). Recent literature has also emphasised the everyday practices performed by dwellers in response to such disruptions (Brown 2014, Desai, McFarlane, and Graham 2015, Yatmo and Atmodiwirjo 2018). Available resources tend to be shared between households, or organised at community level (Iossifova 2015, Yatmo and Atmodiwirjo 2018). Community initiatives sometimes also lead to the strategic creation of shared facilities (Yatmo and Atmodiwirjo 2018). In Kampung Pulo, floods often damage, at least temporarily, structures such as public toilets and the waste disposal facility, jeopardising the community effort and leading to less investment into them in the long term.

In such an unstable context, access to infrastructure works through bricolage connections including 'improvisation and a range of intermediary providers as key partners to interruption' (McFarlane 2010: 136). Dwellers seek to secure multiple options of access from a variety of dispersed sources to be used alternatively according to availability. The connection may be appropriated by the neighbourhood from public networks (McFarlane 2010). Understanding the passages that emerge from the process of connecting with such a variety of resources for domestic needs arguably demonstrates how domestic territory is constructed by an assemblage of agents (Brighenti 2010).

Dwellers may use sanitation facilities besides their own, including toilet spaces in other dwellings, communal toilets available in the neighbourhood, and toilets in public spaces near the neighbourhood, such as in the nearby market. At their own place, some dwellers only have bathrooms without toilets, or have broken toilets, which they cannot afford to repair. Other dwellers prefer to use others' facilities because of better quality, for example an elderly person chooses to go to her daughter's house every time she needs to take a shower, since her daughter's bathroom is larger. The passage territories created this way vary accordingly. Usually, dwellers only feel comfortable to ask permission to use neighbours' toilets who live very close by, for example in the same alley. Dwellers who use their relatives' services may live nearby, but they may also take a slightly longer path, walking 50–100 m to the next block. On the other hand, since the provision of communal toilets in the neighbourhood is limited, dwellers might have to walk even further, up to 200 m. In some cases, where there is no access to any toilet within the neighbourhood,

Figure 10.5 Two bamboo platforms used for cloth and dishwashing, with toilet box equipped on the edge of the platform. The platforms are also used for river crossing, surrounded by heaps of waste at the dumping spot on the edge of the river (photograph by author).

some dwellers may walk outside the neighbourhood to access toilets in the nearby public spaces, which can be more than 500 m away.

Another infrastructure-driven pattern of passage territory emerges from waste disposal facilities. Dwelling spaces are small and dwellers must invent their own way of managing waste. Informally designated dumping areas are set up in multiple spots inside and on the outer boundary of the neighbourhood. Dwellers might use multiple dumping areas, depending on the type of waste and the route they need to take on that day. For example, some dwellers separate their dumping destination for wet waste (such as food ingredients or leftover food) and dry waste (such as paper or plastics). Wet waste is usually disposed of closer to dwellings. Other dwellers use the nearest dumping spot along their route in and outside the neighbourhood, either going to the market, to school, or to work. The sanitation and waste disposal spaces often interweave with each other in relation to the dwellers' movements across the neighbourhood (see Figure 10.5).

This infrastructure bricolage demonstrates that dwellers' domestic territory can stretch beyond the neighbourhood, far from their dwelling space. Besides close social relationships, a variety of dwelling conditions and access to public networks becomes important to generate more options of infrastructural resources in times of disruption.

Passages for managing safety

The fourth pattern of passage territory concerns safety from the recurring environmental hazards. Urban planning literature on flood-prone urban kampung settlements often focuses on the mitigation of environmental risk, by either improving existing structures or attending the wider environmental setting (Marschiavelli et al. 2013, Vollmer and Grêt-Regamey 2013). However, residents have already developed a variety of spatial strategies to cope with floods. Two of their primary concerns include finding a safe refuge to run to, and keeping on with business while their dwelling is flooded.

Since the neighbourhood varies in terms of altitude, and some parts are never flooded, dwellers seek to strengthen extended family and acquaintance bonds so as to be temporarily shielded during these difficult times, which are especially challenging for elderly people. During the flood, dwellers move to the least impacted locations in the neighbourhood. Some extended families occupy homes at different altitudes, and dwellings located in the highest position are used as a safe refuge during the flood. Some dwellings might not be entirely safe, but as discussed in the beginning of the chapter, dwellers can also move to the second floor in their own houses. Dwelling is thus reconfigured to support subsistence practices during water inundation (see Figure 10.6).

In an interview, one resident stated that when the water level starts to rise, she picks up her elderly parents and moves them temporarily to her house

Figure 10.6 Some transformation of the dwelling to create a safe refuge during an extended period of flood through heightening the water tap position to ensure access to clean water (photograph by author).

uphill. Another dweller did the opposite, and moved back with her family to her parents' house that is safer. Since available space is limited, such forms of sharing only take place within families and close acquaintances. Nevertheless, some dwellers may not have any relatives in the area, or they are all living in the same unsafe space. In such conditions, some dwellers will either take refuge in public shelters, or rent another dwelling outside of the neighbourhood.

As discussed above, home-based enterprises are key to Pulo's local economy. Accordingly, prolonged floods significantly threaten daily earnings. Food sellers then seek to rent spaces in the upper parts of the neighbourhood, in order to continue working and earn money during flooding times. A sweets maker, for instance, told us how, as soon as the weather news came, she loaded her basic ingredients (flour and sugar) and instruments on a lorry. She would then evacuate to other dwelling spaces in the periphery of the neighbourhood with her family, where she could continue to bake her sweets. A meat-soup maker said he rents a small kitchen in the upper part of the neighbourhood, while also maintaining a two-story house in the slightly lower part of the neighbourhood as his main living space. His plan for the flood is to move to the upper floor, while still commuting to the unflooded upper part of the neighbourhood for work.

Such scattering of working and living spaces thus becomes a safety net against the economic uncertainty created by natural disasters, ensuring the livelihood of the community. Taken together, these scenarios show the importance of adaptability and resilience of a community (Brand 1995, Karimah and Paramita 2020).

Sketching the domestic territory of the urban kampung: entanglement of passages

Entanglements between passages in a domestic territory

Depending on their needs, some dwellers potentially deploy more than one passage pattern. Each domestic territory of a particular household may therefore create multiple patterns of passages, which entangle with each other throughout the dwellers' domestic life, solidifying their domestic territory. Ingold (2007) explores the notion of entanglement in his discussion of the meshwork of lines as follows:

> For inhabitants, however, the environment does not consist of the surroundings of a bounded place but of a zone in which their several pathways are thoroughly entangled. In this zone of entanglement – this meshwork of interwoven lines – there are no insides or outsides, only openings and ways through. An ecology of life, in short, must be one of threads and traces, not of nodes and connectors. And its subject of inquiry must consist not of the relations between organisms and their external environments but of the relations along their severally enmeshed ways of life.
>
> (Ingold 2007: 103)

Instead of fixed boundary, domestic territory is shaped by the process of entangling passages in a living environment. The entanglement animates and weaves together inside and outside spaces, instead of differentiating them (Atmodiwirjo and Yatmo 2021). Simmel (1994) has advanced a similar take on entanglement in his discussion of the idea of a bridge. Different than a door that is a border that detaches and separates between the inside and the outside, it can be argued that a passage resembles Simmel's articulation of a bridge, in that it recognises the dispersal of entities, but still considers the entities as part of a single field connected by the paths traversing it.

The notion of entanglement also explains why the passages dwellers take between their dispersed living spaces are not necessarily the shortest ones. Dwellers may take a slightly longer path to a space, when going through such a path enables them to attend multiple needs at once. Such occurrences defy discussions of routes and movement in urban literature, which often aim to demonstrate the quickest path (Ballantyne and Smith 2011, Petrescu 2007). An example can be found in space syntax literature (Hillier 2015), driven by the search for optimisation and determination (Till 2013). By doing so, similar approaches tend to neglect those paths that convey the rich, often 'hidden gestures and "delinquent" routes' (Petrescu 2007: 95).

A similar contrast between optimised and 'delinquent' routes can be found in Ingold's (2007) description of the wayfarer experience. Ingold distinguishes between routes and trails: routes are destination-oriented, while trails create a mode of inhabitation as one wanders along them. The trails of passage between dispersed spaces enable dwellers to inhabit the neighbourhood, although it may not be the shortest nor most comfortable route. Instead of distance-driven, the selection of such passages may reflect Certeau's (2011) 'tour,' with its focus on movement and the lack of a totalising overview.

The domestic territories created by passages represent how each passage signifies a mode of inhabitation and a reality of experience. Such reality of experience can be seen in Petrescu's (2007) investigation of the route drawings by child psychiatrist, Fernard Deligny, which explores the autistic individual's experience along a walk. Drawing their movements reveals their discomforts due to sensitivity to magnetic fields around the area, which is shown by a pause and a concentrated movement along the way.

A similar experience of inhabitation is demonstrated in the kampung by the movements along passage territories enabling dwellers to better understand their living spaces. Residents who work, care for younger children, or cook regularly, tend to move more frequently around the neighbourhood; in turn, enhanced movement gives more chances to dispose waste, find refuge during flood, and to keep one's business open. One passage may influence the possibilities of other passages, creating a traversing constellation that illustrates the complex and unique exchanges between dwellers and their living environment.

Entanglements between passages across domestic territories

The entanglements between passages across territories of different households emerge when multiple dwellers share domestic roles in a single domestic environment, or when they use similar passages to connect to dispersed spaces. Multiplicity of roles can be seen in dwellers who connect to other dwellers for multiple needs, such as those who rely on their extended families for child-rearing and sanitation facilities. Such multiple roles potentially increase the frequency of movement through the territories, affirming that dispersed dwelling spaces of extended relatives, or neighbours, are a connected territory. Depending on the position of these dwelling spaces in the neighbourhood, the multiplicity of social roles may create a potential spill-over, transforming the spaces around the dwelling, and potentially also the path, as part of the same domestic territory.

An entanglement between passages across territories can also be seen when one passage can be used for multiple needs of dwellers from different households. Different residents may appropriate one passage to activate multiple spaces, which may be adjacent or en route to one another. For instance, as we have seen, some dwellers may dispose of their waste on the way to work, or on the way to the toilet. Various residents may take the same route to work or to the toilet, and thus also use the same waste disposal area. However, such entanglement depends on the timing and possibilities of such activities, which may vary. As discussed, it is thus all the more important to have a portfolio of options towards different spaces and resources at one's disposal, to be used depending on changing needs, or when services are disrupted.

Another scenario of entanglement occurs when dwellers' passages and dispersed spaces intersect, reflecting Ingold's (2007) discussion regarding the space of activities (nodes) and space of circulation (connectors). For example, some dwellers trespass other dwellers' spaces to access other points of the neighbourhood, such as a leisure or sanitation space, demonstrating how one's space of activities can be another one's space of circulation. Intersections also occur during collective appropriations, such as the neighbourhood path that is being used for playing and gathering together.

Entanglements of passages mirror the connection between different passages for different dwellers. Digital mapping of everyday stories in another urban kampung in Jakarta by Atmodiwirjo et al. (2019) demonstrates an example of such entanglements in the way residents occupy multiple spaces for leisure, such as playing or exercising collectively. The event of leisure does not happen only at a destination, but also en route and through momentary interactions (Adams and Marlor 2019). In Kampung Pulo, a resident recounted how during a stroll in the neighbourhood with her grandchildren she would often stop at a neighbour's or relative's house, picking them up to have a stroll together to the market or to other places; sometimes, she would just stop and have a chat at the neighbour's' before going on her way.

These scenarios of entanglements of passages across territories demonstrate a fleeting and contingent quality: passages only exist as long as there are social, spatial, and economic relations that generate possibilities of passage. The entanglement of passages reveals a type of domestic territory that is not limited to a particular spatial scale or spatial ownership. A passage can unfold between and across dwelling, neighbourhood, and city. The relations that enable the entanglement of different passages are often valued more than spatial ownership, creating a possibility of use open to multiple dwellers.

Conclusion

This chapter has sought to reconstruct an understanding of domestic territory as practiced in an urban kampung. The complexity of domestic territoriality matches with a context plagued by instability, due to political and environmental uncertainties. Throughout, I have employed the notion of passage territories, defining domestic territory as consisting of dispersed spaces used for domestic activities. This conceptualisation potentially expands the understanding of territory beyond a bounded expanse, thus contributing to the growing literature that recognises the complex and multi-layered nature of territory (Brighenti and Kärrholm 2020, Massey 2005, McCarthy 2005).

Domestic territories created by passages link together different actors and different dwellings through various scenarios of uses, which we have illustrated in the cases of child-rearing, performing economic activities, accessing infrastructure, and managing safety. Reallocation of space and resources enhances connections between spatial scales, linking the individual experience to the city process (Poot, De Vos, and Van Acker 2018). These linkages blur the dichotomies so often associated with domestic life, fostering the interplay between inside and outside, living and working, and public and private. Such interplay demonstrates how passage territories reject fixed classifications, identifying spaces dynamically based on the performative presence of dwellers. Domestic territory is no longer positioned as a bounded territory, but is instead distributed through multiple agents and networks.

Passages interweave and construct a dweller's domestic territory, which creates modes of inhabitation through the richness of experience and relations between these passages as an entangled mesh of lines. The frequency of movement enables dwellers to activate more spaces inside and outside of the neighbourhood, thus increasing passages and consolidating the entanglement. Spatial ownership becomes less important than the spatial system activated by passages. This illustrates how territory is constructed more from the ever-evolving inhabitation process than from pre-existing conditions.

The entanglements of passages across different domestic territories highlight the intersection between passages shared by dwellers in their domestic life. This intersection influences the intensity of collective appropriation of certain spaces in the neighbourhood, transforming its spatiality when more people are using space more frequently; when use and intensity wanes, this contributes to a transformation of relations and the conditions of agents. The intersection between passages and their dynamic influence reveals how domestic territories in urban kampungs are tightly positioned in relation to the neighbourhood and the surrounding city.

Passage territories thus contribute to the literature on how a sense of belonging can evolve in the context of tumultuous change and displacement (Briganti and Mezei 2012). The dispersed, performative, transgressive, and contingent character of passage-driven domestic territories mirrors the different ways in which one may belong, according to the political and environmental instability of kampung. A thorough analysis of domestic territory in informal settlements challenges the assumptions of territorial stigmatisation: in the context of the Global South, architectural and planning practices can be informed by this insight.

Acknowledgements

The research on which this study is based was funded by the Overseas Graduate Education Scholarship (*Beasiswa Pendidikan Pascasarjana-Luar Negeri*) granted by the Directorate General of Resource for Science, Technology, and Higher Education (DG-RSTHE) of the Ministry of Research, Technology and Higher Education of Indonesia from 2013 to 2016.

References

Adams, R. and Marlor, L. (2019) 'Breaking the Binary Oppositions of the Interior: A Momentary Permanence.' *Interiority* 2 (2), 113–128.

Atmodiwirjo, P., Johanes, M., and Yatmo, Y.A. (2019) 'Mapping Stories: Representing Urban Everyday Narratives and Operations.' *Urban Design International.* [online] Available from <https://scholar.ui.ac.id/en/publications/mapping-stories-representing-urban-everyday-narratives-and-operat> [1 April 2020]

Atmodiwirjo, P. and Yatmo, Y.A. (2021) 'Animated Interior.' *Interiority* 4 (2), 135–138.

Atmodiwirjo, P., Yatmo, Y.A., and Ujung, V. (2015) 'Outside Interior: Traversed Boundaries in a Jakarta Urban Neighbourhood.' *IDEA Journal* (Urban Interior).

Ballantyne, A. and Smith, C. (eds) (2011) *Architecture in the Space of Flows*. Abingdon, Oxon, England; New York, NY: Routledge.

Brand, S. (1995) *How Buildings Learn: What Happens After They're Built*, reprint edition. New York, NY: Penguin.

Briganti, C. and Mezei, K. (2012) 'Introduction,' in *The Domestic Space Reader*. Toronto; Buffalo: University of Toronto Press.

Brighenti, A.M. (2010) 'On Territorology: Towards a General Science of Territory.' *Theory, Culture & Society* 27 (1), 52–72.

Brighenti, A.M. and Kärrholm, M. (2020) *Animated Lands: Studies in Territoriology*, illustrated edition. Lincoln: University of Nebraska Press.

Brown, S.T. (2014) 'Kampala's Sanitary Regime: Whose Toilet Is It Anyway?' in *Infrastructural Lives: Urban Infrastructure in Context*, Graham, S. (ed.). Abingdon, Oxon; New York, NY: Routledge.

Certeau, M.D. (2011) *The Practice of Everyday Life*, 3rd edition. University of California Press.

Chatterjee, P. (2006) *The Politics of the Governed: Reflections on Popular Politics in Most of the World*.

Deluchi, C. (2018) 'Urban Interiority and the Spatial Process of Securitisation in Medellin: A Speculation on the Architectures of Reassurance.' *Interiority* 1 (1), 37–48.

Desai, R., McFarlane, C., and Graham, S. (2015) 'The Politics of Open Defecation: Informality, Body, and Infrastructure in Mumbai.' *Antipode* 47 (1), 98–120.

Dovey, K., Cook, B., and Achmadi, A. (2019) 'Contested Riverscapes in Jakarta: Flooding, Forced Eviction and Urban Image.' *Space & Polity* 23 (3), 265–282.

Dovey, K. and Polakit, K. (2012) 'Urban Slippage: Smooth and Striated Streetscapes in Bangkok,' in *Loose Space: Possibility and Diversity in Urban Life*, 1st edition. Franck, K. and Stevens, Q. (eds). London; New York: Routledge.

Ellisa, E. (2016) 'Coping with Crowding in High-Density Kampung Housing of Jakarta.' *Archnet-IJAR* 10 (1), 195–212.

Hamanongan, J. (2015) 'WC Umum Digusur, 400 Warga Kampung Pulo Sulit Buang Hajat.' [online] Available from <https://wartakota.tribunnews.com/2015/09/25/wc-umum-digusur-400-warga-kampung-pulo-sulit-buang-hajat> [1 June 2021]

Hawken, S. and Sunindijo, R.Y. (2018) 'City of Kampung: Risk and Resilience in the Urban Communities of Surabaya, Indonesia.' *International Journal of Building Pathology and Adaptation* 36 (5), 543–568.

Hillier, B. (2015) *Space is the Machine: A Configurational Theory of Architecture*. CreateSpace Independent Publishing Platform.

Ingold, T. (2007) *Lines: A Brief History*1st edition. London; New York: Routledge.

Iossifova, D. (2015) 'Everyday Practices of Sanitation under Uneven Urban Development in Contemporary Shanghai.' *Environment and Urbanization* 27 (2), 541–554.

Jakarta Post, The (2016) 'Dozens of Kampung Pulo Evictees at Risk of Losing New Homes.' [online] Available from <http://www.thejakartapost.com/news/2016/04/12/dozens-of-kampung-pulo-evictees-at-risk-of-losing-new-homes.html> [21 April 2017]

Jakarta Post, The (2015) 'Violent Eviction of Poor in Kampung Pulo.' [online] Available from <http://www.thejakartapost.com/news/2015/08/20/violent-eviction-poor-kampung-pulo.html> [1 April 2018]

Jones, P. (2017) 'Housing Resilience and the Informal City.' *Journal of Regional and City Planning* 28 (2), 129–139.

Karimah, A. and Paramita, K.D. (2020) 'Investigating the Domestic Layers Adaptation During Pandemic.' *Interiority* 3 (2), 185–200.

Kompas (2014) 'Sudah Lelah Mengungsi dari Banjir, tapi Belum Ada Solusi Segera…' [online] 7 February. Available from <https://megapolitan.kompas.com/read/xml/2014/02/07/0813181/Sudah.Lelah.Mengungsi.dari.Banjir.tapi.Belum.Ada.Solusi.Segera.> [31 May 2021]

Kusno, A. (2020) 'Middling Urbanism: The Megacity and the Kampung.' *Urban Geography* 41 (7), 954–970.

Kusno, A. (2015) 'Power and Time Turning: The Capital, the State and the Kampung in Jakarta.' *International Journal of Urban Sciences* 19 (1), 53–63.

Marschiavelli, M., Lye C., Pramono Hadi, M., McCall, Michael K. and Kingma, Nanette C. (2013) 'A Community-based Vulnerability Assessment of Floods in Urban Areas of Kampung Melayu, Jakarta.' *The Indonesian Journal of Geography* 40 (2)

Martinez, R. and Masron, I.N. (2020) 'Jakarta: A City of Cities.' *Cities (London, England)* 106, 102868

Massey, D.B. (2005) *For Space*, 1st edition. London; Thousand Oaks, Calif: SAGE Publications Ltd.

McCarthy, C. (2005) 'Toward a Definition of Interiority.' *Space and Culture* 8 (2), 112–125.

McFarlane, C. (2010) 'Infrastructure, Interruption, and Inequality: Urban Life in the Global South,' in *Disrupted Cities: When Infrastructure Fails*. Routledge.

Meilasari-Sugiana, A., Sari, D.A.P., and Anggraini, R. (2018) 'Housing and Resettlement of Jakarta's Urban Poor: Case Study of Kampung Pulo's Slum Revitalisation in Jakarta, Indonesia.' *Human Geographies* 12 (2), 191–208.

Newberry, J. (2008) 'Double Spaced: Abstract Labour in Urban Kampung'. *Anthropologica* 50 (2), 241–253.

Paramita, K.D. and Schneider, T. (2018) 'Passage Territories: Reframing Living Spaces in Contested Contexts.' *Interiority* 1 (2), 113–129.

Petrescu, D. (2007) 'The Indeterminate Mapping of the Common.' *Field Journal* 1 (1).

Poot, T., De Vos, E., and Van Acker, M. (2018) 'Thinking beyond Dualities in Public Space: The Unfolding of Urban Interiority as a Set of Interdisciplinary Lenses.' *Interiors: Design, Architecture, Culture* 9 (3), 324–345.

Putri, P.W. (2019) 'Sanitizing Jakarta: Decolonizing Planning and Kampung Imaginary.' *Planning Perspectives* 34 (5), 805–825.

Putri, P.W. and Moulaert, F. (2017) 'Spatial Practices and the Institutionalization of Water Sanitation Services in Southern Metropolises: The Case of Jakarta and Its Kampung Kojan.' *International Journal of Urban and Regional Research* 41 (6), 926–945.

Roy, A. (2011) 'Slumdog Cities: Rethinking Subaltern Urbanism.' *International Journal of Urban and Regional Research* 35 (2), 223–238.

Sack, R.D. (1983) 'Human Territoriality: A Theory.' *Annals of the Association of American Geographers* 73 (1), 55–74.

Sennett, R. (2006) *The Open City* [online] available from <http://urbanage.lsecities.net/essays/the-open-city> [26 May 2021]

Simmel, G. (1994) 'Bridge and Door.' *Theory, Culture & Society* 11 (1), 5–10.

Simone, A. and Rao, V. (2012) 'Securing the Majority: Living through Uncertainty in Jakarta.' *International Journal of Urban and Regional Research* 36 (2), 315–335.

Sumardi, S. (2015) Personal interview.

Thrift, N. (2005) 'But Malice Aforethought: Cities and the Natural History of Hatred.' *Transactions of the Institute of British Geographers* 30 (2), 133–150.

Till, J. (2013) 'The Broken Middle: The Space of the London Riots.' *Cities* 34, 71–74.

Tilley, L., Elias, J., and Rethel, L. (2019) 'Urban Evictions, Public Housing and the Gendered Rationalisation of Kampung Life in Jakarta.' *Asia Pacific Viewpoint* 60 (1), 80–93.

Tunas, D. (2008) *The Spatial Economy in the Urban Informal Settlement*. Netherlands: International Forum on Urbanism.

UN Habitat (2003) *The Challenge of Slums - Global Report on Human Settlements* [online] Available from <https://unhabitat.org/the-challenge-of-slums-global-report-on-human-settlements-2003> [1 June 2021]

Vollmer, D. and Grêt-Regamey, A. (2013) 'Rivers as Municipal Infrastructure: Demand for Environmental Services in Informal Settlements along an Indonesian River.' *Global Environmental Change* 23 (6), 1542–1555.

Widyaningsih, A. and Van den Broeck, P. (2021) 'Social Innovation in Times of Flood and Eviction Crisis: The Making and Unmaking of Homes in the Ciliwung Riverbank, Jakarta.' *Singapore Journal of Tropical Geography* 42 (2), 325–345.

Wilson, I. (2015) 'The Politics of Flood Alleviation in Jakarta.' [online] Available from <https://www.thejakartapost.com/news/2015/09/05/the-politics-flood-alleviation-jakarta.html> [31 May 2021]

Yatmo, Y. and Atmodiwirjo, P. (2018) 'Collective Spatial Strategies in Urban Kampung Communal Toilet.' *Asian Journal of Environment-Behaviour Studies* 3.

Yatmo, Y.A. and Atmodiwirjo, P. (2013) 'Spatial Strategies for Domestic Service Activities in Urban Kampung Houses.' *International Journal of Technology* 4 (1), 24–33.

Yuliastuti, N. and Sukmawati, A.M. (2020) 'Creative Urban Kampung Based on Local Culture, a Case of Kampung Bustaman Semarang.' *Journal of Architecture and Urbanism* 44 (2).

Chapter 11

Dodging rocks and baseball bats

Stories of territory, tourism and trespassing in Detroit neighborhoods

Paul Draus and Juliette Roddy

Introduction: Get Out of the Car (Paul)

When I was in graduate school, we were assigned a slender book to read, called *Maps Are Territories: Science is an Atlas*, by David Turnbull (1989). It was towards the latter part of our survey class on sociological theory, taught by the late Peter Whalley, and the book was a bit of an odd selection, after Weber, Durkheim, Marx and some of the other classical theorists. I still have the book, and it made a lasting impression on me, because it emphasized the extent to which knowledge is embedded in the experience of places, and how theories, like maps, seek to abstract that knowledge upward and place it in some kind of objective plan, outside of territory, as it were. Turnbull made a particular point of contrasting Western or so-called scientific maps and theories with what we might today call the indigenous way of knowing:

> Aboriginal maps can only be properly read or understood by the initiated, since some of the information they contain is secret. This secrecy concerns the ways in which the map is linked to the whole body of knowledge that constitutes Aboriginal culture. For Aborigines, the acquisition of the knowledge is a slow ritualized process of becoming initiated in the power-knowledge network, essentially a process open only to those who have passed through the earlier stages. By contrast, the Western knowledge system has the appearance of being open to all, in that nothing is secret. Hence all the objects on the map are located with respect to an absolute co-ordinate system supposedly outside the limits of our culture.
>
> (Turnbull 1989, p 42)

My own work as health care worker at that time had brought me into the daily lives of tuberculosis patients living in different neighborhoods in the city of Chicago, and the book spoke to my own experience in navigating the complex social terrain, and all the ground-level particularities that maps did not quite convey. In response to Turnbull's book, I wrote an essay entitled 'Get Out of the Car' that emphasized the importance of experiencing the social landscape

DOI: 10.4324/9781003196365-11

directly, through encounter and relationship. The idea of indigeneity, applied to the contemporary city, positioned long-term residents of neighborhoods as authorities on their environments by virtue of their relationship with the territory and its human and non-human habitants.

There was one man, named Cornelius, who I saw almost every day in the West Side neighborhood where he lived and where I visited for work. I had learned a good deal from him about daily life there, which was fundamentally different from my own social reality, even though my apartment was probably only about a mile from where he stayed. There was a border that I crossed, and my presence on the other side of that border was only provisional, while he seemed as rooted there as the buildings and trees, in spite of his constant housing insecurity. I gave him a small disposable camera and he took photographs, which we then discussed. I audio-recorded the conversations and transcribed them, and these became the basis for a presentation at a sociology conference taking place at a big hotel on Michigan Avenue in downtown Chicago. The experience of doing the presentation became another lived lesson in territoriality.

I had brought Cornelius, who everyone on the street called Neal, and another neighborhood resident, who went by the name of Concho, with me to the hotel for the presentation. They had both dressed up for the occasion, and Concho even put on a tie, but these were two middle-aged African American men, visibly weathered by life, and the aura of the Westside neighborhood surrounded them. We were stopped by security guards – also African American men – in the lobby of the hotel, who wanted to know where we were going – or more precisely, where Neal and Concho were going. As defined by Sack (1983), territoriality consists of the attempt to 'affect, influence, or control actions and interactions (of people, things, and relationships) by asserting and attempting to enforce control over a geographic area' (p. 55). Here we saw a very direct illustration of this principle: territory involves who belongs, and who doesn't, and who has the power to exclude someone else from a particular space.

But these lines were not fixed. I spoke up and explained that these two men were with me, and we were attending a sociology conference upstairs at the hotel. As a young white man, in my late 20s at the time, I apparently had more sway than Neal and Concho, who were decades my senior. The security guards let us through, but the message was effectively conveyed to Neal and Concho that they were no longer on the West Side, and they didn't belong in this downtown space. Concho later gave an impassioned plea to the audience that attended our session, which was on the topic of 'Stigmatized Places,' imploring them to actually go into communities and talk to people. My memories are a little vague, but I recall a rather charged atmosphere in the room, as the presence of these two men from the neighborhood immediately altered the polarity of the discussion, placing all of us, as sociologists, in the role of compromised tourists. It was one of my proudest moments as a young aspiring urban scholar, but it was not comfortable for Neal or Concho, the audience, or me.

I later wrote an article (Draus and Howard 1999) in which I used Neal's photos and words to document the characteristics of the local landscape as he understood it. Since that time, I have carried a sense of responsibility towards any community that I wish to describe or analyze, believing that I need to encounter the land and the people who lived on it, to enter into some kind of direct relationship, in order to write about them. However, I also feel a constant sense of uneasiness about entering and representing communities, which has only been sharpened by my experiences doing research in and around Detroit.

I arrived in Detroit in the fall of 2005, and I began doing collaborative research with my colleague, Dr. Juliette Roddy, shortly thereafter. My daily rounds with tuberculosis patients in multiple Chicago neighborhoods had been invaluable to me as a graduate student in sociology trying to understand the city. Simply by being in the neighborhoods, observing and interacting with residents, I had learned many lessons that books and articles couldn't teach. When I first came to Detroit it therefore made sense to me to try to do the same thing, and I looked for opportunities to do so. Julie, who at that time was more comfortable with numbers than people (in her words), was open to these types of excursions. These scenes set the stage for our ruminations on the nature of territory, tourism and responsibility in urban field research.

What am I doing here? (Julie)

In August of 2004 I was working at a methadone clinic as a post-doctoral fellow with the Great Lakes Regional Node of the National Institutes on Drug Abuse's Clinical Trial Network. I had spent 1994–2002 in Wayne State's Ph.D. program in Economics. When I graduated in 2002, I had no clinical training. My fields were Health Economics and Urban Economics. My dissertation was written on rational addiction to cigarettes and I wanted to study addiction to other drugs. Heroin seemed like a logical place to start in Detroit. The logic wasn't fully embraced by everyone. I had been at the clinic since October of 2002 and was given very little access to the population. Most of my encounters happened in the parking lot as I was entering or exiting the building.

On this day in August, my oldest daughter had called my cell phone. She needed her health forms in order to participate in a pre-season athletic practice at her school. She was requesting that I fax them to the school. If you knew my oldest daughter, as those who are close to me do know her, you would know that I was compelled to respond immediately. I headed to the parking lot, to my car, and to the health forms that were somewhere in the trunk end of my SUV.

The clinic faced Jefferson Avenue, a fairly famous street in Detroit because it runs all along the Detroit River and connects the eastern and western suburbs to the downtown area. The parking lot of the clinic contained an education of its own. It was fenced off with a sliding gate that allowed entrance and exit for cars. Entry was done freely. A sensor detected when a car arrived and the gate slid open, slowly, painfully and loudly. Exit from the parking lot was guarded with a code, a four-digit number that had to be typed into a box resembling a telephone key pad in order to initiate the slow, steady, noisy retreat of the same gated entryway. I always thought that it was a bit backward, or telling, that a code was required to leave but not to enter. It reminded me of that Eagles song, *Hotel California*: 'You can check in anytime you like, but you can never leave.'

I typically arrived for work early in the morning, after dropping the kids off at school. There would only be a few straggling individuals in the parking lot when I arrived. No researchers, clinicians or university employees would linger in the parking lot, only the clinic clients. Entry into the building, a beautiful brick three-story structure with surprising architectural enhancements both inside and out, required a magnetized badge. If I forgot my badge, I rode the elevator to the clinic floor with heroin addicts that were feeling the painful edge of withdrawal creeping up on them. Some of the clients didn't smell very good. One memorable morning I forgot my badge and I rode the elevator with a woman whose arm was rotting away. The smell of that wound was so bad in the tightly enclosed elevator that I fought the urge to wretch for the entire elevator ride. I was embarrassed about my reaction and I never forgot my badge again.

The parking lot at any time other than early morning was a bustling enclosed place. When I would leave work in the early afternoons, I would be immediately surrounded as I exited the building. People would offer to carry my briefcase, ask me for money, or try to engage in any way possible. It reminded me of when I went to Mexico and children would follow Americans down the streets, impeding the pathway, almost demanding a donation. This was similar. The parking lot people wanted something from me and they appeared desperate, every day. It was frightening and foreign to me. I feel so much differently today, but this was 2004 and I was much younger and much less experienced.

My daughter's request and the location of the health forms dominated my focus. I had lectured myself about one hundred times in my head to be careful in the parking lot. It is so easy to forget that it is a dangerous place filled with reckless people. At this point in my life I was so used to being the person 'in the room' with the lowest amount of resources. My children attended a very expensive private school in Bloomfield Hills (on scholarship). The other Ph.D.s that I worked with at the clinic were Harvard and Yale trained. The clinic staff were compensated at a higher rate than my postdoctoral fellowship allowed. In my life, at this time, it seemed as if everyone had more money and assets than I did. If I sit down and purposefully contemplate it, I know that the clients milling about in the parking lot would view me as wealthy. But this thought didn't come to me naturally. I was focused and intent on solving the issue of the missing forms. I began to dig in the back of my SUV. I let down my guard and I search for about 3 minutes, digging, focussed.

Someone noticed me. Someone threw three separate firecrackers in my direction. I am not sure where they landed but it felt as if they were very, very close to me. There is no doubt that they were intended to scare me. And it worked. The noise was similar to gunshots (this was Detroit) and it scared the piss out of me, literally. Yes, I mean literally.

My memory post urination is fuzzy. I know I was upset. I closed the car; I don't even know if I locked it. I headed across the lot to back inside the clinic. I would have had to use my badge to enter. I remember arriving in my office on the second floor feeling confident that no one within the clinic had seen me yet but I knew that the parking lot crew had been laughing when I bee-lined for the building. I'm pretty sure they knew how I had reacted.

It's still painful to remember lining my desk chair with a paper towel and hoping that my pants would dry before I had to re-enter the parking lot in order to head home. I didn't go home early. I just sat at my desk and tried to work. I tried to work, but the dominant thought in my mind was this: 'What the fuck am I doing here?'

At that moment, I probably could not have imagined that I would soon be venturing outside of the office facility, into the very communities that seemed so imposing to me then. When Paul and I decided to work together, it was really just a matter of convenience. We were hired at the same time, and we were introduced by our Dean as scholars who did research on drugs. I had been approached by the Detroit Health Department about doing some collaborative research, and I didn't think I could handle it all by myself. I asked Paul if he might want to team up, and to my surprise he immediately said 'yes.'

Riding along (Paul)

It was May 6, 2008. Julie and I were riding in separate patrol cars with the Wayne County Sheriff's Police. We were in the first phase of a study of a court-supervised program for former street sex workers, and we were trying to learn about the program from those most closely involved with it (Roddy et al., 2013). We were in separate cars, but communicating with each other by phone from our respective back seats. 'I'm a firm believer in this program,' said one of the male officers, who I will call Glen, 'because it's such a productive program. Most of the time in jail system there's no treatment. Here you get to see that transformation.'Their job that night was to conduct a sweep, which meant they were looking for women who had 'absconded,' or left the program before completion, without permission of the supervising judge. They had a list of names, photographs, and places that the women were known to frequent. It was thus a literal lesson in territories: the county-wide jurisdiction of the police laid over the much more localized map of neighborhood streets, strolls, corners and hotels. One turf trumping another. Not being from the Detroit area, and having little familiarity with the structure or function of county drug courts, both geographies were new to me.

The other officer in the car, who I will call Gail, spotted a woman walking along the street alone, who she thought she recognized. 'Is that Krystal? Isn't she in the program?' she asked. Although it looked dark and desolate to me, I soon learned that John R was a busy avenue for street sex workers, located close to the Detroit suburban border (Draus, Roddy and Asabigi 2015).

On the radio they called the female officer who was assigned the point person on the program, and they were told that the woman on the street had a warrant out for her arrest. We wheeled the car around to pick her up. She was on the corner wearing jeans, a shoulder-less top, and Timberland boots. I saw Glen take a crack pipe from her and smash it on the ground. The pipe was crudely fashioned from a plastic whiskey bottle. I got to the corner after his boot broke it to bits, but was able to look at the remnants while he explained how they made it, by burning a hole in the bottle, using the steel wool from the hardware store as a screen.

Krystal did not seem particularly surprised or angry to be cuffed and placed into the patrol car alongside an unidentified white male professor. As we continued down John R Street, they spotted another woman, and K said, 'she's working,' and we turned around again and talked to her. They found out that she had been (or was) part of a different program, and decided to leave her there on the street.

Gail asked Krystal, as she sat in the back seat, 'Where you been staying?'

'Here and there,' she replied.

We went to drop her at the Wayne County Jail, in the nearby city of Hamtramck. There I almost got locked up myself while trying to use the men's room; I walked out and found myself among a crowd of other men who were being handed baloney sandwiches with mustard. I was dressed in loose-fitting street clothes, and I guess I blended in with the crowd. Realizing my predicament, I approached the officer with the sandwiches, getting ready to explain that I really didn't belong with that group, that I was a sociology professor doing a ride-along with Sheriff's Police, which seemed like a really absurd escape plan. Luckily, Officer Glen came by and saved me the trouble, though not without getting a laugh out of it. We then found out that K did not have any county warrants, she only had Detroit warrants, so they couldn't hold her there. She was outside their jurisdiction. She and I, for that moment, both seemed to have slipped out of the jail's grasp.

But the night wasn't over. Assuming that she was in the program and had absconded, the main goal of the officers was to have her held somewhere until Monday, when she could go before the judge. This was around 8 p.m. By 8:30, they had pulled her out of the jail and put her back in the car and we were all soon headed back into Detroit. The plan was to drop her at the Northwest Precinct of the Detroit Police Department. In the car, K was laughing and joking with the officers. Gail had told me earlier that 'the girl was slow,' but I wasn't so sure. 'I'd rather go to a jail than a precinct,' she said, indicating her experience with both county facilities and local lock-ups. I would soon see exactly what she meant.

> 'What happened?' asked Gail.
> 'I left the treatment center; I was almost a year clean.'
> 'When was the last time you used?'
> 'This morning.' Crack cocaine.
> 'What you think you doin' to that baby?' Gail asked. Krystal was pregnant.
> 'Burnin' brain cells,' she said.
> 'You know, you're takin' a chance catchin' AIDS, STDs – you don't want that, do you? You're gonna have a crack baby – that baby's gonna be cryin' and screamin.'

This conversation was still unfolding as we pulled up to the NW precinct at Plymouth and Warwick. It should have been a simple drop off, but we ended up spending another 30–40 minutes in the precinct jail area, waiting to get her processed so we could leave her there. They had a whole group of young black men there to be processed ahead of us, and the booking officers weren't giving us any special treatment. They made Glen fill out the paperwork that they required, and he asked, at one point, 'How long is it going to be? Five minutes or five hours?'

The officer's deadpan response, according to Glen, was, 'You pick.'

This statement summarized the situation at Detroit Police Department local precinct with its casual, bureaucratic brutality. We finally just left her there in a chair – meanwhile, she had a chronic cough; she said she had bronchitis and 'needed an inhaler bad,' and she was freezing in the flimsy top, there in the unheated jail area. There was another woman there who had been locked up for the night for fighting ('to calm me down she said). Krystal asked, 'Anybody else in there? The woman said, 'no.' Krystal said, 'I'll be in there in a minute.'

When asked if she had any tattoos or evident scars, K said 'I have some scars on my shoulders from where my momma used to beat me. No tattoos.'

Through all of this, she did not complain; instead she laughed easily at the officers' joking comments. I seriously considered giving her my outer shirt to help keep her warm; after she asked about a blanket. I asked Glen if they would give her something, and he said, 'Yeah, they'll give her something.' As we rode away in the squad I regretted not giving her the shirt. I doubted that she would get anything at all from the cops at the station. This regret stuck with me long past that night – not that I wanted to be some deluded White Knight, but that in that moment if I could have offered something to take the edge off someone else's suffering, I should have done it. But I didn't.

What are the lessons of this episode? I learned something important while riding along in the back seat of that car. What was my role there? What was my responsibility? Julie and I both saw things that shocked us, but which were treated as perfectly normal and natural by all else concerned. Krystal never questioned getting into the police car, or being left at the jail. The officers, if anything, saw what they were doing as a form of service or protection, which in a relative sense it may have been. This was also important to understand: the places, relationships, and workings of power across and within them. This was part of the territory.

Dodging rocks (Julie)

Another day, another Detroit neighborhood. Paul and I had begun an early career habit of walking through the Detroit neighborhoods to get to know the city and its people. It was summer 2009. On this day, we had decided to explore a declining neighborhood where we heard an urban farm was going to plant its roots. The neighborhood, locally known as Poletown, had a history as a thriving Polish community, when General Motors constructed a massive auto manufacturing plant that cut through the neighborhood and initiated its decline. The history, the urban farm potential, and its current reputation as a rough part of the East Side drew us in. Detroit is often roughly divided into three or four main areas: Downtown, which is dominated by business and entertainment interests; Southwest Detroit, which includes a concentration of Mexican and other Latin American population, and the East and West Sides, which are both predominantly Black but have somewhat different histories and reputations. Generally speaking, the East Side was older, had lost more buildings and population over the years, and was often stereotypically viewed even by other Detroiters as being wilder or more dangerous than other parts of the city.

We parked at the north end of the main street that ran through the neighborhood, an abandoned commercial corridor, and began a stroll down the street. This is usually how we met residents from the neighborhoods that we explored and gathered stories. On this street there were a number of abandoned structures in various stages of disarray. We would stop and examine spaces and talk about what we were missing. I remember seeing trees growing in the doorways (with no door present) of commercial properties and a long conversation about the re-wilding of previously populated and urbanized space. We examined weeds and discussed how hearty and resilient they are. And we spoke about the similar resilience of the substance-using populations that we studied. We spoke about their participation in the 're-wilding' of urban spaces that had once been tamed and law abiding.

We came upon a particular building with gaping open windows and an alley between it and the next building. The space in the alley and the decaying building caught our attention and I can no longer remember why, but we strayed from the sidewalk and began to walk into the alley and open space. The open space was clearly once a part of the property, but now seemed more public, a courtyard whose boundary to the street had eroded. Paul was ahead of me, which was not typical, and I was following about twelve feet behind. I felt something drop just to the side of me but I ignored it. Then I felt two more drops, each one heavier. 'Hey Draus, c'mon. Turn around. Someone is throwing rocks at us.' Paul was not quick to acknowledge what I said, but a second or so later, he turned around and caught up with me back on the sidewalk. 'Really?' he said. 'Maybe we are trespassing?'

We continued down the street, wondering aloud again, but this time about all that we may *not* be seeing. Perhaps the neighborhood was more populated than we originally thought. We never saw anyone, and there was no one else on the street to ask. It was not something we had experienced before, and it never happened again. It remained a mystery. We speculated that we might have disturbed people who were involved in illegal activity, but we had no evidence for this. Precisely because it was an unexplained anomaly, it never made it into our formal research. But it became embedded in our memories as a reminder of the contested nature of urban territory, even or perhaps especially that which appeared to be 'empty.' The one thing of which we were fairly certain was that the rocks were directed at us.

Around this time, we had several funded projects underway, each in various stages and each with some level of overlap. It seemed as if every exploration we began led to another idea or question that could be crafted into a unique research opportunity with community partners. During 2008 and 2009, we investigated and evaluated a public health program in Detroit that promoted recovery and reintegration of street sex workers. This involved riding along with police through Detroit's streets and interviewing sex workers about their routines, as described above by Paul. Geography and neighborhoods became a theme and that inquiry took on a life of its own. Detroit had several neighborhoods that were on the cusp of change.

One neighborhood, on the West Side, had a large non-profit in the center of it. The non-profit was intent on having a positive change on the neighborhood with specific programming for early childhood through senior living. We proposed a baseline study for the neighborhood to gather social and behavioral variables on the residents of the neighborhood *now*, before the slate of programming took hold. This would allow the nonprofit to understand the impact of their work. A second neighborhood, in Southwest Detroit, was in the process of a de-populating. A major corporation had planned for a phased buy-out of the residents, offering a minimum price or market value to purchase the homes. Most residents took the offer and left; however, there were several that decided to stay and see how the de-population affected the quality of life. We proposed a study that consisted of interviewing those who planned to leave and those who planned to stay. How did they expect their quality of life to change?

Finally, there was the aforementioned Poletown neighborhood, which was actually the first area that we sought to study in this way. Historically, it was densely inhabited by Polish and other European immigrant groups, but the population at the time of our research was majority African American, or Black. The oldest Black community in the city, known as Black Bottom, had been located just to the south of Poletown, but was demolished in the age of so-called 'urban renewal.' The community that remained in between these two demolished 'ghost' neighborhoods was fragmented and historically traumatized but also full of relationships and memories (see Draus, Roddy and McDuffie 2013, 2018; Draus et al. 2019). Again, we focused on establishing a baseline of social and economic life in the neighborhood prior to the anticipated arrival of the large urban farm. We were interviewing both residents and businesses in the area to understand the life of the neighborhood today. I was leading the business interviews. There were limited for-profit businesses still in operation in the neighborhood, so I stretched a bit and included storefront churches and schools in my recruitment.

We would usually secure the interviews with both businesses and residents by walking through the neighborhood on wonderful Michigan summer days. We could stop by and talk to people who began to grow used to us roaming their neighborhood. Both Paul and I look white. Paul identifies as Polish and German American and I am half Ojibwe and half Irish. We stuck out in the neighborhood, as few of the remaining residents were white. And we walked around observing and curious, each visit it seemed we saw something new and we likely resembled tourists some days. On some days, I went to the neighborhood on my own, especially when I was trying to secure a specific business interview.

There was one small service-oriented business that was prominent in the neighborhood that I hadn't even stopped by yet.[1] To be honest, I was a little intimidated. I was unsure whether they would appreciate my presence and purpose in their space. I was alone on this warm August day, and it was a younger crowd of African American men and women in the business. When I walked in, I was not greeted warmly. There were two young women who looked as if they worked there, though I didn't even get far enough to verify that. I told them that I was interviewing businesses owners in the area and asked if I could speak to the owner. In guarded language that was not rude, but was also not friendly, they told me that the owner was not present. I handed them my University business card with my cell phone number on the back and asked them to pass it along to the owner and have him call me. As I turned to leave the shop, one of the young women muttered that the owner was likely down the street at a mysterious building that I had passed by many times. In a challenging tone she said "You can ***try*** to catch him there." I was intrigued.

My interest was elevated and my mind was racing because I had been hit with the overwhelming smell of marijuana when I walked in. There was no smoke in the business so I was pretty certain that there was a garden nearby. Medical marijuana had become legal in Michigan in 2008 and we had another funded project that interviewed users in order to determine racial and spatial differences among users. We were in the beginning stages of recruitment and making progress with urban African Americans – a population I initially thought might be reluctant to talk to me about their marijuana use. On this August day I was very excited, no longer thinking about a business interview, but imagining an informative

1 For purposes of protecting confidentiality, we do not identify what type of business this was.

marijuana interview. Maybe the person would even talk to me about the growing operation that I suspected was in their place of business.

I walked down to the mysterious building. The windows were barred and the face of the building was painted black. There were cars out front and I knew there were people inside. I knocked and knocked and knocked. Finally, someone came to the door. I explained that I was doing research in the area and that I had just come from the business down the street, directed to this spot by the women in the business. After some shuttling of information between myself, the person at the door, and some others inside, I was eventually invited in. There were seven African American males inside and they were friendly but slightly cautious. It was awkward, but I brought up the marijuana research. To my absolute delight, every one of the young men agreed to an interview appointment the next day at the half-way house. Before I knew it, I had booked seven interviews for the marijuana research. I didn't secure the business interview or even find out which of the young men might own that business (if any of them). I think that I just forgot or maybe I had planned on bringing it up during the marijuana interviews. I can't remember. The marijuana research had an urgency, due to the law just passing and maybe due to the risk involved, that the neighborhood research didn't have. In any case, I left the neighborhood feeling lifted. My mind was mulling over how integrated my research projects were and as an economist I naturally valued the efficiency of the integration. I couldn't wait for the interviews the next day.

The guys showed up on time and in sequence. They gave me information freely. Although the question was not a part of the instrument, I asked each one of my seven new participants about local grow operations. The fifth and seventh interviewee told me about a large grow located in a building in the neighborhood. I asked both of these participants to allow me to tour the grow. Neither committed right away, but both gave me their phone number and promised that they would consider taking me through the grow.

My recollection is that I called each one of them several times before they agreed to take me through the grow. I might be imagining or misremembering how many times I called. I always feel like a pest calling research participants and this time I was clearly asking for a favor that went beyond the research. I was just really interested in how these gardens could exist in spaces that were completely hidden and secretive. I had toured other gardens in people's basements and garages, some even outside and on roofs, but I had not toured a large grow in a commercial space and I imagined that this might be one.

I drove down to the neighborhood around midday, parking in front of a storefront church and walking to my destination. The tour of the facility was everything that I had hoped it would be. It was a commercial space. There was a chain link fence in front of the building and we entered through a side door. There were three full floors of growing space. There were grow lights that were glowing on the second floor and some weed drying on the third floor. Pots of plants were elevated on milk carts. For the life of me, I cannot remember the watering system or set up. I don't remember any windows. The smell, as always, was overwhelming. I only spent about fifteen minutes inside, but it was a fascinating fifteen minutes.

I was so happy with my work and the overlap in research projects. And then came trouble.

Late the next day, I learned that the grow had been busted. Wayne County Sherriff's police raided the place and, on the news, reported that over $2 million in marijuana was seized. Mayor David Bing suggested that people from the neighborhood were likely not the ones to set up the grow, as it was a very sophisticated operation. The electric utility had discovered that a large amount of power was being pirated from the grid. Reports in the media suggested that the raid was the result of a 'tip' and that surveillance that had begun three days prior to the bust. If that was the case, the surveilling police might have witnessed my visit. Of course, I began to think about what I would do if I was present during a bust. Would I wind up in jail? That was the extent of the risk that I contemplated upon hearing the news about the bust. That thought was bad enough. At this point, I had been inside of Detroit jails to interview research participants and it was not a place that I wanted to spend any time.

Maybe a week or two after the grow had been busted, I showed up back in the neighborhood. I had an interview scheduled with a business owner there. My mind was on the baseline research and why a business owner would stay in this depopulated neighborhood. I hadn't completely forgotten about the marijuana grow, but it certainly wasn't on the forefront of my mind. I parked my car at the storefront church and began to walk to the place of business. I was early. I am always early. I was walking down the street when I saw two of the men that I had done marijuana interviews with. They were walking toward me but it didn't seem like it was with any intent. However, once we got closer, it was clear that they knew who I was and these two were not happy to see me.

I can no longer remember the exact words that were said, but I remember that it caught me completely by surprise. They called me 'bitch' and let me know that I was at risk being in the neighborhood. Although they were not the two that had led me through the grow operation, it was clear that they thought I had something to do with the bust. They told me to leave.

I remember feeling shaken, scared and hurt. I turned immediately to head toward my car. As I turned to walk away, one of them said something to the effect that I had better destroy their interviews too. I remember turning around and saying "All seven?" It was a ridiculous reaction, but the loss of all seven interviews was disappointing and I was wondering if the body governing research at the University would agree that two participants could insist that I destroy all seven interviews. I don't recall how they responded to my question, but I remember the two men making it clear that they didn't want to see me in the neighborhood again. Ever.

I drove home, now lamenting the integration and overlap of my research projects, irritated by the loss suffered in both of them. I made a quick note to self: call the business owner and apologize for not showing up for our interview, begin writing up the adverse event for the Institutional Review Board, and be more careful next time.

Talking Back to Baseball Bats (Paul)

In October 2013, I was back in the same neighborhood with Anthony, my research assistant. Anthony was a graduate student of sociology at another university, who Julie and I met while working on a project that focused on the lives of returning citizens. Anthony was older than I was, a lifelong Detroiter who had spent his share of time on the streets, and he had a good way of relating to people we met in the community. One day we decided to try to connect with a particular man, named Tyrone, who had taken an oppositional stance in relation to the urban farming project. I wanted to learn more about his perspective, but we did not know exactly how to find him.

My years as a health care worker had taught me that the streets could be more effective than Google at finding people, especially in a neighborhood where everyone knew each other going back years or even generations. From a previous interview, we were able to find out the approximate block where he lived. On that block we saw a man sitting on the porch, and I said hello from the other side of the street. He acknowledged me and seemed friendly, so I walked across the street and asked if he knew where we might find Tyrone. He asked us if we had Tyrone's phone number, and if so, why didn't we call him? He said 'I've been living here since 1959 and I have never known anything.' I said, 'I hear ya' and we kept on walking. It was a bit of a tense moment, but I didn't think much more about it after we got off the block.

We walked south a block and headed east. I wanted to introduce Anthony to another gentleman in the neighborhood that we had met earlier that summer. On the way down the road, we saw a woman sitting on her porch smiling, and another man asking us if we had a light. I chose this moment to try to tell them who we were and what we were doing, but the woman on the porch just kept smiling and nodding, and the guy also approached us from the other side. In the meantime, a third man walked past going the other way, and Anthony tried talking to him. As we talked a little more, it became clear that he recognized Anthony from somewhere, either from the shelter downtown or from a treatment setting or someplace, and we were trying to figure out where they might know each other when we saw the two figures approaching with the sun behind them, walking up the street with dully glowing objects that soon resolved into aluminum baseball bats that were shining in the afternoon sun.

They were walking up the middle of the street, but then they approached us on the sidewalk, shaking hands with the man that we were talking to (who I think also asked them for a light). When I made a comment about the baseball bats, the taller, older guy said, "There are a lot of stray dogs around here." It soon became clear that this man was in fact Tyrone, and that our passing through his block had triggered a chain reaction that resulted in him and his son walking through the neighborhood with baseball bats, apparently looking for the white guy and black guy who they had heard were looking for him. This was evident to Anthony right away, but as usual it took me a minute to put two and two together.

We stood and conversed for a while, with the bats present but lowered. I gave Tyrone my card with our phone numbers on the back. He said that he might be willing to do an interview at this point, since time had gone by, and the implementation of the urban agriculture project was no longer imminent. Finally, we told him we would give him a copy of whatever papers we wrote, and we soon concluded our fieldwork for the day.

After the 'baseball bat conference' was concluded, Anthony and I talked it over in detail. He said that he knew from the moment when I asked for Tyrone that it would raise an alarm on that block. I responded that it worked – we wanted to get a message to Tyrone, and we did, almost immediately. In this case, it was by disrupting an unseen, locally understood boundary that we came to understand something about the lay of the land. Anthony didn't disagree, but he was seriously worried about a beat-down with the baseball bats, and he knew that at his age he couldn't run away fast enough.

We eventually wrote that paper (Draus, Roddy and McDuffie 2013) – but we never saw Tyrone again. The whole episode got me thinking about the ethics of what we were doing, and how we felt okay walking through other people's neighborhoods and approaching them in the name of research. Would I accept that in my own neighborhood? I wondered how Tyrone and his son would be treated if they were walking around on my home block in Dearborn, Michigan, asking for me. In that case, they might stick out as much as we did, and it's possible that the police might be called. If that happened, and the cops were to tail and question them, it wouldn't be so different from them following us with baseball bats. In fact, as recent events in the United States suggest, it might well turn out much worse for them. As with so much else, the consequences of trespassing varied with the territory.

In the Shadow of the Refinery (Julie and Paul)

On Wednesday, September 11 of 2013 we met in the parking lot in the Southwest Detroit neighborhood, which was in the process of being de-populated because Midwest Oil Company was buying out homeowners to create a 'green buffer zone.' We were there to learn the perspectives of the residents about this process. Julie had already called the company's chief of security on my drive to the neighborhood. It irritated her that she had to call a private security agency to enter a city neighborhood, but we complied with this request in order to minimize distractions while we were in the field. They would stop us if we didn't call and the alert was supposedly for our own protection.

Regardless, the security guards that patrolled the neighborhood for Midwest Oil were typically respectful and non-intrusive while we walked. We stopped at a couple of abandoned houses. One house was owned by Midwest Oil and marked with one of their standardized NO TRESPASSING signs, while the other was visibly abandoned but not properly secured. The doors and windows were missing and the house was completely open to the elements. As was typical, we were approached on our walk by a Midwest Oil truck with two men inside, a security guard and a real estate agent who was working on the property purchase program. The security guard told us that the abandoned house was called the "cat house" because so many stray cats and kittens lived inside.

We dropped in on Reginald, one of the few African American residents in the area, who told us that he would stay in his home even though almost all of his neighbors had sold to Midwest Oil and their homes had been leveled. At one time he had owned the lot adjacent to his home, but he was delinquent with the property taxes and Midwest Oil paid the back taxes and took over title of the property. There were pear, peach and plum trees on the lot and he regularly harvested the fruit and consumed it. The peach tree, he said, came from Cambodia and used to belong to a Hmong family that lived near him when he resided on the East Side of Detroit. When they moved they left the tree, and when he moved to Southwest Detroit he brought it with him. Lastly, Reginald told us about different industrial smells that waft through the neighborhood. At times, they made him nauseous.

We then stopped in to see two sisters who lived in the house around the corner from Reginald. There were piles of cat food along the sidewalk on the way to the home, and two birds in cages hanging from the porch ceiling. There was a "Beware of Dog" sign in the window as well as stickers listing the pets present inside (dogs, cats and birds) in the event of a fire. One of the sisters answered the door. We spoke a little about the piles of food, cats and kittens. She told us that there had been a marked increase in the number of stray cats as people exited the neighborhood. She was trying to feed them but was having difficulty affording it, and she felt she could no longer leave her dogs in the yard untended, for fear they would injure a cat. The house and the yard were well kept. We snapped a picture of the cat, but felt it was disrespectful to do much more.

Discussion: On trespassing, tourism, and responsibility (Paul and Julie)

In the tradition of the Chicago School of Sociology, we sought to map neighborhoods of Detroit experientially by walking every block of the sub-areas or neighborhoods that we were trying to understand. But this was an elusive goal, because these neighborhoods were not stable entities. A neighborhood became a demolition zone and then an empty space and then a green landscape emerged. The territory itself was transformed and therefore what we were trespassing on was no longer the same: now it was more of an industrial province, patrolled by corporate security on the one hand and flocks of geese on the other, both requiring negotiation of space. In each of these cases, we sought to make legible the lines of territory that were meaningful to those living within them.

Our patchwork stories convey a sense of territory that shifted even as we walked upon it: the residents, the industrial landlords and their private police

Figure 11.1 Signs for a 1950s fictional bowling alley painted while converting the neighborhood to a movie set on top of a mural done by a local nonprofit that sought to rejuvenate the neighborhood through urban agriculture (photograph by author).

force, and the plants and animals were all making their claims upon this piece of turf. In later work we explored this further, resituating the framework of urban ecology to encompass all of these actors that we witnessed, or disturbed, in our often-clumsy research forays (Draus and Roddy 2018; Draus et al. 2018). From the residents' perspectives, it was difficult to know where to place us, but it would not be surprising if they saw us merely as an extension of the larger shadow cast over what was once a thriving community.

As the 2000s rolled on and waves of foreclosure washed across Detroit, the East Side increasingly resembled a ghost town or a war zone. The area had lost significant population since its heyday in the 1950s. This impression was enhanced when the neighborhood was used in 2016 as a live sound stage for a scene from one of the Transformers films, where they actually painted the crumbling storefronts with faded signs of bakeries and bowling alleys, to make them appear to be remnants of a small town from the 1950s. After the film crew left, the alterations remained, creating a kind of visual disconnect between the actual legacy signs that still stood in the neighborhood and the ones that had been added for cinematic atmosphere (see Figures 11.1 and 11.2).

Figure 11.2 Business advertisements painted on the side of an abandoned building to make it seem like a Western ghost town. The sign facing the street is an actual relic of the neighborhood's past, when this was a bustling commercial district (photograph by author).

Years before the Transformers arrived, we were active as researchers in the neighborhood, due to a proposed urban agriculture project which also promised to transform it. We set a goal of walking each block in the proposed project's footprint area, meeting people as we went and engaging them in casual conversations and potentially more formal interviews. Our purpose was fairly straightforward: we wanted to get a sense of this community as a place, in terms of its history, its identity, its physical bones and its lived relationships, before this proposed transformation took place. In social science terms, this would form a baseline against which we might measure the changes that took place as a result of this project. However, it was not something that neighborhood residents had necessarily asked for. Therefore, our presence had to be explained.

In most of the urban contexts that we enter as researchers, we are *choosing* to be there, when we don't have to be. To the extent that we are able to exit the scene, to return to a place of comfort, this is certainly a form of privilege and power. Insofar as we seek to truthfully report what we have seen, to serve in the role of witness, then it may be seen as a form of ethical commitment or responsibility. This was certainly the promise of each of our research studies – that it would be used to improve the conditions witnessed by the researchers. But this certainly didn't happen automatically. The impacts of research are rarely direct, and they are often not perceived by residents at all. In our view, therefore, this commitment is always suspect – hence the uneasiness about whether we should be there at all.

These internal conflicts reflect an enduring tension between the role of social scientist as *explorer* versus *colonist*: someone who is *describing* the territory versus someone who is actively seeking to *control* it, or enabling others to do so. It might be more accurate to simply call us *tourists*. The term 'tourist' is often used as an insult in urban research, being equated with gentrification and exploitation (Fuller and Michel 2014). Scholars debate the potential of a *hopeful tourism* that may contribute to social transformation as opposed to reinforcing colonial relations (Chambers and Buzinde 2015, Boluk and Carnicelli 2019). But in our case, it was probably a more honest depiction, even if it did not paint us in a particularly noble or heroic light. We may imagine ourselves as being on the side of the people in the community, but that might not be what is perceived. Like respectful tourists, we seek to learn, appreciate, report honestly, possibly bring some benefit, without doing any damage – but we are guests in someone else's territory, bringing an outsider's lens as well as a web of power relations with us.

This power, though real, was largely limited to what our presence signified. As Detroit was moving into the twenty-first century, we could see something new was being born out of the shell of its twentieth century urban form. The Detroit we saw from the squad car and the jail was a reminder of the real drag exerted by criminal justice institutions, which intervened somewhat arbitrarily in neighborhoods without altering the dynamics of damage and decline that had set in, instead often reinforcing them (Draus 2009). As researchers who had previously focused on illicit activities and marginalized groups in and around Detroit, we were interested in how changes taking place at the level of local landscape might benefit the daily lives of those particular groups – be a lift, not a drag. While some landscape interventions, especially those related to urban agriculture, promised to promote social inclusion through the building of human and social capital as well as economic self-sufficiency, critics have questioned whether such efforts truly benefit the most marginalized urban residents (Alkon and Cadji 2018).

Like Madden (2014), we came to view these neighborhoods not as static containers of identities or simple transmitters of downstream effects, but as complex bundles of 'contested, contingent' processes (p. 491). This perspective aligned with the concept of urban assemblages as 'fluid entanglements of entities whose power is a temporary achievement that must be continually reasserted through complex co-ordination practices' (Ureta 2014, p. 245). This echoes Brighenti's (2010) assertion that 'territory is better conceived as an act or practice rather than an object or physical space' (p. 53). In Detroit, we observed a number of spatial projects that expressed goals of ameliorating social and physical environments, through gardens, farms, parks or expanding green space, sometimes with the added promise of economic development in the form of increased investment or employment opportunities. However, we also saw that without deliberate efforts to protect the interests of long-term residents, expansions of green space in low-income areas could produce a paradox, displacing the very people who were supposed to benefit from environmental intervention (Wolch, Byrne and Newell 2014).

Conclusion: Whose Territory?

By the turn of the twenty-first century Detroit as a whole had been symbolically stigmatized and actually devalued, with very material consequences for its residents (Draus, Roddy and Greenwald 2010). Our own research (Draus, Roddy and McDuffie 2013) had shown that the concept of neighborhood could be defined as much by its absence as its presence. Likewise, the use of 'neighborhood' as a mobilizing concept may contribute to the exclusion of those who are not connected to the right assemblage. White newcomers to the majority-Black city might attend community meetings, assert their belonging in 'the neighborhood,' and soon become the dominant voice, shunting aside the views of those long established on the block. This was in fact what Tyrone had foreseen, what he resisted in the urban farming project. The nonprofit foundation, the university, the jail, the sheriff's department, the refinery, the security guard, the city government: the institutions that moved behind the scenes would all support and favor them, the newcomers, who were in fact the same old colonists, the white settlers, come again to take the land, to usurp our home. As much as we wished to be on the right side of the struggles we witnessed, we were often equated with the forces of domination.

This fear emerged as a consistent undercurrent in interviews that we conducted (see Draus, Roddy and McDuffie 2013, 2018). We saw this fear reflected in the reactions to our own visits – the idea that we might be bringing a new assemblage of power that could suddenly rearrange the territory under peoples' feet. Once, while walking on a quiet side street on the East Side, we encountered a Black man with dreadlocks and a White woman, both on bicycles. We tried to engage them in conversation, but while the woman seemed responsive, the man wheeled his bike around and rode off. Before he departed, he cried out that all the Black people would soon be in prison or the graveyard.

These encounters both instructed and humbled us. The rock flying from a darkened doorway of an apparently abandoned building, the brandished baseball bats – these were not aggressive, but defensive measures. They weren't so different from the cry of a flushed pheasant or the snarl of a dog guarding pups, meant to buy time and fend off danger. From those willing to tolerate our intrusions, we learned more than we could hope or promise to return. We were the tourists, the trespassers, after all.

References

Alkon, A.H. and Cadji, J. (2018). Sowing Seeds of Displacement: Gentrification and Food Justice in Oakland, CA. *International Journal of Urban and Regional Research*, 44(1): 108–123.

Boluk, K. and Carnicelli, S. (2019). Tourism for the emancipation of the oppressed: towards a critical tourism education drawing on Freirean philosophy. *Annals of Tourism Research*, 76: 168–179.

Brighenti, A.M. (2010). On Territorology: Towards a General Science of Territory. *Theory Culture & Society*, 27: 52–72.

Chambers, C. and Buzinde, C. (2015) Tourism and decolonisation: Locating research and self. *Annals of Tourism Research*, 51: 1–16.

Draus, P.J. (2009). Substance Abuse and Slow Motion Disasters: The Case of Detroit. *Sociological Quarterly*, 50(2): 360–382.

Draus, P., Haase, D., Napieralski, J., Roddy, J. and Qureshi, S. (2019). Wounds, Ghosts and Gardens: Historical Trauma and Green Reparations in Berlin and Detroit. *Cities*, 93: 153–163.

Draus, P. and Howard, C. (1999). Spying on an Eyesore: Space, Place, and Urban Decay. In Hutchison, R. (Ed.) *Constructions of Urban Space* (Research in Urban Sociology, *Vol.*5), Emerald Group Publishing Limited, Bingley, pp. 59–79.

Draus, P., Lovall, S., Formby, T., Baldwin, L. and Lowe-Anderson, W. (2018). A Green Space Vision in Southeast Michigan's Most Heavily Industrialized Area. *Urban Ecosystems* 22: 91–102. doi:10.1007/s11252-018-0765-7

Draus, P., Roddy, J., and Asabigi, K. (2015). Streets, Strolls and Spots: Sex Work, Drug Use and Social Space in Detroit. *The International Journal of Drug Policy*, 26 (5): 453–460.

Draus, P., Roddy, J. and Greenwald, M. (2010). A Hell of a Life: Addiction and Marginality in Post-Industrial Detroit. *Social & Cultural Geography*, 7(11): 663–680.

Draus, P., Roddy, J., and McDuffie, A. (2013). We Don't Have No Neighborhood: Advanced Marginality and Urban Agriculture in Detroit. *Urban Studies* 51(12): 2523–2538.

Draus, P., Roddy, J., and McDuffie, A. (2018). "It's Like Half and Half": Austerity, Possibility and Daily Life Inside a Depopulated Detroit Neighborhood. *City, Culture and Society* 14: 37–46. doi:10.1016/j.ccs.2018.01.001.

Draus, P., and Roddy, J. (2018). Weeds, Pheasants and Wild Dogs: Resituating the Ecological Paradigm in Postindustrial Detroit. *International Journal of Urban and Regional Research* 42(5): 807–827.

Fuller, N. and Michel, B. (2014). 'Stop Being a Tourist!' New Dynamics of Urban Tourism in Berlin-Kreuzberg. *International Journal of Urban and Regional Research*, 38 (4): 1304–1318.

Madden, D.J. (2014). Neighborhood as Spatial Project: Making the Urban Order on the Downtown Brooklyn Waterfront. *International Journal of Urban and Regional Research*, 38(2): 471–497.

Roddy, J., Draus, P., White, E. and Asabigi, K. (2013). Moving Parts and Balancing Acts: Building and Maintaining a Collaborative Partnership in Detroit. *Advances in Applied Sociology*, 3(1): 26–36.

Sack, R.D. (1983). Human Territoriality: A Theory. *Annals of the Association of American Geographers*, 73(1): 55–74.

Turnbull, D. (1989). *Maps are Territories: Science is an Atlas*. Chicago: The University of Chicago Press.

Ureta, S. (2014). The Shelter that Wasn't There: On the Politics of Co-ordinating Multiple Urban Assemblages in Santiago, Chile. *Urban Studies*, 51(2): 231–246.

Wolch, J., Byrne, J., and Newell, J.P. (2014). Urban green space, public health and environmental justice: The challenge of making cities 'just green enough.' *Landscape and Environmental Planning*, 125: 234–244.

Index